Comparative ethnic and race relations

White talk black talk

Comparative ethnic and race relations

Published for the Centre for Research in Ethnic Relations at the University of Warwick
Senior Editor
Professor John Rex, *Associate Director & Research Professor of Ethnic Relations, University of Warwick*

Editors
Professor Robin Cohen, *Executive Director & Professor of Sociology, University of Warwick*
Mr Malcolm Cross, *Principal Research Fellow, University of Warwick*
Dr Robin Ward, *Head of Ethnic Business Research Unit, University of Aston*

This series has been formed to publish works of original theory and empirical research on the problems of racially mixed societies. It is based on the work of the Centre for Research in Ethnic Relations, a Designated Research Centre of the Economic and Social Research Council, and the main centre for the study of race relations in Britain.

The series will continue to draw mainly on the work produced at the Centre, though the editor will consider manuscripts from scholars whose work has been associated with the Centre, or whose research lies in similar fields. Future titles will concentrate on anti-racist issues in education, on the organisation and political demands of ethnic minorities, on migration patterns, changes in immigration policies in relation to migrants and refugees, and on questions relating to employment, welfare and urban restructuring as these affect minority communities.

The books will appeal to an international readership of scholars, students and professionals concerned with racial issues, across a wide range of disciplines (such as sociology, anthropology, social policy, politics, economics, education and law), as well as among professional social administrators, teachers, government officials, health service workers and others.

Other books in this series:

Michael Banton: *Racial and ethnic competition*
Tomas Hammar: *European immigration policy*
Richard Jenkins: *Racism and recruitment: managers, organizations and equal opportunity in the labour market*
Richard Jenkins and John Solomos (eds.): *Racism and equal opportunity policies in the 1980s*
Frank Reeves: *British racial discourse*
John Rex and David Mason: *Theories of race and ethnic relations*
Paul Rich: *Race and empire in British politics 1890–1962*
Robin Ward and Richard Jenkins (eds.): *Ethnic communities in business*

White talk black talk

Inter-racial friendship and communication amongst adolescents

ROGER HEWITT

Research Officer, University of London

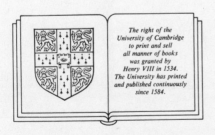

The right of the University of Cambridge to print and sell all manner of books was granted by Henry VIII in 1534. The University has printed and published continuously since 1584.

CAMBRIDGE UNIVERSITY PRESS

Cambridge

London   New York   New Rochelle

Melbourne   Sydney

Published by the Press Syndicate of the University of Cambridge
The Pitt Building, Trumpington Street, Cambridge CB2 1RP
32 East 57th Street, New York, NY 10022, USA
10 Stamford Road, Oakleigh, Melbourne 3166, Australia

First published 1986

Printed in Great Britain at the University Press, Cambridge

British Library cataloguing in publication data

Hewitt, Roger
White talk black talk: inter-racial friendship and communication amongst
adolescents. – (Comparative ethnic and race relations)
1. Youth – Great Britain – Attitudes 2. Social interaction – Great Britain
3. Great Britain – Race relations 4. Great Britain – Social conditions – 1945–
I. Title II. Series
302.2′242′088055   HN385.5

Library of Congress cataloguing in publication data

Hewitt, Roger.
White talk black talk.
(Comparative ethnic and race relations)
Bibliography.
Includes index.
1. Sociolinguistics – England – London. 2. Creole dialects, English – England – London.
3. Youth – England – London – Language. 4. Blacks – England – London –
Communication. 5. London (England) – Race relations.
I. Title. II. Series: Comparative ethnic and race relations series.
P40.45.G7H48   1986   401′.9′094216   86–6146

ISBN 0 521 26239 9

CE

For Louis and Winnie Hewitt

Contents

relations; 'private linguistic arrangements' in inter-racial friendship; white-with-black creole use, its modes and contradictions; 'black language' use by other minorities; black/white sociolinguistic relations in the United States and the Caribbean.

Acknowledgements

Although his unfailing enthusiasm and support for research are widely recognised, I must acknowledge that I have been granted an abundance of both by Professor Basil Bernstein. As head of the Sociological Research Unit at the University of London Institute of Education, he gave me the space and opportunity to pursue my work, and as a friend he has given generously of his time and intellect. To him I owe a unique debt. I would also like to thank Professor Robert Le Page of the University of York for his early encouragement and constant support. Frank Parkin and Margaret McLure were both instrumental in getting my research off the ground, and I thank them for their help. To Euan Reid I would also like to extend my thanks for his benign interventions. Lorraine Hewitt's moral support was always strongly felt and very welcome. With very deep gratitude I thank Private Robert Taylor of the 3rd Battalion of the Parachute Regiment for his patience and unflagging assistance. Through his perceptive commentaries I came to understand much that would otherwise have remained obscure to me. I also thank, especially, Simon Luxford. Others who have helped me, and to whom I owe a debt of thanks, are Aston Campbell, Brian Wallen, Sandra Smart, Valery Pennant and Paul Eliot. To the many youth-workers and teachers who were my colleagues at times during the research, and to my many young informants, I also extend my thanks. The Research and Statistics Branch of the Inner London Education Authority made possible my research in schools. To Patricia Thomas of the Nuffield Foundation, whose advice and help were generously given, I wish also to say a special thank-you. To the trustees of the Nuffield Foundation, whose kind support made the research possible, I also extend my sincere gratitude. Finally, to Anna Russell, who has patiently read and commented on every word in this book – and many that didn't make it – and whose criticisms were always useful if not always heeded, I wish to acknowledge a debt that is impossible to measure.

Typographical conventions

Square brackets around words in passages of quoted material indicate that those words are the author's, and intended as a clarification of the text.

[...] indicates material omitted.

[*] indicates an inaudible part of tape-recorded text which seems to be a single syllable. Hence

[**] indicates two inaudible syllables, and so on.

Where inaudible speech extends to more than a few syllables, the word [inaudible] has been inserted.

/ indicates tooth-sucking.

Introduction

Unlike the United States, Great Britain has only comparatively recently come to have a native-born black population of any numerical significance (Fryer 1984). Over half of all black British people whose parents were born in the Caribbean are at present under the age of twenty, and the vast majority of these were born in Great Britain. This, together with the growth in the number of British children of South Asian parentage, has provided white British children, especially in English cities, with the possibility of an experience of inter-racial contact quite different from that afforded to previous generations. The impact of that experience has taken a number of social and cultural forms, and is itself mediated by other important influences. Hence the urban white adolescent responses, and those of black adolescents which are the subject of this book, do not easily yield simple answers to questions posed in terms of 'attitudinal change'.

The impact of inter-racial friendships on *black* British youngsters is, of course, of special importance in that it has a potential relevance to the way in which racism is or is not experienced in close association with white peers. Of importance here too are not only the *social* terms within which adolescent inter-racial contacts operate but also the *cultural*. Black youth culture in Britain has, since the 1960s, become increasingly well defined. This has had a significant part to play in determining the nature and terms of black/white adolescent contact, for it is often through the more oblique means of cultural affinities and oppositions that adolescents come to live out and enact what remains unarticulated in more conscious ways.

This area of cultural relations is the principle theme of this book, and, within that area, the role played by language in registering, influencing and providing a medium through which relationships are acted out. In the context of adolescent race relations, the use of Caribbean-based

1

creole speech by young blacks and the acquisition and use of those same forms by *whites* are examined from a perspective which draws on sociology and that anthropological part of sociolinguistics which has gone under the name of the 'ethnography of speaking'. It deals with communicative practices between adolescents in specific urban settings, and its starting point is the actual friendships between young British blacks of Afro-Caribbean parentage and white working-class adolescents in two areas of South London. It is based on research conducted between 1980 and 1983 which used qualitative, ethnographic techniques involving extended serial interviewing, participant observation, and the tape-recording of spontaneous speech in natural settings.

At the outset it is necessary to stand back a little from a tangentially related set of issues surrounding what has been called the 'contact hypothesis' – a hypothesis which broadly posits that an increase of contact between racial groups reduces 'prejudice'. This hypothesis has been 'tested' in the United States from the 1940s onwards with mixed results (Allport 1954; Wilner *et al*. 1955). The same mixture of findings has also been true of British studies (Butler and Stokes 1974; Studlar 1977; Husbands 1979). There have also been difficulties with the hypothesis at the theoretical level, for it is an issue which has awkwardly straddled sociology and social psychology and its exact terms of reference are variously defined. Furthermore, the effects of 'contact' are far less frequently considered for the nature of their impact on the black minority, which is treated more often as the constant and impassive stimulus to white responses. The majority of studies under this rubric are, therefore, generally lacking in theoretical or empirical concern for the interactive dimension and qualities of 'contact'.

Within the clearly sociological version of the hypothesis, two kinds of finding have been most common in British studies, and both appeared in the reports of early research carried out within the Colour and Citizenship Survey (Deakin 1970). The first, as set out by Deakin, resulted from a comparison of 'a representative sample of the whole white population with a more limited group who were more likely to have experienced day-to-day contact with coloured people'. This indicated that, 'over a series of key questions . . . no significant difference was found between the views of the two groups' (Deakin 1970: 318; see also, Husbands 1979: 156). The other finding, which resulted from an examination of 'degrees of contact' within racially mixed inner city areas, was that 'those who said that they have become more favourably disposed towards coloured people tended also to be those who had spoken to and got on well with them' (Deakin 1970: 328). This second type of finding led writers such as Bagley (1969) to see in contact itself a 'hopeful' sign for race relations, and it is one that is also reflected in even the more impressionistic accounts of official and policy-related bodies. Thus the Select Committee on Race Relations and Immigration (1977) reported:

> The committee are encouraged by their impression that within the neighbourhood where West Indians are concentrated there is now much less evidence of racial prejudice than there was a few years ago. (xxxix)

This relation between official perspectives and such findings as have been made in relation to the 'contact hypothesis' has been examined by Henriques (1984) who has argued that its negative formulation – i.e. that unfamiliarity creates 'racial prejudice' – has, through such books as Patterson's *Dark Strangers* (1963), been absorbed into British official policy dealing with race, and that during an important period following the early 1960s a laissez-faire approach became apparent which 'paralysed' initiatives that might have addressed more effectively the question of racism.

The research reported on in *this* book, while having inter-racial friendship as its starting point, attempted to go far below the surface of the kinds of answers put forward by studies based on the 'contact hypothesis'. In contrast, it initially examined the kinds of influence which friendship *patterns* (rather than individual friendships) have on the flow of racist ideas and practices within socially located adolescent groups. Racism is not, therefore, treated here simply as a quality of individual personal relations, but as an attribute of societies and cultures which may be manifested in particular instances. Although produced and reproduced in various economic and institutional locations, it is examined here through its appearance in specific local adolescent social networks as it is registered in the social life of signs exchanged and manipulated within a particular cultural terrain.

Another group of studies which appears to be close to the present research is specifically concerned with inter-racial contact between children and adolescents. Here, again, the United States has inevitably a somewhat longer history of academic interest than has Great Britain (Carter *et al*. 1980). These studies are predominantly concerned with the effect of racial contact and mixing on white pupils, with the effect on black pupils being treated as a consequence of the moderation or otherwise of white 'racial attitudes'. Insights into black views of contact, such as occurs almost in passing in Cayton and Drake's famous study of Chicago, *Black Metropolis* (1946: 123) are rare in the literature, which for the most part displays a 'progressive liberal' viewpoint and involves a psychological or social psychological research framework. The desegregation of schools has especially been a stimulus to North American studies (Rist 1978; Gerard and Miller 1975; McConahay 1978; Schofield 1978) and studies of 'ethnic preferences' in young children, through sociometric studies and experiments involving photographs and dolls, have also been conducted (Koslin *et al*. 1969; Porter 1971) following the work of Clark and Clark (1947).

In Great Britain, the same predominance of studies from psychology and social psychology has been evident in the area of 'ethnic choice' and young people (Kawwa 1963; Durojaiye 1970; Puskin 1967; Bagley and Verma 1975; Braha and Rutter 1980; Milner 1983; Davey 1983). With increasingly sophisticated measurement techniques, social psychologists have repeatedly proved beyond a shadow of doubt – if such a shadow existed – that children tend to choose their own racial kind as friends far more than they choose members of other racial groups. Much of this work has looked at primary school children, although some work on secondary school children has also been conducted. Most studies have not involved the actual observation of behaviour, a fact which some authors lament (Milner 1983: 124) while others apparently applaud on the grounds that, 'one cannot know by observation how children would like to associate' (Davey 1983: 132).

Although social psychologists attempt to deal with what they see as human *group* relations and group identification in 'inter-group behaviour', methodologically there is a considerable gulf between the aims on the one hand of sociology/anthropology and on the other hand of the social psychologist, for whom an interest in measurement and experiment heavily outweighs an attention to explanation and theory. Disciplinary differences, therefore, are responsible for the gap between many of the works cited above and the present study, which is not concerned with measures but with mechanisms, and with 'friendships', 'social groups', 'race' and 'ideologies' as they are located in everyday life.

Despite the early recognition of the fact of children's racial mixing in British cities (Hiro 1971: 236), it is a curious fact that no *sociological* studies were undertaken of this specific area. Even as late as 1979, Rex and Tomlinson could request: 'We would like to see a study undertaken of white youth from immigrant majority schools, and white youth on the margins of immigrant areas' (Rex and Tomlinson 1979: 239); yet even now, at the time of writing, no such study has been undertaken, and the present work only obliquely answers the suggestion. Certainly the issue of adolescent racism has been addressed, in passing, by several of the studies appearing in recent years concerned with the sociology of youth and youth culture (Daniel and McGuire 1972; Mungham and Pearson 1976; Cohen and Robins 1978); but it is only occasionally (Pearson 1976) that the sociology of youth has directly addressed itself to this matter. The same is also true of those studies conducted by the Centre for Contemporary Cultural Studies at Birmingham University (Willis 1977; Hall and Jefferson 1976). While some of this influential centre's work on youth has included allusions to the racism of white adolescent boys, little attempt was made to subject it to any sustained ethnographic or theoretical attention.

The prominent exception at Birmingham to this lack of interest in black/white adolescent relationships was Hebdige (1976; 1979) whose research, although not primarily concerned with patterns of adolescent racism, into black and white youth cultures led him to build significantly on hints in Cohen (1972), and to construct a speculative but suggestive account of the impact of black cultures on white youth in the 1960s and 1970s. His interest in the semiotics of style and his emphasis on black music and speech in relation to whites indicated an area hardly attended to elsewhere (see also Chambers 1976; Root and Austin 1978). Hebdige's approach was partly influenced by French structuralism; and it is in relation to this, with the more clearly *anthropological* approaches of ethnography, the semiotics of culture (Geerz 1973) and anthropological linguistics, that a methodological ground, if not a specific area of interest, can be found which accords with the interests which underlie the present study.

It was from within this anthropological tradition that David Parkin addressed the question of language and its relationship to ethnicity and adolescent gangs in Nairobi (Parkin 1977), drawing urban anthropology, multi-lingualism, and the sociolinguistic work of William Labov on pre-adolescent gangs in New York into the theoretical debate over cultural categories and social order. A similar nexus of interests, although without specific concern with adolescents, has also marked the work of American anthropologist John Gumperz, who has consistently addressed the question of 'inter-ethnic' relations from the standpoint of linguistic anthropology, and has also conducted such studies on British soil (Gumperz 1978; 1982) Gumperz' work and the theoretical landscaping performed so effectively by Hymes (1962; 1971), together with the sociolinguistic research into 'black language' conducted by Mitchell-Kernan (1971), Labov (1972), Wolfram (1974), Heath (1984) and others, built upon a tradition which is, however, almost restricted to North American researchers.

This kind of approach has no sustained parallel in Great Britain, despite the useful incorporation of social network theory into sociolinguistic analysis by Milroy (1980) and the concern with 'language, ethnicity and inter-group relations' in the publications of Giles and his colleagues (Giles 1977), working within the specialised framework of social psychology. The attempt here, therefore, is to bring the kinds of issues, interests and methods that characterise the ethnographic approach to language and culture into relation with a concern with racism, its manifestations and oppositions in adolescent life as it is found in the British context.

A fundamental concern of this research was the cultural study of black/white adolescent friendship and contact patterns, and the relation these had to the formation and non formation of racist ideas and practices. Although, as has been indicated, the extent to which racial mixing occurs has been investigated within other disciplines, no study had taken as its starting point apparently successful inter-racial friendships themselves, or tried to examine the exact nature of such relationships or the way in which issues of racism manifest themselves and are processed within them. A longitudinal approach was needed, in order to examine the *course* of particular friendships, and to isolate, at least to some extent, the social pressures brought to bear upon those friendships. Thus, studying friendship and looking at those instances where racism appeared to be absent, or at a low level, would make it possible to see more clearly some of the factors which contribute to the existence of racism more widely amongst young people. In paradoxically seeking where racism appeared not to be, one could learn more about its mechanisms of reproduction.

A balance of data was essential to capture the *interactive* quality of the relationship between black and white youngsters, whilst still focusing on white adolescents. While both black and white sides of the friendships were to be reviewed, it was the white side that was to be treated as problematic, because white adolescent racism appeared to be common, even 'normal' in South London and more widely. A popular explanation of this has been 'rising youth unemployment' (Cochrane and Billig 1984) although, other than the linking of the presence of 'immigrants' with unemployment in the propaganda of the National Front and other extreme right-wing groups, no convincing account of the precise connections between these phenomena has been published. (In fact, without explicit connections being made, almost anything might be asserted as linked to unemployment after the late 1970s.) However such an explanation might be framed, it would need also to account for the apparently growing affinity between some sections of black and white working-class youth over the same period, as glimpsed, for example, in the numerous references in the press to the presence of white adolescents in the disturbances in Bristol and Brixton in 1980–1, which were ostensibly spontaneous black protests against policing levels and practices.

The framework within which researchers seemed at first to choose to work were potentially ambiguous: the question (reflecting the dominant literature on the topic): 'What is the connection between inter-racial friendships and levels of prejudice?' would seem to suggest that 'levels of prejudice' within *individuals* was the focus. It is obvious, however, that no necessary connection can be established between these two aspects in any individual case. What emerged as a clear possibility, on the other hand, was that there might be a connection between the level of racism within a particular social locale and the local *patterns* of inter-racial friendship found in the adolescent community. On the basis of this possibility, individual friendships became less interesting for their own sakes and more interesting to the extent that processes within them were both part of and contributed to wider patterns of association and the relay of ideas and practices within and between peer groups. In a manner characteristic of ethnographic method, in looking at individual cases the research was to focus on the social dimension of adolescent existence, and to seek where possible to situate it within the wider context of social structures. Of especial importance were the interactive mechanisms, including sociolinguistic ones, by which the evaluative/ideological elements in the culture led, or did not lead, to an avoidance of racism.

A further reason to avoid being drawn into any estimation of individual 'levels' or 'degrees' of racism was that direct questioning regarding racial attitudes is very difficult where young people are involved, for they are at an age when they are only beginning to establish the relationship between their lived experience and social 'opinion' and 'knowledge' about it, even though it may be argued that the process itself *begins* with earliest socialisation. What, as a *processing* of social experience and social 'knowledge', comes more naturally than reasoned accounting, are the tentatively developed interactive cultural forms in which these matters are acted out rather than clearly articulated. Young whites are especially vulnerable to the apparent battery of ready-made, culturally available opinions and attitudes which come to occupy the space between their experience of race and their conceptualisation of it. A constant danger is that adolescents are over-impressed by the inquisitive attention of adults such as researchers, and like to be seen to have 'opinions' and to debate as adults have opinions and debate. When asked directly about race, there is a certain pride in giving adult-sounding, 'firm' views, with little regard for specific content. What is often provoked from young whites are formulaic responses, either prominent and racist ones they have heard 'validated' by adults or, less common but equally uninformative, those of the 'there's good and bad in all' kind. Such formulae, being only imitations of 'thoughtful' opinion, do not touch upon the complexities which few adolescents have the conceptual vocabulary truly to represent in the discourse of 'opinion'. The unerring uniformity of results in 'racial attitude' studies of young whites – which earnestly report the 'worryingly high levels of racial prejudice' – is clearly related to this fact.

What *is* true of such 'prejudice level' studies is that they do reveal racism in the culture because they reveal the formulaic corpus most readily available to young people and, possibly, the extent to which that corpus has, at the time, been nationally highlighted through media and other attentions. What such studies reveal or imply about young people beyond their recourse to this cultural 'resource' during an interview is, however, difficult to evaluate. This is not to say that young people researched in this way may not in fact *be* highly racist; but the way in which they are, and the particular form of racism in which they engage, may not be captured by explicit interview or by other techniques where 'the race issue' is approached directly. The social reality they live is not properly reflected in the narrow formulaic terms in which the issue is socially aired, and even less in the quantifiable units of research schedules which compress even more these limited terms.

If, however, it were true that the 'issue of race' did not exist outside of some such terms – terms which themselves constitute activated ideologies and fragments of ideologies – it would be more important to the formulation of this research to get at how these were acted out in daily life, and to establish how, on the one hand, racism was performed and transmitted and, on the other, what interactive features, types of social arrangements and communicative practices subverted or interrupted this. It was also important to write into the equation the surfaces of adolescent social life that moved obliquely around the edges of 'the race question' – now coming into prominence, now fading – that is to say, the social and cultural life within which young people were situated. In all these aspects, the place of language and the specific cultures of youth were of central importance.

Pilot work had indicated that black/white friendship was less common after school-leaving age, which, for most of the youngsters with whom I was concerned, meant the age of sixteen. Furthermore, the communicative aspect in which I was especially interested – the use of creole by whites – tended to occur in early teens. Informants were, therefore, recruited from the thirteen to seventeen age-range. In practice, most informants were fourteen or fifteen at the time of their first interview. By interviewing the same informants at three intervals of not less than six months in each case, four interviews, spread over an eighteen-month to two-year period – and sometimes over a longer period – were elicited from each. Thus, by the last interview, most had left secondary school or were on the verge of doing so. A few were as old as eighteen.

Informants were secured through personal contact, mainly by myself as a youth worker (part of the research involved participant observation in which I worked as a part-time youth worker in four different youth clubs) or through other of my informants on a 'snowball' basis. A total of seventy informants, black/white, male/female, were secured, of whom forty-four constituted the core group. The remainder gave only one or two interviews each, either individually or within group discussions. A further factor determining inclusion in the sample was residence. The research was divided between two areas, one of low Afro-Caribbean settlement, Area A, the other of comparatively high settlement, Area B, and care was taken to keep the black/white, male/female cells distributed as equally as possible within the two areas. Because of the areas chosen and, within these, the youth clubs selected as sites of participant observation, the samples from both areas are very predominantly working-class. A majority lived in local council-owned flats, and the parents of only a few were home-owners. Most of the youngsters left or expected to leave school at sixteen, although high levels of youth unemployment encouraged some to enrol at colleges of further education or to stay on in the sixth form to take or re-take examinations. Some had unskilled jobs, a few apprenticeships. Some were unemployed.

A necessary condition for the selection of white informants was that they had at least some black friends. Black informants were also chosen on the basis of their friendship with whites. There was no concern to measure the 'typicality' of my sample, nor what percentage of black/white friendships there was in each of the youth clubs. Clubs, in any case, had changing and fluctuating attendance and membership. The concern was simply to examine those cases where friendships *were* inter-racial, and to relate substantial interview material to observations of behaviour in the clubs and in other settings such as school and street. It was here that typicality was evaluated. Further contextualising ethnographic work was conducted with gangs and other groups of adolescents who were *not* part of the sample (see Chapters 1 and 2), and interviews were conducted with youth workers, teachers, area youth officers and others involved with young people in both areas. This contextualising ethnography, together with very long periods of participant observation, permitted an evaluation of what was said *about* the course and nature of inter-racial friendship and communication in the interviews.

Separate from this sample of interviewed informants, an additional thirty adolescents, distributed between three schools, volunteered to wear radio microphones during their school lunch periods and to have their speech monitored and tape-recorded. All three schools were within Area B, for reasons that are explained in Chapter 4. The objective of this was the examination of naturally occurring speech with regard to the *interactive* aspects of creole use. The speech of some additional subjects were recorded in other settings, including youth clubs and the street.

The areas of South London in which the research was conducted are not far apart from one another, but are somewhat different both socially and culturally. Area A is a varied, predominantly working-class area with lower-middle-class and professional enclaves. It is rather a patchwork of occupational levels, types of housing and political allegiances and has, for a number of reasons, always been something of an anomaly in South London. Removed from the inner city to the extent that it is sometimes disparagingly referred to by inner city dwellers as 'the country', it has, nevertheless, one of the oldest and strongest traditions of working-class industrial and political organisation in London. This tradition was founded upon a wide range of industries and crafts which flourished in the second half of the nineteenth century and earlier, when skilled workers predominated and the older trade unions, like the Amalgamated Society of Engineers, the Amalgamated Society of Carpenters and Joiners, and the Operative Bricklayer's Society established a firm base for the working-class movement which later developed locally with such vigour. Indeed, the late-nineteenth-century working class of Area A included a substantial artisan elite, deeply committed to radical reforms and strongly influential in the Co-operative Movement. The area was also very important in the early development of the Labour Party.

Although the area suffered from many of the same housing problems as much of London in the late nineteenth and early twentieth centuries, and was certainly not without its own poor and 'disreputable' quarters at that time, the problems of over-crowding and slum conditions were never as acute as in many parts. The high number of large (and some very large) industrial employers also meant that unemployment was usually on a par with London as a whole, and sometimes actually far less of a problem.

The early decades of the twentieth century saw an expansion of industry, with electrical engineering becoming particularly dominant. Furthermore, the local Labour council, strongly committed as it was to a public housing policy, did much to improve the living conditions of the local poor during the 1930s, when unemployment and hardship were particularly acute. This same commitment to public housing was also evident immediately after World War II, when an energetic building policy was pursued in response to the housing shortage. Throughout this period and up until the mid-1960s, the population steadily increased, and local industries remained strong; and in 1965 unemployment stood at only 0.8%. In the late 1950s and early 1960s, too, the old town centre was entirely rebuilt and modernised. The cost of such modernisation and the subsequently higher local rates meant that many smaller businesses were forced to move outwards towards the fringe, and the traditional shopping area became dominated by multiple firms and big businesses. These modernisation programmes, and the building of high blocks of flats, transformed both the feel and the appearance of the area at a time when social and economic conditions were also particularly buoyant. In the late 1960s, however, the structure of employment began to change radically, with a major exodus of manufacturing firms. Several of the large electrical manufacturers moved out of London altogether, as did a number of other major employers in the engineering trade. Beside manufacturing, there were also reductions in construction, transport and distribution between 1966 and 1971, causing an overall decline in the number of local jobs available. This was offset to some extent by increases in jobs in retailing, public administration, education and health, and, indeed, a trend from manufacturing towards service work continued into the 1980s, although manufacturing was still an important part of the local economy.

In some respects the skilled workers, who once formed such a significant part of the workforce, were being replaced by a new army of lower clerical and other service workers, many of whom also worked outside the area. Thus, in the late 1970s, 42% of all school leavers who found employment went into clerical work, while only 13% entered manufacturing and 8% construction.

The community itself was predominantly white. Up until the mid-1970s people from the Irish Republic constituted the largest ethnic minority, although the majority of these had entered before 1955. In the early 1950s, however, immigrants from Asia – mainly Jats – had begun to settle in small communities in parts of the area; and in the late 1960s, Gujerati small traders and Sikh artisans from East Africa had also followed. During the 1970s these groups increased by some 40%. Immigrants from the Caribbean were (and continue to be) far less numerous and, unlike the Asian groups, did not settle in distinct districts but remained fairly scattered throughout the local population. Apart from very small numbers of immigrants from Africa of non-Asian origin, Caribbeans constituted the smallest significant ethnic minority. Thus in 1981, while 14% of the population of Area A belonged to households where the head of the house was born in the New Commonwealth and Pakistan (NCWP) – with a few wards where the proportion was a little over 20% – approximately 80% of these people were of Asian origin.

Young whites in Area A grew up, therefore, in a largely white area, although one where hostility to Asians was extremely common and, especially in the late 1970s, attacks on Asians and racist graffiti were frequent occurrences. Afro-Caribbeans and their children were less disliked; but amongst whites generally, blacks and Asians tended to be regarded with hostility, and extreme right-wing political groups, although always small, were at times very active. In the late 1970s and early 1980s, these groups held a particular attraction for some young whites, especially those adopting skinhead style. Young black adolescents, by joining together socially, generally fared somewhat better than did young Asians and tended to make certain cafes and youth clubs their own, while young Asians suffered in isolation far more.

In 1981 unemployment amongst those under nineteen years of age was 11.74% (9.22% for males and 18.53% for girls), figures slightly below those for London as a whole. Thus, although following the national trend economically, Area A was by no means a uniquely depressed area nor, apparently, experienced as such by the young. Area B, however, the centre of which was a little over three miles from the centre of Area A, had rather different characteristics.

Situated in the north of a South London borough, Area B comprises a cluster of inner-city wards with a population of about 60,000. From the late nineteenth century until 1931, the population of this area stood at just under 110,000 and overwhelmingly consisted of working-class families. The rapid expansion of the population between the 1850s and 1880s was through the classic growth industries of the mid-Victorian economic boom. The Great Depression, however, brought unemployment and poverty on a large scale. During the last quarter of the century, the conscious development of housing for the working classes by local estate owners, led to the creation of an upper area of town houses for the better off, and a lower area of smaller terraced dwellings for working families and the poor. Such was the development of the area, however, that already by 1900 even these town houses had been given over to multi-occupation, and the middle classes moved steadily southwards.

The resident population included both what Charles Booth termed 'comfortable working-class families' and an equally substantial 'poor working class' of semi-employed people living in overcrowded slums and appallingly insanitary conditions. Limited slum demolition at the turn of the century caused inhabitants to resettle in other nearby slums, adding further to the overcrowding. By 1900 the area was notorious for its poverty, street crime and prostitution. Such social conditions were, however, only part of the story for the area also supported a substantial and well organised labour force. Indeed the workforce contained a large number of exactly those skilled workers, also found in Area A, who had formed the backbone of the Victorian 'labour aristocracy'. Especially prominent were the engineers, whose Amalgamated Society was the most visible and influential trade union in the area. Largely through the activities of this 'labour aristocracy', here as in Area A, friendly societies, co-operatives of various kinds and political societies were well established before the turn of the century. Dockyard and industrial development, including a strong engineering industry, came to provide major sources of employment, and metal trades and transport also developed as important employers in the early twentieth century.

Community identity appears to have always been very strong, and late in the nineteenth century Booth observed that there was an 'old-established solidarity about the conditions of life even amongst the poorest of the area'. With its narrow streets of terraced houses, corner pubs and working men's associations, it was and long remained a classic working-class neighbourhood. Like Area A, too, it was amongst the first of the London areas to have its own Labour member of parliament and local council, a tradition which persists today.

During the 1920s more slum clearance and a resettlement programme marked the beginning of a large-scale diminution of the population. Between 1930 and 1950, the local population dropped by almost 25%, a trend which continued through into the 1960s and 1970s, when much of the area was affected by demolition and re-building programmes. By 1980, only a few isolated terraces of old houses remained in the original working-class district, dotted about between the large local authority-owned residential estates, but this development came much later than it had in Area A. The period since the 1920s also saw a steady decline in the manufacturing industries, with no compensatory growth in other sectors of employment, a process which – consistent with the trend for London as a whole – accelerated greatly from the mid-1960s onwards and added momentum to the decline of the area.

Against the tide of population movement out, and in response to the plummeting value of property, immigrants from several countries began to move in during the 1950s. Small numbers of Pakistani, Indian, African and Turkish immigrants settled at this time, as did slightly larger numbers of people from the Republic of Ireland. The largest single group, however, came from the Caribbean, principally Jamaica. In the late 1950s and early 1960s a 'Caribbean quarter' developed, as West Indians bought up houses, initially in a single street, and sublet them to other West Indians as well as to whites. The Council, at first torn between the notion of brotherhood and the conservatism of community closure, bent to political pressures both locally and nationally and attempted to contain the Caribbean community through its housing policy. Indeed, there was much local hostility to black settlement both outside and within the local Labour Party, and it brought to the fore important contradictions in the politics of the local white community. Anti-immigration and repatriation platforms of far-right parties consistently stimulated upwards of 1,800 votes in local elections.

After the reorganisation of local government in 1964, the new, much wider borough authority followed a similar policy with regard to housing and black people but, to 'protect' its more middle-class white areas, consistently directed black applicants to the wards of Area B as a whole. By 1971 approximately 20% of the population of Area B were people whose parents were both born in the Caribbean. By 1981, blacks constituted a little over 25% of the overall local population, and between 40% and 50% in many localities within the area.

From its earliest days when black people, such as those of the Pentecostal Church who were unable to find a hall of their own in which to worship, struggled to secure a foothold in the area, the Caribbean community gradually built up a strong local profile. As the old white working-class community declined in numbers and in local economic and political coherence, the new black population came to impress itself with increasing strength on the area. Shops and market stalls catering for Caribbean households mushroomed, while black churches, social clubs, educational and other self-help projects came to co-ordinate and give visible identity to the black community, and in some respects to superimpose new networks of kinship and association on the older, fading, white working-class patterns.

Due to stark differences in the age structure of the Afro-Caribbean and white populations, amongst the total population of those of fifteen years old and under in 1971, nearly 45% were black – a fact of special relevance to the issue of inter-racial friendship, for this greatly influenced both the school and neighbourhood experience of young people. Many of these young people were entering the labour market in the early 1980s, during the period of my fieldwork, when unemployment generally, and amongst the young especially, had begun to increase to alarming levels. These conditions were far worse for black youngsters than for whites, for even in 1977 black school leavers were three times more likely than whites to be unemployed six months after leaving school. By 1981 the local rate of unemployment amongst sixteen to nineteen-year-olds was over 30% and amongst blacks unemployment was 'considerably higher' than amongst other groups.

Thus, while the racial composition of the area had changed considerably since the 1950s and the derelict appearance of the neighbourhood had been transformed by local authority residential development, the poverty and unemployment which had contributed to its notoriety a hundred years before remained the same, but without the economic securities of earlier years. It remained as it had been for most of the century, a depressed lower-working-class district, albeit one with a strong sense of identity.

The differences between Areas A and B, for the young people whom I interviewed and recorded, were, in experiential terms, considerable. Young blacks from Area B, although in little doubt about the nature of racism, could at least feel relaxed in their neighbourhood, while those in Area A were forced to create their own adolescent community and for self-defence assume a certain wary posture towards the whites – placing perhaps even more stress on the signs of their cultural and racial identity than did the more numerous blacks of Area B. The Asians of Area B were very few, but those of Area A were generally conscious of the common white hostility towards them, while their parents did their best to create, in the family and through local Asian religious and other institutions, a supportive structure.

For young whites, and especially for those young whites with black friends, the differences between the areas were also clearly marked. Young whites in Area A with black school friends and acquaintances – and friends and acquaintances amongst youngsters of Asian parentage – were common. The same was true for the whites of Area B. Where the differences between the areas lay, however, was in the out-of-school patterns of friendship within which in-school friendships existed. As will be seen, friendship itself is not simply equatable with an absence of racist views amongst whites; and in this respect, purely school-located friendship is, although far preferable to lack of friendship, certainly not on its own a solution to white adolescent racist ideas and practices. The impact of black youth culture on the white adolescents of these areas was also quantitively different even though the mechanisms of such cultural relations are a somewhat different matter from the issue of friendship itself.

In what follows, Chapters 1 and 2 deal predominantly with inter-racial friendship and its social setting in the two research areas; Chapters 3, 4 and 5 deal with language issues; and Chapters 6 and 7 address certain ideological issues arising from the cultural and social relations between black and white adolescents. The question of the relationship between white and Asian youth, while clearly of great importance, was not included in the research, and constitutes a separate area which awaits investigation. It is only dealt with here in passing. This is in no way a reflection on the relative importance of Afro-Caribbean and Asian relationships to white youth, but of the necessary limitations on any single piece of research. To protect the identity of my informants it has been necessary to use pseudonyms throughout, and to assign to the research areas the names Area A and Area B. Similarly, letters have been substituted for the names of actual places and persons referred to in quotations from interviews. However, where place names occur in such a way as to give no indication of the research locations themselves, such names have been retained.

1

Inter-racial friendship in Area A

I

The process by which ideas and values concerning social groups become established and relayed within the adolescent community is in part related to the forms of adolescent association, including the friendship dyads, primary peer groups and extended groups which, like the family, provide a vehicle for cultural transmission varying in relation to their wider social and economic contexts. In this connection I found that certain of the patterns of association which I observed, and which have been documented by writers specifically concerned with the structure of adolescent peer groups (Savin-Williams 1980; Douvan and Adelson 1966: 174–228; Ausubel 1954: 341–89) were amongst the factors affecting the distribution of ideas and practices concerning race within the adolescent community. Specifically, I found with regard to white adolescents in Area A that, although expressions of racial hostility were widely apparent, they were far less prominent amongst girls than boys; and that a significant arena for the transmission of racial hostility amongst boys were the extended groups commonly found amongst boys but not amongst girls. Furthermore, the overlap of school-age and post-school-age sets characteristic of both boys' and girls' out-of-school friendship groups meant that links with post-school-age male extended groups, within which racist ideas and practices were especially evident, penetrated down into the culture of younger school-age boys to some degree. These factors significantly contributed to the nature of the social terrain within which particular inter-racial friendships were situated.

Amongst the differences in peer association attributable to gender which are commonly remarked on in the literature on friendship groups, strong dyadic friendships and small primary peer groups are usually attributed to girls; larger primary peer groups and extended groups are

17

observed more often for boys (Spiro 1965; Suttles 1968; Savin-Williams 1980; Henry 1963: 150). This generalisation was partly supported by my research, although the size of girls' primary groups was not always as small, by comparison with boys, as is often suggested. While girls' groups which conformed to the stereotype of dyadic 'best friends', or associations of threes and fours, were common, larger groups did also occur, especially within the institutional framework of school or youth club. Although girls' 'gangs' are notoriously uncommon (Suttles 1968; Thrasher 1927; McRobbie and Gerber 1976; Campbell 1981), they certainly existed within my research areas. Many schools experience 'trouble' with third and fourth-year girls' groups of this kind, and the establishment of 'girls' nights' in youth clubs have, by eliminating the predominance of 'boys' activities', capitalised on the often quite large girls' groups which are apparent on 'mixed' nights (Inner London Education Authority 1980). Beyond such institutional contexts, white girls' groups of any size are rare, although a small number of the black girls of Afro-Caribbean parentage whom I observed did associate in groups, of anything from five to ten members.

The principal difference between girls' and boys' friendship groups lay less in their size than in the existence or non-existence of effective links *between* groups. I found some boys' groups to be situated within quite large networks of male groups, whereas such networks were not paralleled by similarly linked girls' groups. Although boys' peer group networks contained only a minority of the boys' groups within the localities studied, their existence had a significant effect on inter-ethnic association, and on the promotion of racial hostility in the wider adolescent population.

The most extensive, although not necessarily the most bonded, were those organised around youth cultural styles such as 'soul boys' and 'skinheads'. However, style-groups were not the only way in which cultural continuities were related to organisational ones. Some groups of male adolescents who avoided any clear style identification also had extensive links with other groups which clearly promoted the flow of values, and which may well represent a form of male adolescent social organisation stretching back far beyond the postwar emergence of visible youth styles.

At the same time, the patterns of association between school-age and post-school-age adolescents also provided a basis for the relay of ideas and values. In school, adolescent friendships tend to form themselves within the strata of school year groups, while out-of-school school-age groups are usually based on a wider range. Adolescents who have left school also commonly associate within a wider age-range, often extending up to nineteen or twenty. Thus, although school-age and immediate post-school-age sets may be differentiated by the informal status accorded by school-leaving and by the rhythms of life after school at work, Further Education (FE) college or on the dole, in practice some overlap of these sets is common in the composition of out-of-school friendship groups. As will be seen below, this overlap also contributed to the flow of racial hostilities.

The effective flow of racism within the adolescent community is, however, both partial and inconsistent. The extent to which boys are affected by it depends on the extent of their contacts with the circuits within which racism is relayed and acted out. Indeed, some boys resemble girls in being relatively isolated from the direct impingement of such male networks, and it is more often amongst these boys that those having close black friends are found. Nevertheless, the attitudes and practices of both girls and boys of this kind are best seen in relation to the boys' networks. For this reason I conducted a limited amount of background ethnographic research which served to contextualise the information on inter-ethnic friendship gathered in the interviews and in the course of participant observation. The following account of two boys' groups is derived from the results of that ethnographic work, and is presented here to provide some idea of the context within which the inter-racial friendships which I investigated were situated.

Group 1 (non-style based)

This group of eleven friends met every Friday night to drink at a pub called 'The Swan'. They were not a 'gang'. They were simply a drinking fraternity, although (with the exception of some members) they did, as a group, occasionally become involved in fights. They were not, however, a 'conflict group' in the sense intended by Cloward and Ohlin (1960: 20).

The core of this group consisted of five close friends who referred to themselves as 'The Five'. These were Kevin (17), an apprentice chef; Martin (19), a post office counter clerk; Derek (19), an electrician; Peter (17), a fitter; and Mick (18), a sixth-former still at school. They did not live near to each other but were spread out within a two-mile radius. They were not, therefore, a friendship group growing out of a single close neighbourhood.

This core group attended parties, discos and pubs together within Area A independently of the other members of the group, and were also bound by the mutual exchange of help related to their different skills. Martin would help any of the others with advice over such things as car tax, driving tests, passports etc.; Derek would help with any electrical work, usually on cars; Peter, who had the necessary contacts, obtained any soft drugs required by the others, especially for use at parties; Kevin would provide catering for his friends' family functions and was also something of a 'father-confessor' for the group. Mick, regarded as the 'boffin', was occasionally consulted about such things as the meaning of words or information that required knowledge about how to use books for reference.

'The Five' were connected to two senior age-set groups through the older siblings of two of them. Mick had an older brother in a large group of young Irish Catholics in the twenty-one to twenty-eight age range, known as 'The Mulligans', and Kevin had two half-brothers in a similar group known as 'The Family'. The Family comprised about fifteen members, all white English, who were mainly qualified tradesmen – painters, bricklayers, scaffolders, etc. All, with the exception of one or two, had been skinheads in the early 1970s. They were strong supporters of West Ham football club and they were given to frequent fighting. The Family had a history of fierce feuding with the Mulligans, but this had died down in recent years. The fact that the younger age-group had kin in both senior groups was, in any case, insignificant, as Mick had little to do with his brothers and his friends. Kevin, however, was regarded as one of the group at West Ham, and did have strong ties with his older half-brothers.

Because of the age of this senior group, they were prone to some diminishing of their numbers through the effects of marriage, employment migration or simply a 'softening' with age. Hence a slow but discernible transformation took place over the research period, in which some of The Five would begin a kind of apprenticeship through example, as junior acolytes of The Family. They would occasionally be invited to join the older group on drinking nights or even attend their parties. This process was partially one of replenishment of The Family from below, although they also grew into a separately constituted (if junior) group in their own right. Indeed, they were sometimes referred to by The Family as the 'under-fives team'. It was assumed that they would in time come to constitute another similar group themselves, deriving some of their practices and values from this informal tutelage, underscored by numerous anecdotes and accounts of fights, drinking bouts and so on.

The wider group of eleven of which The Five were the core also contained James (18), Jim (18), Trevor (18), John (19), Alan (19) and Del (19), who were, like The Five, mainly in trades or apprenticeships. The lending of money between the members of this group was a regular occurrence, although with certain differentiations related to the closeness of association *within* the group. With the exception of Jim,

Trevor, John and James, any of the group would lend amounts of up to about £20 to any other until pay day, or some other fixed date. Jim, Trevor, John and James were not lent, and did not lend, amounts above about £5. Thus The Five, plus Del and Alan, were closer in this respect than the other four. This economic pattern coincided with a quite separate division related to reliability in fighting. Each of the four who were most weakly integrated into the economy of the group were also regarded either as poor fighters or as likely to run away in a fight.

The exchange of mutual support in fighting was very important to the cohesiveness of the group. The degree to which members expected support from each other in fighting was directly related to the extent to which they gave it, and different members had different expectations regarding the support they might receive. Thus John, who consistently ran away from fights, actually failed to call out to the others when he was set upon outside a pub because he was not sure that they would respond to his call. Others would have known that they would have received help.

Loyalty in fighting was highly valued by the core members, and its realisation effected powerful ties. As one of them expressed it, 'What brings you really close is when you see a geezer risking his neck for you in a fight.' Fights were common, caused by numerous petty incidents involving potential loss of pride, and, regardless of detail, any one of the group who gave such support could legitimately ask any or all of the others for help if needed. In their terms they would 'die for each other'. They fought, they said, principally because they enjoyed fighting, and they looked down on style-groups like skinheads who offered social or political explanations for their actions: 'It's not rebelling or anything like that. We fight because we enjoy it.'

> If someone phoned me up and said, 'We've got some trouble,' I'd enjoy it. You're giving it the Big One. You're going along with the crowd. It's a row. 'Old Kev was there, he done this, he done that.' You talk about it afterwards, 'Cor, Derek went in good.' After a week it's forgotten. Spur of the moment . . . and you're a big hero afterwards. If you've done all right, that is . . . I'm just a fuckin' hooligan but I *admit* it.

Their links with other groups also meant that if a feud developed to a degree beyond what they could handle themselves, they could call upon outside support and in turn be called upon. The other lateral groups to whom they were occasionally allied were drawn principally from the other pubs where some of them drank (the King George, the Jolly Farmers, and The Ship), although there were other 'firms' of youngsters who were not necessarily associated with any one pub. Although the support was, in effect, of one group by another, or by several others, the actual request for help was made between individual contacts because not all members of a group could have equal claims on all the members of another group. In some cases favours were owed, even stretching back to school days, in others help was offered merely to demonstrate friendship. Because of this pattern of group association, it was often the case that several members of one group would not even know some of the people for whom they would be fighting:

> If it was a bad punch-up you're talking about the seven or more of us, all the Farmers, all the George mob, all the Ship mob. If it was really heavy I could get my brothers' lot and so on. You see, Derek and Martin would do the business with all the George lot. They'd say, 'We're having a bit of trouble. Do you fancy coming up "The World" for a drink. There might be a bit of trouble.' And Del would tell Paul Williams and his mates, 'We're going up thing tonight. Kevin's havin' a bit of trouble.' So they'd go up there. We'd all sort of stroll in, in threes and fours, and gradually all the Farmers would say, 'What's the trouble, Kev?' and I'd go, 'It ain't me, it's me mates there' – who they don't know – 'We're having a bit of trouble with this geezer's mob.' They'd just ask me who're we with and where's the enemy, like, and that's good enough, if we're in trouble, and vice versa.

Although there is an element of assumed network support in this imagined scenario, the following account of a real event shows sufficient closeness to it:

> The mob from 'The Ship' had some trouble down 'Two Thousand and One' [a disco club] about a month ago. So last week they all arranged to go down there. A message came to one of our lot. Micky comes to me, he goes, 'The Ship mob are goin' down "Two Thousand and One". They had a bit of trouble down there last week.' The governor's son, Mark, who's our age, asked if our lot could go down there. So we went up The Ship that night. There was a load of people from the Talisman there too. About a hundred, I'd say, were there.

Thus they were brought together with a group with whom they had had little direct contact, 'the lot from the Talisman', in an alliance effected by 'The Ship mob'.

This network of groups was mobilised to fight through selected contacts on the basis of already established ties, debts and friendship histories. The same network also functioned as the relay for information about parties, goods for sale in the black economy, jobs etc., as well as gossip about people and the establishment of individual reputations.

A significant function of this relay was the dissemination of information about girls. Indeed, within the network there was an 'intelligence service' available to any male adolescent wishing to know the 'pedigree' of almost any girl in the district, and, unlike requests for help in fighting, no special selection of informants, made on the basis of close ties, was needed. Questions about girls could be asked of even quite remotely known network members with no sense of awkwardness or embarrassment:

> I wouldn't feel embarrassed asking another boy about a girl even if I'd only ever nodded to them, 'cos its *the* subject isn't it? Easier [as a subject] than fighting really. You don't walk up to a geezer you don't really know and say 'I've got some trouble, come and help me.' You don't *do* things like that. But birds, it's different, isn't it. It's the universal subject.

Some who were especially 'in the know' were, however, better informants than others:

> James Sutton has got the memory of a computer for names and faces. If there's a geezer sees some bird he likes and asks James he goes 'Chris Slater', gives you the name of the road, goin' out with so and so ... You know, you get a computer read-out off James ... It's like a little team really.

Or again:

> One of your mates would know her name or where she goes, or whatever. Most of the time they say, 'She only lives round the corner from me. Her name's so and so', and, 'everyone's been through her', or she does this, or she's a nice girl, or whatever.

There clearly existed here both a relay of information and a common understanding of shared male concerns. Any girl wishing to obscure her past would have difficulty in this setting.

Such mutuality, however, had other dimensions beyond the exchange of information. The process of consultation contained an element of ambivalent nervousness about the opposite sex. As one informant said of such consultations, 'They're mainly worried about boy friends, big brothers, what she's like ... but mainly they're after a boost of confidence.' The need for peer group approval was imperative in relation to

girls, and the balance between personal desires and group opinion –
where personal desires were *shaped* by group opinion, not an uncommon
process – extended into that familiar conflict between life 'with the boys'
– drinking, fighting, having fun together – and the ultimate possibility of
settling down with a girl, ending in marriage and a family (Willmot 1969:
47–8; Daniel and McGuire 1972: 70). Stories of boys torn between the
peer group and the girl friend were common. On one occasion one of The
Five told the others that he was going to have to give up his girlfriend
because he had recently found himself asking her to marry him. When he
'realised what he had done' he thought he must have lost his senses. For
such boys the idea of 'settling down' is in strong contrast to the forms of
masculinity elaborated within the peer group.

These practices regarding gender relations contributed to a definition
of masculinity which is very different to that found in black male
adolescent peer groups, where individual skills with the opposite sex are
taken into the definition to a much greater extent. This is also consistent
with some of the strands of thought found within the black community
regarding the family, such as the view that the production of children is
one of the measures of masculinity, and not, as it is in the view of many
white males, the beginning of its end. Furthermore, a higher degree of
autonomy and independence for marriage partners, rooted in the various
traditional practices of Caribbean family life, means that the family is
seen far less as constricting male personal freedom. Such factors promote
forms of gender relations between black adolescents which, as group
practices, are distinct from those of the white adolescents studied.

For the white male peer group described here, the complex formed by
gender relations and peer group solidarity became related to the question
of race where their territoriality involved competition with black adolescents for cultural space. Here, gender-relation practices of the information network combined with the fear of black encroachment so that
one of the most significant questions to be asked about a girl was 'Is she
nigger-meat?':

> My mate Paul asked me about this girl I know.
> 'She goes to your school, don't she, Mick?'
> 'Yes. Nigger-meat.'
> He goes, 'Oh, right' – 'Cos if I didn't tell 'im and he went out
> with it and then found out what she'd been up to ...

Another of the group, talking about white girls who go out with black
boys said, 'They're fuckin' labelled ... Not many white people want to
know them ... "nigger-meat", you know. Well, it's treason, isn't it?'
Here again, group approval was central. The boy quoted here said, when

asked what would happen if a boy went out with a girl who had in the remote past been out with a black boy, 'If your mates knew she'd went out with a wog then you'd get some stick.'

During the early part of the research period there was a reported increase in the number of white girls going out with black boys. This was referred to as a current 'fashion' by the girls themselves, as well as by black boys and girls. White boys felt it particularly acutely, and the issue became intimately bound up with the question of territoriality. Referring to a local youth club which for a while attracted both black and white members in large numbers, one boy said, 'Down St Mary's it was always the whites who took a back seat . . . with the birds and everything. The blacks all thought they was tough.'

Here, where colour rendered the male 'universal subject' less than universal, 'masculinity' was threatened, while territoriality was increased. The territoriality was not based on local geographical boundaries, although it had at times a purely topographical expression: 'Why should they [young blacks] walk through the High Street at half-past eleven, having superiority over our territory just 'cos we drink up town? This is *our* place.' 'Place' in this simple sense of territorial possession was, however, something of an abstraction, and the boundaries between black and white adolescent groups were more commonly construed as cultural rather than geographical:

> Race? All the politicians, socialists, serious people get it
> wrong. It's just like mods and rockers, teds and punks. Their
> fashion [that of black adolescents] just totally disagrees with
> us. And it's a fashion. They're not Rastafarians. They don't
> even *believe* in God. It's just a big image and it's a shit fashion
> as far as I'm concerned. Their fashion is just anti everything
> that we're sort of thinkin'. It's a fashion but you'd never get
> them to admit it. 'I-man, I dread, mi music, mi colour, my
> background, my roots.' Fuck their roots – it's a fashion.

There is in this statement a clear attempt to deny political or social meanings that might be derived from conceding to black youth style any authentic claims to ethnic integrity. It is also noteworthy that the statement comes from a member of a group which itself eschewed visible youth styles, and regarded as spurious the interpretative social gloss placed on such styles by their users and by popular sociological commentators.

Although some elements in 'mod' style (of the late mod revival) did occasionally inflect their dress – in keeping with Phil Cohen's (1972) observation of the mod style of the 1960s that it reflected an upwardly aspiring 'respectable working class' orientation – this group did not see themselves as mods, and would have regarded conflicts with other groups purely on the grounds of style as beneath them. This strategic reduction of black youth style to the level of fashion was principally a denial of the advantage that an authentically ethnic youth style might be seen to bestow. The motive force behind this strategy lay in their actual experience of contacts with black adolescent *groups*, as distinct from contacts with individual blacks at school or work.

The 1970s had produced a significant increase in the numbers of black teenagers, and a rapidly developing black youth culture which gave a confidence to black adolescents in relation to the white community. In Area A, where Afro-Caribbean families represent the smallest distinct ethnic group, adolescents participated in this confidence but remained merely a cultural enclave, geographically dispersed within a racially mixed but predominantly white environment. Black adolescents tended either to opt for an integrationist tactic, keeping a low ethnic profile in small black or even largely white friendship groups (where they often gained a reputation amongst whites for mildness), or they chose to emphasise their ethnicity in black groups which stressed the blazonry of black youth culture in dress and speech.

Far from accepting the inferiority ascribed to them by whites, many despised the white community for its cowardly racism and what they saw as its cultural insipidness, in contrast to a vigorous black culture with its continuities in both England and the Americas. Amongst boys there was also evident a strong sense of pride in their traditions of prowess displayed in the field of sport, and in their reputation for effective street fighting. Something of this inevitably carried over into their dealings with white boys, who grew resentful of the disdain to which they were sometimes subjected.

Incidents in which the assertiveness of black boys challenged white male dignity were commonly relayed as news, interpreted through a framework of 'knowledge' about black youth derived both from local white adolescent folklore and media representations. The following account of just such a challenge may serve to illustrate the point. On this occasion Kevin recalls how he was on the top deck of a bus together with Martin, Derek and Derek's girl friend. The bus stopped at the Lord Harlow (a pub with an almost exclusively black clientele) and a large group of young blacks got on. According to Kevin they were very noisy, and several argued with the conductor about paying their fares:

> Then they all came upstairs and gradually worked their way
> down filling up the seats. And I'm sitting there with Derek and
> his bird to me left, and Martin sitting in the corner on the back

seat (he's got a fractured wrist where he spanked a couple of blokes last week) and there's one seat between me and them, and I'm just sitting looking forward, like . . . And this cunt come up to me an' he goes striking down the seat 'Come on! Move it! Move ya rass! Com on ya white man, move yer fuckin' rass!' And I just looked up at him, you know. The fucking' fury! If *any* man does that to me, let alone *this* cunt! And I thought, Derek's got his bird there, Martin's got a broken arm. I'd love to do it, just to spank that cunt. And I'd do it before I got murdered, but then I thought I'd be cut to fuck. I mean I'd be stabbed. I knew it. I mean you're talking about fifty geezers – blacks – one of 'em's sure to have a blade and they'd love some of that. So I thought, 'Here goes another Terry, mate,' so I just moved me leg, like that . . .
[demonstrating a gesture of grudging compliance]

The one-to-one insult was obviously deeply felt, and was for Kevin one of the absolute certainties making middle-class liberal arguments for a generalised racial tolerance seem 'soft' and devoid of any real experience of street life. However, in the process of narration, this event becomes embedded within the pre-existing local and national discourses which obtain with regard to race. The remarks, 'One of 'em's sure to have a blade' and 'they'd love some of that', were clearly derived from local 'street knowledge', while the reference to Terry May, whose death by stabbing by one of a group of black assailants was dramatically covered in the national press, guaranteed the place of such 'knowledge' within a wider framework. Like the racism which is enacted whenever phrases like 'nigger-meat' are employed, this kind of lore, with its implicit meanings and cultural underpinnings, becomes transmitted, albeit patchily, beyond the friendship network in which it is initially consti-tuted, into the surrounding adolescent social terrain.

Expressions of hostility to young blacks were commonplace for this group (although by no means commonplace as far as older blacks were concerned). The influence of national events – or, more accurately, media representations of national events – significantly contributed to the interpretations of local interactions, and frequently a shadow of national issues was cast across the purely local ecology of relation-ships.

Although only one or two of the core group had black acquaintances, the older group had all, when younger, known and been on good terms with black boys. Changes at the local and national level had since contributed to the erosion of those friendships. As one of the younger group put it:

> The older lot used to live and talk and play and fuck with
> black people. Now cos of all the tensions and the mounting
> thing, and all the black friends they used to have are going
> away into their little Rasta world . . . talkin' all this shit [i.e.
> creole] . . . but they still see 'em, talk to 'em.

And again:

> They've seen Brixton, they've seen Bristol, they've seen Terry
> May, they see all the Carnivals. They don't like it. It's not
> black[ness that they're against], it's taking liberties in their
> own territory.

Here 'their own territory' clearly becomes transformed into England
itself.

Although this group of friends would, through such instruments as
attitude surveys, appear to be highly racially prejudiced, in fact their
'attitudes' were rather complex formations, derived from a number of
sources, some of which were very stable, others of which were more
volatile. In view of the interventions in youth culture by racialist political groups that will be discussed below, it is worthy of note here that
such explicit political ideology as this group subscribed to was not of the
far right. The majority of them came from traditional Labour-voting
families, voted or said they would vote for the Labour Party themselves,
and regarded the National Front with considerable scorn. Several were
also committed trade union members. Furthermore, the senior age-
group were also strong Labour supporters, with the exception of one
who proselytised for Trotskyism, and who would insist on the unity of
black and white class interests to his friends whilst still engaging in mild
forms of racial abuse on and around the football terraces. Besides the
majority of Labour supporters, the younger group also contained one
enthusiast for Margaret Thatcher, and even a stray National Front
supporter. Indeed, despite the Labour majority, there was a high degree
of tolerance for, and even lack of interest in, the *explicit* political and
broad social philosophies of members. What varied far less were the
group practices and beliefs surrounding loyalty, and the values of personal and group pride to which racialist ideas and practices became
attached. It is therefore necessary to discriminate between racial ideology as an explicit philosophy, and racial ideology enshrined in a set of
behavioural practices which knitted with the overriding mores of the
group.

That the racial attitudes of this group cannot simply be reduced to the
effects of their territoriality, the 'stridency' of black youth culture, or the

relationship between the two, is evident from the impact of *external* factors on the defining processes of racial interactions. Besides the effects of media representations commented on above, the racial attitudes absorbed in early childhood were also an important element in how interactions were interpreted. The contrast between the confidence of black adolescents in their dealing with whites and white 'social knowledge' of black 'inferiority' was occasionally invoked by the boys when attempting to explain their feelings of dislike for young blacks. Furthermore, attitudes to Asians, *never* restricted simply to young Asians, were by no means derived from adolescent inter-group experiences. As one boy put it:

> Even in primary school my racialist feelings about Pakistanis were I just didn't like them. And that has been so pounded into you, 'Paki is bad' . . . I know its wrong but nothing's going to change me. I just don't like 'em. I hate them.

However, Asian/English youth did not pose the kind of challenge posed by Afro-Caribbean/English youth, and therefore these racial hostilities were not elaborated through the vocabulary of adolescent rivalries. By contrast, early knowledge of the imputation of racial inferiority to Afro-Caribbeans – and indeed to all black people – *did* articulate with conflicts in the adolescent community, and did contribute to the process which served to justify and explain hostilities.

While there did emerge what some writers might regard as a 'culture conflict', the form it took was predicated upon pre-existing notions of the social status of blacks, received from the dominant culture. The idea that blacks *in general* were fundamentally inferior was part of what was 'known' and accepted unquestioningly about the social status of particular black acquaintances. Such black acquaintances were able to be accepted as even 'quite good friends', just as unskilled or unemployed adolescents from lower-working-class homes might be. When black adolescents began collectively to challenge the basis of this classification, however, and to emphasise their ethnicity to the extent that it rose to prominence above the broad class definitions, then racism became activated in explicit forms.

The significance of the network in which this group was situated lay especially in that network's capacity, under certain conditions, to relay and boost these 'racial' attitudes and practices within itself, and to achieve a consensus of meanings and terms which spread beyond the network to penetrate, although unevenly, the wider and less formally coherent structures of adolescent association. This aspect will be returned to below.

Group 2: a skinhead gang

In distinct contrast to the friendship group and their network described
above were the associations of adolescents based on 'skinhead' style
which had first emerged in the late 1960s and early 1970s. The revival of
skinhead style began in 1977, but was not at first associated with racialist
politics. Indeed, like its precursor, it actually drew on black youth
culture, especially with regard to musical taste. By early 1980, however,
the popularity of the 'two-tone' bands had begun to wane. The racism
with which the style later came to be associated, and which had been
present in the initial skinhead movement with regard to Asians, gradually asserted itself. This was not merely an impromptu internal development but the result of a conscious attempt by the neo-Nazi political group
known as the British Movement to subvert the exaggerated working-
class imagery of skinhead style to its own ends. This attempt to forge an
associative link between racialist politics and skinhead style was largely
successful. Stickers were produced reading simply 'Skins Hate Wogs',
and skinheads were characterised in British Movement literature as
representatives of a working class oppressed by police and the Home
Office for 'fighting for a white country'. When it became clear that
skinhead style had become almost synonymous with racialist politics, the
National Front organisers also directed their attention more vigorously
toward the young.

Racialist attacks on black and Asian people increased to alarming
proportions in Area A over this same period, and a lengthy dossier of
such attacks was compiled by an Asian advice centre and handed to the
local police commander. But it was not until the press began to carry
feature articles on the skinheads and their Nazi connections that the
police started to take concerted action against skinheads. The form
which this action took was essentially that of 'stop and search' tactics
applied very generally to any youngster who could be identified as a
skinhead. Reports of racial attacks were, according to black and Asian
community workers, still not investigated vigorously, and workers within
these communities felt that the 'harrassment' of skinheads in general was
something of a substitute for the proper measures that should have been
taken in specific instances of racial attack. Such tactics did, however,
have the effect of driving many youngsters to abandon skinhead style,
while others became even more committed, seeing themselves as pitched
against both the institutions of the state and the 'immigrant' communities.

By no means all adolescents who chose to adopt skinhead style were
involved with racialist politics or with racial attacks. Many merely liked

the style and the music and had no real objection to the wider social meanings with which it became associated; but the existence of the style did provide the basis for the formation of gangs whose ultimate social identity was largely predetermined by the most prominent group ideology available, that of racism.

Between September 1980 and May 1981, I conducted research by interview and participant observation into the activities and composition of a skinhead gang whose numbers grew from five to thirty at the height of its most active period. The gang's members were drawn from a larger geographical area and a wider age-range than the group described in the previous section. The youngest was fourteen years old, the oldest was a council worker in his late twenties, and the majority of the group were between sixteen and nineteen years old.

The gang began to take form when a bus shelter which contained benches became adopted as a 'hang-out' and meeting place for five skinhead boys. They were gradually joined by several others, and, with the use of graffiti and numerous acts of vandalism, they began to mark out a clear territory in the surrounding streets, with the shelter as its centre. The graffiti they employed consisted of the names of bands, and abuse directed at anyone following the mod style, which was also enjoying something of a revival at the time. Recruitment to the group took place casually and was based not on any pre-existing friendship ties but principally on the adoption of skinhead style, although new members tended to join in groups of two and three. Barry (nineteen), for example, was standing on a street corner with Mick (eighteen) when three of the gang approached them and asked if they wanted to go 'mod-bashing'. They agreed, and thereafter joined the gang regularly in the bus shelter. On another occasion, one of the gang told me, 'Some skins came round the corner and said, "We heard there's a lot of skinheads coming about." So they stuck with us till the Old Bill split us up, so we didn't see 'em again.' The gang was essentially formed as a conflict group, with mods conceived as the opposition.

The initial members were Jerry, the fourteen-year-old, who was living away from his mother in a children's home and who had been expelled from two local schools for misbehaviour. No other school was prepared to take him, so he was on the streets all day. A child welfare officer had occasional contact with him, but Jerry disliked living at the home, and was repeatedly running away and being returned by the police. His sprightly and resilient personality made him popular with the welfare officials I interviewed who had dealings with him, while his 'cheekiness' towards adults in general made him popular with youngsters of his own age. Another of the initial members was Terry, who was in his last months of school when the gang was first formed. He was tall and well-built for his age (fifteen) and presented a clean, stylish appearance, with very short hair rather than the almost total baldness of most of the others. His father was a carpenter, but when Terry left school with a few CSEs he joined an East End firm of painters and decorators. A third member was Rich (seventeen), who was unemployed. He had often been in trouble with the police for petty theft and taking and driving away cars. He had for a while worked for the local Co-op supermarket, but had been discharged, and had not managed to get another job. Dave, a council labourer, claimed to be twenty-five, although it was believed by some that he was nearer thirty. His short, stocky build, vociferous support for racialist politics and firm commitment to 'go on being a skinhead for as long as possible' enabled him, with some awkwardness, to fit in with the younger members, and to be regarded by some as the gang's effective leader. Two brothers, Jake (nineteen) and Warren (eighteen), knew Jerry from the children's home, where they too had lived for a while. Jake worked on a building site as a labourer, and Warren was formally unemployed, although he supported himself by housebreaking and petty theft. He was arrested for burglary and the possession of firearms in December 1980 and was subsequently imprisoned. Although the gang did bring together people such as Barry, mentioned earlier, and Steve (seventeen) who then worked together on thieving expeditions, these activities were extra-curricular to the recognised activities of the gang itself.

While this heterogeneous group constituted the initial core of members, over the last months of 1980 it gradually attracted others, many of whom were refugees from areas where the police had become particularly active against skinheads. A large proportion of the gang were unemployed, while those who were in employment were exclusively in unskilled, menial jobs. A few were still at school. They lacked the cohesiveness and multiplicity of ties which characterised the friendship group described above, although the style itself provided an instant and synthetic, if limited, version of those ties, and was capable of extending to any number of male adolescents and of forming the basis of many alliances of varying durability.

The identification of the gang with racialist politics was initially weak. Through the influence of Dave, 'NF' signs soon became a feature of their graffiti, and Jerry chose to dub himself 'Jerry the Gasser' in his wall inscriptions. Warren, however, acquired a swastika armband from a stall in Petticoat Lane, wearing it at all times, and others also followed him in this. It was not until the British Movement organised a march and rally in Welling, in October 1980, which the gang attended in force that they came to extend their vandalism and violence to the Asian and black community. Soon after this march, an attack on an Asian shop was made by eight of the gang, who sprayed swastikas on the walls and kicked in the windows. This was followed by three similar attacks over the following months. They also turned their attention to black adolescents from a nearby school, ambushing a group of black boys and attacking them with half-bricks. These events, and the self-publicity which followed on walls and on the seats of buses, initiated several waves of new membership and helped to replace the style-group conflict with a strongly racialist purpose.

Dave, who was a member of the National Front, provided one source of information about political rallies and marches, although Terry had also developed contacts with members of the far-right group Viking Youth. However, the British Movement was very active in the area, and the boys were usually well supplied with leaflets and stickers. On one occasion Steve and Terry went to the house of a local British Movement 'manager'. This man gave them a supply of leaflets and American Ku Klux Klan papers, which they showed me with obvious pride. On another occasion Jerry told me:

> I saw this geezer in a tee-shirt going round puttin' up stickers saying, 'Niggers Watch Out the Race War is Coming Soon'. It had at the bottom, 'White Independent Nationalists' – which is WIN. I called out, 'All right' to him and we had a little chat. He said 'e used to be a skinhead once.

I was also told by one of the gang who was still at school that a boy in his class was always disseminating British Movement leaflets and news-papers.

The racialist identity of the group, fed from such sources, actively transformed even those who had not previously considered racialism. Terry, for example, had had black acquaintances at school with whom he was on good terms. His involvement with skinhead style had initially been because he liked the music and the style of dress. He commented, however, that 'Since I've been hanging around with this lot I've become much more racialist ... That changed me, being a skinhead. I wasn't racialist when I wasn't a skinhead. I was a skinhead 'cos of the music, then I got more involved. Got more involved in the clothes and the politics came along with it ... I'm working-class and I'm proud of working-class.' The connection between skinhead racialism and class pride seemed obvious to him: 'I've always thought of myself as working-class and since I've been a skinhead I'm more proud of being working-class.' His notion of class, however, was unrelated to anything to do with the terms of employment: 'Don't like the unions, especially big ones, TUC and all that – goin' over to Russia for their holidays.' But he did not like to discuss class politics with reference to work: 'I don't talk about politics like that. The only politics I talk is racialist and anti-commie.' He had also developed a keen sense of which groups of people he did not like: 'I've built up a hate against upper-class and all that. Can't stand their voices. And somehow I've got a hatred against Yanks. Went to France, don't like the French. Don't like Commies. Don't like Italians ... The only thing I like, I like the Irish but what I hate is the IRA. Scottish are all right. Welsh are all right ... I've just built up a hate for every other country 'cept England.'

The semiotics of class and politics were written into their involvement with skinhead style at many levels, from the outward display of 'White Power' badges down to the colour of their bootlaces, where white laces were worn to show National Front support, red laces indicated British Movement support. The same colour-coding also extended to socks and braces, and, as Terry told me, 'braces mean working-class'. Despite this colour-coding, support for the two racialist political groups was not regarded as divisive but merely a choice between complementaries. There was, however, a strong preference for the British Movement amongst the group, partly because the BM demanded little from their members, while the NF liked them to attend meetings and read pamphlets. In fact, only five of the gang actually joined the BM and one the NF, although a number of them did volunteer their services to the local NF candidate in the Greater London Council elections in March 1981 and subsequently went out leafleting.

Although derogatory references to blacks were common, their strongest feelings were reserved for Asians. Their hostility was fed by numerous myths propagated, it would seem, by the newspapers of the racialist parties. I was told with passionate certainty, 'When they come to this country, the Pakis, the government give them a thousand pounds. That's right. A family comes in, they give them a thousand pounds. They say, "We'll bring our parents over" – another thousand pounds. "We'll bring our kids over" – another thousand pounds. And then they've got enough money to buy their shops.'

The spraying of Asian shops became commonplace for the gang and on at least two occasions they beat up young Asians in the street. They admitted to no qualms about this behaviour. When they were discussing their first attack on an Asian shop with me on one occasion, one said that the shopkeeper was lucky that they had not used a firebomb. Although they never did, to the best of my knowledge, extend their activities to anything on that scale, they regularly fantasised along such lines. I asked them on this occasion whether they would not feel mean about doing such a thing. They all replied that they would not. The interview continued:

What if someone got killed?
STEVE: Well, it's one less isn't it?
DAVE: That's their problem, innit?
What if a kid got killed?
STEVE: I wouldn't care. Couldn't give a toss really. It's another one, innit?

They were considerably less vocal about black adolescents, whom they clearly feared, although they justified their attack on the black school-boys on the grounds that they were acting to redress what they claimed to be the 'bullying' of a white boy by a black boy in the school. As a result of this incident they saw themselves as a vigilante group protecting whites against blacks, although in fact they did not engage in such activities again:

> Face the facts. Some of our skinheads have been beaten up round here, right? And the word gets around amongst the skinheads round here and they go out for revenge. And the blacks don't like it when we hit back at them. We don't go around deliberately provoking them. It's only when they start picking on white blokes. I mean you've got schools where blacks pick on the white guys now and we get to hear about it and we come down and have a bash at them.

Apart from the single occasion referred to above, this self-characteri-sation was entirely fantasy. As a gang they avoided further confrontation with local black boys, although some members did take part in attacks on blacks made by aggregations of other gangs with the same racialist orientation.

The police were repeatedly credited with protecting blacks and Asians whilst victimising skinheads. Indeed, their hatred for the police was often just as vehement as their dislike for blacks and Asians, and was given expression in gory fantasies of massive skinhead revenge. William Whitelaw, as Home Secretary, was particularly singled out for criticism on a number of occasions. 'I think William Whitelaw is black', one commented, while Dave added, 'He's talking about he's going to bring in anti-race units, police units. Now basically to us skinheads that means against us. That's how we look at it. They're trying to intimidate us.'

Although this gang did not attract all of the adolescents who adopted skinhead style within the vicinity of their territory, and while many kept their distance because of the gang's reputation for 'trouble', they were not unique. Gangs like them, and aggregates of such gangs with as many as one and two hundred members, had been involved in racialist attacks which were widely reported in the local press. Furthermore, following the disturbances in Bristol and later in Brixton and Toxteth, self-styled vigilante gangs, such as one that called itself 'The Bench', containing adolescents in their late teens and early twenties, also responded to the attention black youngsters were receiving in the press by setting on black adolescents whenever the opportunity arose. Following the events in Bristol in particular, a gang of about sixty white boys patrolled the town centre in Area A calling out a challenge to fight any black youngsters they saw in 'reprisal' for Bristol. A group of about twenty black boys did assemble to fight them and were badly beaten.

This 'political' phase lasted for only about two years, and such violence was not permanent throughout the research period. It did, nevertheless, contribute to the background of racialism against which adolescents who were not involved either in racialist politics or in skinhead style grew up. Furthermore, because skinhead style attracted adolescents from a wide age-range, its racialism penetrated directly into schools more keenly than did that of the largely post-school adolescent networks described in the previous section.

The skinhead gang differed from Group 1 in a number of respects. Firstly, they were drawn from a stratum of the adolescent population within which unemployment was especially common, and they lacked any relation to the (albeit declining) traditions of Labour Party and trade union support which provided some background coherence for Group 1. Secondly, their method of recruitment to the gang, based less on pre-existing friendship ties than on style-group allegiance, meant that the nature of their association and the means by which their group identity was expressed was significantly different. Notably, there was a gap between the individual functions which gang membership served for each of them and the social identity of the gang *qua* gang.

What was achieved by the linking of skinhead style with an explicit racialist philosophy was a conceptual framework in which a unified 'working class', conceived of as without internal divisions, was starkly opposed to the 'middle-class' representatives of authority, and to the 'foreigners' whom those representatives were regarded as protecting. Much publicity was given by the racialist political groups to what they called 'commie teachers'. At the same time, the police were characterised as implementing the much-hated Race Relations Act to the impoverishment of white youth. The growth of interest in multi-cultural education in the schools, and the focusing of police attention on skinheads, provided them with an apparent proof that, at several levels, the state and social groups of more power than this imaginary 'working class' were allied against their interests. In the translation of this formula into the everyday iconography of skinhead style, these oppositions were enacted and bestowed with an apparent coherence at the cultural level that was clearly evident in the gang I studied.

By contrast, the adolescents of Group 1 had affinities which provided a different basis for their friendship associations. Their closest ties were with white adolescents who were occupationally similar to themselves, and while they accepted members of certain contiguous social groups as part of the same broad community, they simultaneously believed in their own superior status within it. Hence their attitude to skinheads had some features in common with their attitude to black youth. The skinheads were mainly lower-working-class or dislocated from any class community. They had most to gain from membership of a mythic 'working class' in which internal divisions were ignored in the interests of presenting an unbroken 'ethnic' front. They were highly dependent on the politicised racism of fascist propaganda to sustain this stance. But it was not surprising that the 'respectable working-class' adolescents of Group 1, while agreeing with skinheads in most of their racial attitudes, did not wish to be associated with their proletarianised version of working-class identity, and would have regarded skinhead self-presentation and racial politics with some scorn. It was also perfectly consistent that this same group should wish to reduce black youth culture to the level of a 'fashion', and to place it alongside what they called the 'silly little skinheads', for to accept *either* group on that group's own terms would have implied a reduction of their own status.

Both of the groups described here engaged in that aggregation of primary peer groups which has been observed for male adolescents in many cultures (Thrasher 1927; Eisenstadt 1956; Mead 1928; 1930; 1935; Mirsky 1937). The *ways* in which they did so, however, differed markedly, and were influenced partly by differences in class location and partly by the concepts concerning the collectivities of which they felt a part. Nevertheless, both contributed something to the level of racism amongst adolescents locally and to the normative status of that racism. Although the racism relayed within such groups extended unevenly into the local adolescent population, it provided a ubiquitous context to the inter-racial friendships which I investigated, provoking in black youngsters suspicions of latent racism in their white friends, and tensions of allegiance and awkwardly distorted behaviour, designed to allay such suspicions, amongst whites.

II

The process of diffusion could be seen most clearly in its impact on white adolescents who had a few black friends but most of whose friends were white. It was particularly apparent (*a*) in the way racist group practices provided an interpretative mechanism for the assessment of the everyday problems that occur in friendship, when those friendships were inter-racial, and (*b*) in the way direct pressure, in the form of explicitly critical comments, was applied to whites with black friends. The first of these factors was particularly apparent in male interview subjects who were not yet part of the kinds of white groups described above, but for whom such groups provided a reference point in the creation of their own social identities.

As has been seen, some members of both Group 1 and Group 2 had some black acquaintances, if not close friends. Beyond these groups it was also not uncommon for boys who had once had black friends, in school and out, to cease to have black friends and to begin to express racist opinions in certain contexts. When white adolescents told me, as many did, that they had once had black friends, but that when they reached a certain age their black friends had suddenly changed, and that hence their own attitude to blacks in general had changed, a number of different processes seemed to be converging. First, they had reached an age at which lateral *groups*, as well as individuals, became noticed and related to the self. Thus groups which may well have existed for some time were suddenly registered for the first time. This increased importance of 'group perceptions' often also entailed, if not membership of an extended peer group, certainly an awareness of such groups and of the racism enacted within them. Secondly some black adolescents were, like some white adolescents, coming together in groups and demonstrating a street presence that had not previously existed so obviously.

The weight that might be given to either of these factors was always difficult to assess, but such reports of the 'unaccountable' changes in black boys were common amongst the white boys I interviewed and any single explanation – including the interpretations offered by the boys themselves – was clearly inadequate. The following is a fairly typical example:

> I've grown up and I've known a lot of black people, you know, at school. Then when you come fourteen, fifteen, suddenly there was crowds of black geezers roamin' about town givin' you abuse, dressing fuckin' stupid, talkin' a load of shit, carrying knives, goin' '/ You rassclaht!', walkin' along, their heads up high as if everybody's against them and so I've disliked it.

This recognition of black adolescents as a group was repeatedly explained as the recognition of a new phenomenon, not as a recognition of something that had always existed, and was usually offered as an explanation for a change in their attitude to black youngsters in general.

Under the influence of this form of perception, the unique conditions of particular friendships became subtly blurred in many of the first-person descriptive accounts which I elicited. One boy who had black school friends, and some black acquaintances out of school, gradually came to turn against blacks during his last year in school. Finally he joined the British Movement. I had interviewed him twice before conducting the interview from which the following quotations are taken. On neither occasion had he expressed any hostility towards blacks – indeed he had been a close friend of several of the black boys in his year, and had expressed anti-racialist views to me. On the third occasion, however, just a few weeks before he was due to leave school at the age of sixteen, he told me that over the previous six months he had come to 'hate' blacks. When I asked him why he replied:

> The one main reason for my hatred is that they didn't want to recognise you no more. That was the one main reason and it just boiled up inside me. For months and months it's been boiling up inside me.

However, when pushed to specify particular friends who had acted in this way, the underlying group reference of this personalised explanation began to appear:

> No, it wasn't anyone particular. Still there's a couple that I like, you know what I mean. All the Eltons, Horace, and that, and there's one or two outside of school. One or two, but there ain't many out of the hundreds that I know, hundreds.

Towards the end of the same interview, the attempt at a personal, reasoned explanation had given way to one framed in terms of involuntary reactions:

> You have the feeling that you're going to go against them, the friends that you thought was friends. They walk along the street, you know what I mean, don't move out the way for no-one. All along the street. Right Flash Harrys.

At the same time, the contact necessarily provided by the school made it impossible for him to disentangle himself from his longstanding friendship with certain black boys. Indeed, he had no desire to do so. He overcame the inconsistency constructed within the interview by suspending judgement on his school friends:

> *But you don't 'hate' your school friends?*
> I can't hate them can I? 'Cos I've been going to school with
> 'em. I spose it might change when I leave school and I ain't
> seen them for a while. They might go the way the others went.
> Can't say now 'cos I see them every day.

Thus the adequacy of his generalisation about black adolescents was not
undermined by his friendly contact with particular individuals – a very
common condition, of course, long familiar in accounts of diverse race
relations contexts. But it was not only in the artificial situation of an
interview that the inconsistency was in danger of being exposed and
needed remedial action to suppress it, as here in the 'suspended
judgement'. Within the school he was driven to secrecy about his newly
articulated racialism, carefully keeping such opinions from his black
friends and taking trouble to hide his British Movement membership
from them. His BM membership, which was effected by a white
out-of-school friend, allied him with a 'white power' ideology which was
attractive to him largely because of its adoption by, at that time, an
increasing number of white adolescents. Although the stance and his
membership were shortlived, because he did not like the association
which the movement had with skinhead culture, it did temporarily
expose him to a stream of racialist propaganda in the form of leaflets,
stickers and newspapers which he subsequently received as a member,
and provided him with a broad rationale for his feelings of hostility
towards black people.

  The acknowledgement of differing 'racial' group allegiances could
enter into interpretations of particular friendship interactions at the most
minute level. Another boy, who subsequently experienced the same
transition as the boy quoted above, came to interpret difficulties in his
friendship with a certain black boy by reference to the fact that his friend
had a close black friend who was very involved in black youth culture.
His black friend was seen by this informant as turning against him
simultaneously with his induction into the culture. Again an individual
friendship became contextualised by reference to group relations:

> He made snidey little remarks, piss-taking, meant as a joke
> between him and Clive, but it, you know, gets home.
> *So you felt cut out?*
> No. I'm not cut out at all because I don't *need* him. If a white
> friend done that to me I'd feel bad about it.

The boy in question was this informant's last close black friend. By the
time he left school this white boy, too, had developed a strong generalised hostility to young blacks.

The emergent use of racial group categorisations by young white boys, derived from the convergence of racial categories in the prevailing culture and adolescent group perceptions, was further strengthened by the explicit criticism of whites with black friends by their white peers. The borderline of racial groups – continually attended to, as will be seen, on *both* sides – was strongly reinforced where group allegiances were thought to be in doubt. Where the majority of a white boy's friends were also white, the need to comply with group pressures was strongly felt. Little comment was usually needed to inform a friend that he was in danger of being thought a 'traitor' and to demand, in full confidence of a reply, an explanation for public displays of friendliness towards blacks. One boy illustrated the compromise he sometimes felt placed in by telling the following anecdote:

> Yesterday, when I was in the car with Steve, Rodney and Denis [two black friends] walked up. They go, 'All right, Al?' I goes, 'All right.' Steve goes, 'Who're those cunts?' And just to make it all happy for him, you know, 'cos he's a right fascist, I just said, 'They're my brother's pill-head friends. He scores off them.' He goes, 'That's all right then. Long as they're good for something.'

Through such small but socially informative incidents, boys with black friends were subjected to the pressure of peer group influence, and warned about the possibility of conflicting ties.

The appearance of racial group identities posed choices of identification which made difficult the maintenance of friendships unmediated by considerations of group allegiance. However much white boys might wish to choose friends on an individual basis, the pulls of group allegiances intervened constantly. Where most of their friends were white, the pull of white group allegiance, with its strong thread of articulated racism, was obviously stronger.

I found no evidence that the location of group identities was effected for girls through the lateral pressure of same-sex peer groups in the way it was for boys. While girls might be influenced towards racism by their immediate peer group and, in specific ways, by boys, their parents, the media and other sources, the powerful forms of same-sex peer group pressure, relayed and extended from group to group amongst boys, did not seem to exist for girls. As was suggested earlier, the actual *structure* of girls' peer groups was a significant factor here. The tendency towards smaller primary peer groups and the absence of extensive networks of groups may well have been important in inhibiting the relay of racism amongst girls' groups. It may also go some way towards accounting for the fact that expressions of racist attitudes were far less common amongst girls than amongst boys. Certainly the absence of such networks deprived girls of one of the contexts in which racism could be embodied in inter-group *practices*.

Linked to this question of peer group structure is that of territoriality. Although white girls I interviewed who held racialist views frequently employed the conventional vocabulary of racism in referring to Britain as a 'white people's country' and spoke disparagingly about districts of dense black population, such expressions were not mapped onto the immediate local territorial concerns which characterised some boys' groups. Equally absent were expressions of unease about the encroachment of black youth culture. This may have been related to the fact that amongst boys the competition for cultural space was often elaborated through perceived sexual rivalries. White girls did not compete with black girls for white boyfriends, even theoretically, and sexual rivalry, which apparently exacerbated the hegemonic struggles amongst boys, was totally absent. Furthermore, although girls' primary peer groups were much more open to changes in composition than boys' groups, 'falling out' with particular black female friends did not lead to the formulation of generalised group hostilities based on colour that were found amongst boys.

The adoption of skinhead style by girls was characteristically in association with boys, and highly dependent on identification with this essentially male culture through association. While the skinhead girls I interviewed, who were attached peripherally to Group 2, all expressed racialist views in discussion, they remained uninterested in racialist politics, and the boys did not attempt to involve the girls either in their political activities or in their racialist violence. It was readily accepted by the boys that girls were not interested in that level of commitment, and that, as the boys' politics was likely to be expressed in violence, girls were best 'out of the way'. A similar attitude in skinhead boys was described by Ian Walker (1982: 14) with regard to skinhead girls and the National Front, while the few girls I interviewed who were members of the National Front and attended marches did so independently of any wider group of male or female acquaintances. British Movement marches were also almost exclusively male. The racialist views of such girls who were involved did not appear to be relayed through any group practices beyond their immediate female circle.

In addition to this lack of female inter-group pressure, and the weakness of the appeal of the racialist political groups, girls who had black girl friends did not report the same kind of direct criticisms of their inter-racial friendships that many boys reported. Girls seem more content to 'live and let live' in regard to inter-racial friendships. Criticism from boys was, however, occasionally mentioned. White boys were primarily, but not exclusively, concerned with white girls' involvement with black boys, rather than with black girls. As gender mixing is almost as much a minority pursuit as racial mixing, except under the aegis of the boyfriend/girlfriend relation, it was mainly in the context of such relationships that attempts to influence white girls away from black friends took place. Some peer group pressure was therefore experienced by girls who were part of groups mainly consisting of white *couples*, and it was the boys who provided its major source. White boys frequently viewed contact between their girlfriends and black girls as potentially threatening, as this might lead to contact with black boys. It would seem that white boys would often express racist views in the company of girls as part of a preventative ritual of routinised ethnic hygiene. One girl told me how her boyfriend repeatedly referred to the youth club which she attended as full of 'coons'. She had many very good black friends at the club and greatly enjoyed her attendance there. When she replied to her boyfriend's jibes by saying, uncontroversially, 'I don't mind 'em', her boyfriend insisted, 'Well you'd *better* mind 'em'. The same informant told me that since going round with her boyfriend and his group she had come to hear a lot of expressions of racism:

> That's all I hear, the crowd I'm with at the moment. That's why I think it must be the 'in' thing to slag the blacks down, sort of thing, hate 'em all. It is getting worse . . . It's definitely getting sort of 'We're here, you're there. There's the river. Don't cross it.' *I* feel it is, in our little lot. And I'm thinkin', 'What way do you go? Stand in the middle and get shot or what?'

Girls who were not part of such peer groups, however, seem to have found it much easier than boys to maintain their inter-racial friendships, and I found many examples of friendships that were quite unharrassed by this kind of pressure.

The question 'What way do you go?' in response to white group pressure is difficult for adolescents to answer in a way favourable to inter-racial friendship, when the ideological supports of racism are far more acceptable in the local culture than any non-racist stance. Anti-black attitudes are the manifestation of a set of integrated ideological structures generated by social and economic relations, and supported at one level by stereotypes embedded in ways of perceiving and talking about race, often invisible to their users. At the same time, such conceptual templates may also provide a 'naturalistic' context for articulated racist opinions, which in turn can establish a benevolent environment for racialist politics. Where adolescent racism effectively interrogates whites with black friends, no similarly 'naturalistic' structures of thought and behaviour exist, embedded in the local culture, to support a non-racist or anti-racist stance.

The old liberal ideologies concerning racial tolerance, whilst having the virtue – with respect to easy white to white communication – of maintaining the basic conceptual structure of 'host' and 'immigrant', in which whites are seen as benevolently extending help and friendship to the 'ethnically disadvantaged', in fact have little purchase amongst the young white working class. By their association with the middle class, however, such ideas may constitute an element in upwardly aspiring working-class values, impressed on the young by parents who perceive an association of overt racialism with low status.

More prevalent amongst whites with black friends was the recourse to arguments concerning individual 'rights', contained within a belief in the inviolability of personal friendships over and above the demands of any group pressure exerted by other whites. Thus, one fifteen-year-old white boy with many black friends affirmed, 'It's my life ain't it? I lead it how I lead it. I don't care about no one else. They [other whites] do what they want so I can do what I want.' However, such appeals to an individual's 'right' to choose friends also represents an avoidance of principled formulations which might bring them into conflict with the white adolescent majority view. Such conflict would politicise the meaning of a friendship which they wish to maintain as a low-key personal matter. 'It's best to stay quiet' was a common philosophy of expedience which accompanied this view, and was regarded by many as the only safe response to pressure. Such a strategy suggests that legitimations of inter-racial friendship exist within an ideological vacuum and are felt to do so.

The only specific major initiative made in recent times to provide anti-racism with a coherent ideological support amongst young people was that of the Anti-Nazi League (ANL), which was launched in 1977 in an attempt to counter the advances of the National Front. Ben-Tovim and Gabriel (1982: 162) write:

> Through their imaginative use of popular music, their informal organisational structure, their high and simple propagandist profile ('Never Again' ... 'NF = No Fun' etc.) they seem to have helped win over to anti-racism, or at least to neutralise, sectors of working-class youth who would otherwise be far from the progressive movement, and potentially vulnerable to the appeal of fascism.

This initiative had a significant impact on young people for a while, and did begin to provide a broad cultural challenge which articulated with the rudiments of an ideological framework supportive of anti-racism. However, its narrow focus on opposing the National Front and other groups of the far right tied it too closely to a politics of confrontation which many youngsters, and especially those with black friends, wished to avoid. The initial period of ANL influence was well into decline by the time I began my fieldwork, and none of the white adolescents I interviewed who had close black friends was a member of the ANL. Most said explicitly that they would not wish to wear an ANL badge because they would not like to provoke the hostility of other whites. Some also said that their black friends would not like it, and that the ANL was 'just as bad as the NF' in causing street violence. In this they reflected a view that had been frequently expressed by sections of the press since the ANL's inception (Troyna 1982: 274). It would seem that they wished to avoid any explicit acting out of the conflict between racism and anti-racism because it would make them, and their friendships, even more vulnerable than they were already felt to be.

Such a judgement may have been sound. Some evidence for this, and for the lack of influence the ANL members had with even non-politicised adolescents with racist views, is provided by the comments of white boys I interviewed who saw ANL membership merely in terms of strategies relating to black/white male peer group rivalries:

> The Anti-Nazi League as far as I'm concerned round my district are for kids who can get a membership and walk in St Mary's [a club with a large black membership] safely. 'I'm a member of the Anti-Nazi League.' They're little grovellers. To protect theirselves they join the Anti-Nazi League. I hate it. You get all these kids wearing all these black clothes with badges on all over them. So the white kids, just normal kids like us, that's who they're gonna get a beatin' off now, not the blacks.

Whatever the limitations of the ANL no single populist pressure group *could* provide the kinds of ideological support necessary in the adolescent community which would be able to render anti-racism as 'naturalistic' as racism, especially in a context in which racism is constantly reinforced and regenerated from sources located in the structural relations of the wider society.

Despite the absence of any integrated forms of anti-racist ideology within the white community, within the local *black* population adolescents often combined in defence of their peers who were directly harassed for racist reasons. Black adolescent resistance to racism primarily took the form of action against its *effects*, especially within the schools, when black children had been abused or beaten up by whites. Black girls were no less active in this form of group defence than boys. Where such groups also encompassed white friends these whites might also become involved in this form of anti-racist activity, but in a way directly sanctioned by their immediate (black) friendship group. This form of white involvement in black anti-racist action was inevitably rare, although their position in black friendship groups provided such whites with rather more protection against racist ideas and practices than whites who had one or two black friends but who were also part of small isolated white groups. Positively anti-racist action was therefore sanctioned for the former group to a greater extent.

Of more far-reaching significance for black/white relations was black youth culture. The styles of music, dress and speech which characterised black youth culture had considerable impact on many white adolescents, and in ways different from its reinterpretation through the existing semantics of white youth style described by Hebdige (1976; 1979). Encoded within these black styles were arrays of social meanings related to the history of black oppression, the daily experiences of black youth, and the articulation of a black group consciousness which was generationally specific whilst still maintaining continuities with the parent cultures. However, where at one end the culture and its social coding were indistinguishable, its propagation through commercial channels provided an entrée even to young provincial whites living far from the urban centres where the forms were developed. White enthusiasts for both reggae and soul music were legion. The existence of a healthy and prestigious black youth culture did to some extent serve to counter racism, and would probably have done so even without the articulation of black political and social concerns within the music.

Despite attraction to the music and an acknowledgement of the vigour of black youth stylistics, this culture was, by virtue of its racial specificity, not one which could be enacted by whites. It simultaneously attracted at the aesthetic level whilst resisting white penetration at the level of social meaning. The relation between personal identity and youth cultural forms could not, with any comfort, be established for whites who found themselves attracted to black styles. Nevertheless, for those with close black friends, the prestige of black youth cultural products did provide some external support for their friendship which was lacking in the sphere of articulated ideology. Its presence offered a means by which their personal friendship choices could be accommodated within a social rather than a merely personal context, while nevertheless operating below the level of explicit political ideology.

Some white adolescents in Area A whom I interviewed became immersed in black youth culture and, despite the insurmountable contra-dictions, attempted to establish for themselves a 'black' identity. Cutting themselves off from close contact with white friends and spending most of their leisure time with their black friends, they would appropriate some of the blazonry of black youth style, only listen to black music, and for a while, do their best to 'become black'. Such a strategy depended ultimately on support from at least one or two close black friends who would tolerate and even encourage such an identification. One such white girl had managed to gain a wide acceptance of her adoption of black style through the intercession of her black girl friends, one of whom told me, 'The boys round this area know Stacy as Little Black Girl. They call her "Little Black Girl" and 'cos she sticks out so much, when she's not there they say, "Where's Stacy?" and "How is she?"' She was a close follower of black fashion and peppered her speech with a smattering of creole. Another interviewee, a white boy who customarily displayed Rasta colours on his clothes, was known amongst whites as 'The White Wog'. He was a committed enthusiast for reggae music, regularly going to hear the best known 'sounds'. He was also a member of a group of black boys who were collectively building their own 'sound'. Another seventeen-year-old white boy, who had from an early age always involved himself with black people, was a Rastafarian and wore an enormous woollen Rasta hat. He told me, 'Thursdays or Fridays I go Nyabingi and we talk about Jah Rastafari. But there's many ways to it you know. So some believe in Jah and some take praise to his Divine Majesty . . .'.

It is not surprising that such a degree of commitment should lead to an identification with black social and political concerns. Involvement with black youngsters, for many whites, meant that they would be likely to have first-hand knowledge of the relations between black youngsters and the police. In the course of my research I heard countless eye witness stories by whites of violence by the police to young blacks and arbitrary arrests. Often whites with black friends told me that, although they had been with their friends when a club was raided or a group was picked up on the street, the police had let *them* go before searching their black friends. Such experiences allowed whites to perceive even more strongly reasons for the political dimensions in black youth culture. The girl mentioned above attended the rally in Hyde Park following the inquest into the Deptford Fire and peripherally became involved in other local black campaigns. The white Rastafarian, when interviewed two years later, was reading *The Autobiography of Malcolm X* and informally studying recent black history of the Americas and South Africa. The boy with the 'sound' told me of the political ambitions of his cultural enterprise:

> What I want to happen, I want to see the black and the white unite, like. Come together. That's what I'm tryin' to do, tryin' down the youth club, to get the white people, getting them to like reggae music.

However, despite the adherence to black perspectives by whites who tried to 'pass' culturally for black, such full-throated commitment was, by outward signs, indistinguishable from the merely fashion-conscious appropriations of black cultural insignia by over-enthusiastic white youngsters who failed to perceive the social and political aspects of the culture, or failed to be sensitive to the issue of group boundaries. I was repeatedly told by black youngsters that, while they like to see whites mixing in with black groups, they 'don't like to see them acting as if they're black.' Beyond their immediate circle of black friends, black youth-style postures were difficult for whites to maintain, and black adolescents who were particularly vigilant about the ethnic borderline were not happy to see it breached, even by well-meaning whites. The white Rasta mentioned above was advised by the proprietor of a Brixton record shop to leave the premises when he entered wearing his Rasta hat, even though he was with a group of black friends. The white girl was threatened by a black boy that if she continued to wear a black track suit with red, gold and green arm stripes (Rastafarian colours), she would be beaten up. Such small incidents served to underline the racial specificity of black youth culture.

While all of the black adolescents I interviewed were critical of whites who 'act black', some with white friends who behaved in this way insisted that, where such an adoption of black style was the product of a longstanding closeness with black people, then it was not the product of an opportunistic attraction to fashion but a 'natural' way of being:

WHITE GIRL (15): Some black girls do reject me. When they see me in all nice clothes – reggae clothes – and they haven't got them they say, 'What is she wearing them clothes for?'

Her black friend explained:

> There are lots of white girls . . . with black friends but that's recently. They've only recently come into the black thing and got more into it. But she's grown up with it and people can't seem to see that.

The same black girl told me:

> One time we went to this place. It was the first time she'd ever been. It was where all the black boys play table-tennis and snooker and all that. [We] introduced her and all that, and they say, 'What did you bring her down here for?' And she just look at them and go, / you know?

The white girl added:

> I just said, 'Who dey look pon?' [Both girls laugh]

However, as well as risking the disapproval of black youngsters, those whites identifying themselves with black culture also placed themselves in a contradictory relationship to other whites, as the following account by a white boy, very far from black culture, shows:

> I had a real argument with a girl at college, Carol, a white girl. She was talking to Glenford [a black boy] the other day. They were talkin' and she was sayin', 'Did you go to this blues. Did you go to that blues, and they were talkin' about trouble. Then she says this one thing. She went, '/ Our people are gettin' a lot of trouble down that way.' I went, 'What did you say?' She went all red. She said, 'They got a lot of trouble down there.' 'But you said *our* people didn't you?' She goes all red. I said, 'Carol what *are* you? You're white for God's sake!'

Adolescents who identified with black youth culture so explicitly and then encountered hostility from both sides tended gradually to abandon the more overt signs and settle down into the friendships without feeling the need to display their allegiances. However, the very act of attempting such an identification makes clear the distinction between relating to social groups and relating to individuals. The double role of individual friend and group member is clearly thrown into relief by those white adolescents who chose to exist on the boundary of black and white, truly 'marginal' people, at home in neither world.

They also demonstrate the fact that black youth culture can be contradictorily perceived by white youth. For some, especially those identifying with white group processes, it was perceived as an affront; to others, especially those positioned beyond the influence of those processes, it was profoundly attractive. There is a kind of logical symmetry initiated here which is projected and analysed within the group and individual relations flowing from these contradictory responses. The social logic embodied in those marginal beings – the blonde 'Little Black Girl', the 'white Rasta' – like the ambiguous forms of religion and mythology, creatures formed with the attributes of contrasting worlds, emerged repeatedly in the obscure calligraphy of inter-racial contact.

III

Within this terrain of peer group networks, ideological transmissions and cultural variation, not all inter-racial friendships were so obviously exposed to external pressures as some of the cases cited above. The longitudinal study revealed that the influence and effect of these factors on young whites varied considerably. Unlike the boys described above who suddenly came to express racialist views, or the girl who felt torn by the attitudes of her boyfriend and his group of friends on the one hand and her black friends on the other, some young whites existed in a kind of parallel social world that appeared to have little contact with the sectors of the adolescent community in which explicit racial antipathies were especially salient. Here the diffusion of racism was notably low; and, while the national discourses of race no doubt constituted part of the social and conceptual inheritance of such whites, these were not activated in their immediate social world, were not made explicitly significant by any actual social interactions and local conditions. Indeed, for some whites, the friendships which they developed with black youngsters appeared to present them with few problems to solve or conflicts to resolve of the kind described above.

Such a case was Jane, whom I knew and interviewed periodically over three years, beginning when she was thirteen. As with many white girls with black girl friends, the history of Jane's inter-racial friendships was peculiarly untouched by the racism which at times had become rampant in the local adolescent population. The junior school which she had attended had very few black children. The one black girl in her class, Angela, had become her best friend at the age of six and they remained good friends throughout junior school, although they did not live near each other and did not meet outside of school.

Both girls moved to the same secondary school and remained friends, although they were less close than they had been. However, although Jane had several close white girl friends, from early on the majority of her friends in school were black and she usually went around with a group of about four black girls. Because most of her school friends, black and white, lived some distance from her, she saw them rarely out of school. However, one black school friend, Debbie, lived in the next street to her and was, by her second year at that school, her closest friend in and out of school.

During Jane's first two years at the school she was mildly attracted to black youth culture, and occasionally peppered her speech with the creole words she picked up from her friends. She also said that she sometimes experimented with black hairstyles in the privacy of her own bedroom. She had fairly wide tastes in popular music, which included reggae, but she was not principally attracted to black music. During her third year she stopped using any creole words, concluding that it was 'silly' for her to do so. In this she may have been influenced by what she heard some of her black friends say about other white girls who attempted to use creole forms. Several of them were vociferously opposed to the practice, as they were by other appropriations of black style by white girls. Jane's attraction to black youth culture hardly appeared on the surface at all, and by the end of that year no obvious evidence of it remained.

Her basic in-school friendships remained constant. She had both black and white friends but the majority were black. Out of school she saw less of Debbie, when in the fourth and fifth years, and her closest out-of-school friend became Marcia, another black girl, who was a year younger than herself and who also lived nearby. Marcia, like her other black and white friends, came to her house and she visited Marcia's house. In her fifth year she went on holiday abroad with Marcia and her family.

Both Jane's parents were welcoming to all of her friends and she had never been aware of any expression of racist ideas from them. Her father worked on the Thames barges and her mother worked in a local baker's shop. She told me that her parents thought that 'racial prejudice is stupid'. She said that her older sister was going out with a boy who was 'not white'. She, herself did not have a boyfriend throughout the years that I interviewed her. She said she would go out with a black boy if she liked him, just as she would a white boy, although she was aware of the possibility that some of her black girl friends might not like it. She thought that one black girl in particular might 'talk to [her] about it' if she did. She knew, however, that several of the others would not mind at all. Her parents, too, she felt, would not mind.

She left school at the end of the fifth year hoping to get a job, as her sisters had done, in some form of clerical work, but the employment situation had worsened and, despite quite good grades in her CSE exams, she failed to find employment. She reluctantly re-entered school in the sixth form in an attempt to become better qualified. In the lower sixth only four of the students were black, the remaining thirty being white. Most of her friends had left school, although Angela, her friend since junior school, was there and they saw more of each other. Nevertheless, she also began to grow closer to several of the white girls in her class, and for the first time the great majority of her school friends were white. She saw little or nothing of her old black school friends, except for Debbie and Marcia who lived near to her. Marcia remained her closest out-of-school friend, and they would go to sports events and on shopping expeditions, and spend time together at their respective homes. They also occasionally attended a local youth club, until the skinhead gang described above started to go there too. This appeared to be the extent to which local racist groups affected Jane's life. At this time she also had one close white girl friend out of school.

Throughout her secondary school career, Jane's knowledge of racism remained more or less remote and her attitude to it very understated. During her fifth year she had told me that there appeared to her to be much more racism evident in young people locally, as indeed there was at that time. She said that she had noticed that more young people were joining groups like the National Front. When asked if she felt sympathetic with the Anti-Nazi League she said that she did not, commenting, 'Demonstrations just cause fighting.' She also saw no need to wear an ANL badge. She also felt that a certain white girl whom she knew very remotely 'asks for trouble' in a different way by using a lot of black language and going out with black boys. By her behaviour, the girl in question had incurred the hostility of some black youngsters Jane knew and had also been exposed to violence by some whites. Jane avoided any form of publicly demonstrative behaviour with blacks and whites alike and conducted her friendships without regard for the public debates over race.

Most of her judgements about racial issues were related to personal experience, and her answers to my questions about these matters were not given with much explicit reference to 'common knowledge'. She thought that it was harder for blacks to get jobs than whites because her sister had been offered a job by a woman who did not want to advertise the position because she did not want black people applying. She thought that this sort of thing happened from time to time. Her only reference to knowledge indirectly gained was when asked whether or not blacks and whites receive equal treatment from the police. She said that 'maybe' the police pick more on black kids than on whites 'because lots of black people say they do'. She herself had no direct knowledge of it she said. She was not given to express strong feelings about any issue, however, and, for her, racism was mostly located in the activities of 'stupid people' who did not constitute the majority.

Her friendships with black girls appeared to be very free from direct pressures either from her white friends or from her family. These friendships did not lead her to any generalised recognition of the influence of racism on the lives of black people, although it did appear to be one of the factors serving to diminish the influence on her of the racial attitudes and stereotypes evident in the wider culture. At an early stage she appears to have learned to steer clear of adopting any of the markers of black youth style, quietly internalising the potential dangers of forays across the ethnic/racial borderline. There is no doubt that this circumspection contributed something to the stability and durability of her inter-racial friendships.

In stark contrast to Jane was Stacy, the white girl whom Jane mentioned she knew very remotely and who was the subject of so much criticism from some of Jane's black friends. Stacy lived in a high-rise flat with her mother and sister. Her father lived a few miles distant and had left the family to re-marry when Stacy was twelve. Stacy's older sister had a black boyfriend, and when I first interviewed Stacy her mother had a boyfriend who was 'half Asian'. She had several good friends who lived on her estate, both black and white, but her closest friends were two black girls who lived in her block of flats. One of these had been her friend since the age of six. Stacy got on well with the parents of her black friends and she and her friends were always in and out of each other's houses. The single-sex school she attended was on the edge of the borough, not far from Area B, and there were approximately equal numbers of black and white pupils in her year. She had some white friends in school but mainly went around with black girls. In fact her most consistent and close friendships both in and out of school were with black girls. She claimed to find black friends better company than white friends:

> I'm just more attracted to [black friends]. I ain't used to goin' round with white girls, that's why. 'Cos since I've been goin' round with 'em for nearly nine years and I've stuck to 'em.

She was very keen on reggae music and, with the approval and encouragement of her closest black friends, often used creole expressions and words. She also dressed exclusively in black styles – smart reggae clothes for some occasions, and a track suit with Rasta colours on for others. She was very pretty, and had a succession of black boyfriends, although this she kept from her father, who was strongly opposed to racially mixed relationships. His opposition had apparently been greatly sharpened by the relationship his oldest daughter, Susan, had with a black boy. Indeed, before he had left the family home there had been constant rows about the issue, and ever since he had refused to speak to Susan. The relationship, however, persisted. For this reason Stacy kept her father in the dark about her own boyfriends. This was possible because she only saw him on her weekly visits to his house. Her mother was well disposed to Stacy's black friends, although her own 'half Asian' boyfriend disliked black people intensely, and this also sometimes led to rows. The stresses placed on Stacy's mother first by her husband and later by her boyfriend over her daughter's black friends ultimately became extremely difficult for her to cope with, but throughout Stacy's third and fourth years at school, as had apparently always been the case, she was wholehearted in her support of all of Stacy's friendships.

Stacy enjoyed a great deal of freedom, and at fourteen went drinking every Friday at the Harlow, the pub mentioned above run by, and almost exclusively for, black people. She also went to discos and parties with her friends, and occasionally stayed out all night. Her school work played very little part in her life, although she rarely truanted until well into the fifth year, shortly before she was due to leave. The lack of maternal pressure on her leisure activities and friendship choices at that time was not matched by the attitudes of some of the white adolescents with whom she came into contact. As a white girl who was always out and about with her black friends, she was very conspicuous to local white racist youth, and sometimes came in for verbal abuse from them. Stacy gave me the following account of what she regarded as the worst event of this kind:

> I got beat up by six skinheads [boys] for going round with black people, on the way to school. I was just walkin' down [the] hill and they started to call me 'nigger-lover' and I turned round and I just looked at 'em, you know, and carried on walking and they just come and jumped me. I had a black eye, had a few bruises on my back where they kicked me and my hand where they trod on it.

On another occasion, about nine months later, when the odds were more balanced she actually managed to respond with more effect:

> Me an' Ellen was at Lewisham one day and I went to see these three black boys I knew and I was talkin' to 'em and everythink and I had my tape-recorder with me and I was playin' black people's music, you know. And because I knew these three black boys they got on the same bus as us and there was these two girls on there. One was a skinhead and one wasn't, and they started sayin' 'Look at her! Wogsmeat! Niggerlover!' and all this. So I got hold of her and I pulled her up by her hair and I smacked 'er in the mouth and we was 'avin' a fight on the bus and I kicked her down the stairs . . . The bus conductor threw her off.

At the same time her conspicuous adoption of black style also incurred the hostility of some young blacks, although not from her immediate circle of friends, with whom she was very popular:

> *Did you ever get any trouble from black people who didn't like you dressing in reggae style?*
> Not from people I knew ... I used to get funny things when I used to walk down the road with Valerie and all those. These black people all used to call me, say, 'Look at 'er. She thinks she's black', and things like that. It didn't use to bother me though. Others used to say, 'Oh, take no notice. They're just jealous.'
> *Was that anything of a pressure?*
> No. It didn't really bovver me. 'Cos I knew that I weren't black and that was all there is to it. I wasn't thinkin' I was black. It was just that I went around with black people and I dressed like 'em, an' that. And I liked the music an' everything, so ...

Within the space between skinhead hostility and a certain level of black opposition, Stacy entered the world of black social concerns with – for a fourteen/fifteen-year-old – some seriousness, even if her adoption of black stylistics may have been a little naively enthusiastic. It was she to whom I alluded in section II above as the blond 'Little Black Girl' who attended the Hyde Park Rally following the Deptford Fire, and who also became involved with certain local black campaigns. Indeed, it seemed to me, given the duration and strength of her friendships with black adolescents and her involvement with black concerns at the political and cultural level, that she would continue to keep local cross-pressures at arm's length, and that little change in her friendship patterns would occur.

In this assumption I was mistaken. A few days before her sixteenth birthday I interviewed her again, and found that in the intervening six months a radical change had occurred. Although she still had a few close black friends, most of her friends were white. This transformation had been initiated, it appeared, by her mother, whose personal stresses had reached something of a crisis. Her mother was present at the start of the interview and explained in her own words:

> Her whole life's changed. The whole pattern of her life's changed. 'Cos it got me. I'm not prejudiced but I wanted her to have a few white friends. I'm not prejudiced but it was *all* coloureds, you know. Of an evening I used to come in and

there'd be about eight of 'em sitting in here an' it got me down
in the end, but I didn't want it *all* . . . but I just couldn't . . .
and I was under a lot of pressure at the time with my
ex-husband and this other boy [her oldest daughter's black
boyfriend] and I said, 'For god's sake it's getting . . . It's nice
to have a couple of . . .' I said, 'It makes a change to see a
couple of white faces'. And she's quietened down fantastic,
you know. She's here at ten of a night time, you know?
. . .

It's a different world with them. I don't care what you say.
They're allowed out more, the hours, and their parties are so
different and I nearly had a nervous breakdown . . . Their
parties start at eleven o'clock at night and then go on to six in
the mornin'. You know, and I tried to let her do what she
liked, and I was . . . bein' on me own I was near enough
crackin' up, you know and I was under pressure from the
other two [i.e. the elder daughter and her boyfriend]. I've had
that for four years. My ex-husband and all the family, no one
agreed [with it]. 'Cos she's been goin' with him for four years
and he's a terrific bloke and I was the only one that was on
their side and you know when my husband left he was gonna
do this, beat 'em up and 'no black', you know, so . . . But now
it's all died down, the family's accepted it, which is . . . So I
was under a lot of pressure, but that is the main . . . but she
goes around mainly with white girls now. They're all white
girls now. She's got friends who are . . . Sandra Johnson . . .
but their world is different with their parents an' that, you
know what I mean? . . . But as I say I think she should have a
few white friends . . . a mixture . . . and that's what she's got.

I asked Stacy: 'So was there a day when your mum gave you a talking to?'

STACY: No. She just used to nag me. 'Why can't you get any white
friends' and this an' that. She didn't mind me goin' out with
black boys did yer?

MOTHER: It all depends. I mean I would 'ave died if one of those Rastas
or anything of that lot knocked at the door. Gary was alright
but I thought well, I've been through it all with Susan why
should I 'ave another . . . You know it's not fair. Why pick on
me? You know, *two* of 'em and it's very hard 'cos people are
very . . . neighbours, you know. 'Oh your poor girls, all got
black boys', 'Oh your poor Susan. Must be heartbreakin' for
you to have a . . .', 'What's your reaction?' Oh I've had it all,

you know, 'terrible'. I said 'Look, she's been with 'im four years. She's kept herself straight', I said, 'an' they've both got bloody good jobs, just bought a car and they're gonna get married next year'. But people can be very . . .

She went on to tell me about the pressure she'd had from her ex-husband, her own father and her brother's wife. She then left, and I continued to interview Stacy on her own.

Stacy explained to me that she now went around with a group of three white girls and a larger group of white boys. She also now had a white boyfriend. The transition, she felt, had been fairly gradual, especially as her closest black girl friend now had a steady boyfriend and she had begun to see less of her socially, although they still called in on each other several times a week.

> I was always wiv Sandra. We was best friends ever since we was six years old. 'Cos you know, we've always been together. It's only now that we've just split apart, 'cos Sandra's found a boyfriend and I've found my white friends an' that. But I'd never turn against black people, Never. Not even . . . I wouldn't go around with white people if they hated black people. I couldn't do it.

All of her new white friends, she told me, liked black music, and dressed a bit like black kids. Most of them were between fifteen and seventeen, had black friends themselves, although they mostly attended an all-white youth club on weekday evenings. She told me that she got on well with her new white friends and that the girls all 'also' had strict parents. She felt that she fitted in well with them. 'I don't get funny looks when I walk down the street', she said. It was clear that a knot of pressuring factors had been severed by these changes, and that this had brought about a certain relief:

> I'm feelin' more relaxed. Not to know that I'm gonna be called a 'niggerlover', and all this, and 'wogsmeat', and that . . .

She continued to visit her father every week, but he had turned passionately against black people. He had even begun obsessively lecturing his little three-year-old son by his new wife about how he shouldn't have anything to do with black children. She thought that in fact her father had 'gone a bit mental about it'.

It is not difficult to see the convergence of factors which brought about the transformation of Stacy's friendships a few months before her sixteenth birthday. Although the change took place at about the time when she unofficially left school, it was not the leaving of school which changed the basic pattern of her friendships, as it was for many. It was the convergence of maternal pressure in the aftermath of her sister's relationship – made stressful for her mother by two successive male partners – with pressure from hostile white youngsters, and, to some extent, the opposition and criticism she experienced from some young blacks at the cultural way in which she had attempted to express her social affinity with black people. This last pressure would not have existed had she not adopted black style, but, as for many young whites, such cultural apparatus often did much of the work of situating friendships in a wider context because of the ideological vacuum in which inter-racial friendships existed. It is, therefore, something of a sad irony that the very means of defence which she chose should itself have proved double-edged.

Despite the complexities of Stacy's case, Stacy and Jane were both protected from the relay of racism within local adolescent groups because (*a*) they appeared to have no white friends who directly expressed racist views to them, and (*b*) they had both constantly had black friends from an early age and, by late secondary school, black girls still constituted the majority of their friends. In terms of their direct adolescent associations, therefore, they had no immediate influences towards racism and no context in which racism (of the kind observed above for boys and some girls) might be acted out.

Comprehensible as Stacy's change may be in terms of external pressures and internal familial causes, from the point of view of some of her black friends it may have seemed both sudden and even characteristically 'white'. She did not fall out with any of her black friends and continued to see several of them, but the fundamental pattern that emerged might have seemed to some a 'typical' example of white unreliability, and even another expression of white racism, which indirectly, of course, it was. Certainly it was common for girls like Stacy to be viewed with some suspicion by black youngsters. As one black boy told me:

> At school there were girls [he names three] they used to go out with black boys. They all dress the way black people did, but you see they can't keep up that fashion for a long time.
> They've got to go on to a change and they stop going out with black boys then they just turn on to white boys and they just settle down with the white boys. That's why, not being disrespectful to them but I would regard them as imitation.

This view of the limitations of those who were believed to dabble in black culture was often expressed by black girls too. One black girl described how she liked friends who were open to black culture and 'black ways' without feeling the need to try and 'become black' themselves. Such white friends were rare, she said, and told me about her closest white girl friend from whom she had drifted away by the age of seventeen:

> Ann was different. I used to go round with her since primary school and she used to eat rice and peas [at my house] and want more, eat the soup and want more, you know, but I haven't found another white girl like her. We weren't different. There's no . . . like, I'd go to her house and be family and things like that . . .

Even without immediate and obvious stresses, good friends like these often drift apart after the age of about fifteen or sixteen. Changes in life rhythms after the fifth year of secondary school often alter friendship patterns for adolescents, regardless of the factor of colour. The drifting apart of close friends of differing race is often due to cultural and social factors which, even at the time, are usually opaque and mysterious to the actors themselves. For both black and white this comes to be seen as a 'natural' process. As one seventeen-year-old black informant who had left school told me concerning his white school friends:

> I don't really mix with them. If I see them on the road I say, 'Cool', and everything, you know what I mean, but apart from that . . . you know. I think that's the normal thing, like you know 'em well at school but once you leave school it's just . . . You don't mean to but you just cut off.

When asked about his closest school friend, who was white, this boy replied:

> I don't see Chris so much as I used to, like when we was at school we used to do everything together and now you just . . . It's not you go one way and you go *one* way, but you don't . . . It's not like that but it's like the relationship you had is deteriorating till it just goes, goes, goes, and goes and that's it, you know?

Although this informant is speaking about a friend who was a school friend whom he saw out of school, the same process of decline is also common for out-of-school inter-racial friendships. Some of the pressures on white adolescents that guide them away from friendships with black youngsters have been outlined above. There are also pressures on black youngsters that tend to make black friends preferable to white ones.

Bitter experiences have been productive of a kind of collective wisdom often expressed by both parents and children about some of the possible dangers of having too much to do with white people and even with white friends. In particular, the near-ubiquitousness of racism or its consequences in English social life can turn the most simple activities and exchanges into instances of embarrassment, awkwardness, anger and humiliation which for young blacks can be avoided to some extent simply by not mixing with white people, or by ensuring that their white friends go to the places where they feel socially comfortable and do not unwittingly lead them into potentially embarrassing situations. One seventeen-year-old black girl told me:

> You never forget bad racial experiences even if your
> friendship can cope with it . . .
> If you get hurt once like that you don't want to get hurt again.
> Like you may go to a club, you and your white friend, and
> they'll say to you, 'No blacks', and that kind of embarrassment
> in front of people . . .
> *Does that happen?*
> Yeah, it does happen. It nearly happened to me with Dianne
> [her close white friend] and that kind of embarrassment in
> front of people . . . If you've got a strong friendship you can
> overcome that but you never forget that – 'cos I never forgot it
> – and it sort of marks up a point, you know and then you get a
> collection of these points and you think, 'Cha! I'm safer this
> way' [i.e. not mixing with white people].

For such reasons, black adolescents are occasionally subjected to criticism from other young blacks for having close white friends. As the girl quoted above told me, 'I had to go through a lot of stick because of Dianne . . . Yeah, "What you goin' round wiv a white girl for?" And she had to go through a lot of things.' Reflecting in general on the influence of other black kids she said:

> When you walk past you see 'em and they say, 'Cha! What
> you doin' over dere wi' dat white man', just for fun. Not even
> fun. They might be bored so they think [they'll] pick on you
> and they constantly keep doin' that and you start to thinkin'
> yourself. You feel self-conscious and if you're not strong in
> any case you think, 'I'm safer doin' this'. 'Cos in a way I
> would of been safer not goin' round with Dianne but it's the
> friendship we had that couldn't be broken. That's why I went

to white parties wiv her and she came to black with me. I don't know if it could work now. We were younger then. I really don't know if it could work now . . .

A further influence on black youngsters sometimes comes from parents who attempt to warn their children of the contradictions, difficulties and inequalities that often inhere in black/white friendships:

> *Is there a pressure on black kids with white friends?*
> To stay black yeah. They say, sort of, 'You're safer in numbers' and 'Don't trust 'em'. 'You don't stand a chance wiv 'em' and 'You and them might be friends now but when you get through school they will pull you down', and 'white kids have more opportunities and they take you for a fool, take you for granted. If you've got brains they're gonna be pullin' you down and if you haven't they're going to be leading you astray like thievin' and things like that.' And 'If two of you go out and do the same thing, you're gonna be the one that's got the pressure on you. You're the one that the police is gonna hold and they can go home.' You might even get that from your parents, not really forced into you but just a rhyme, a slang [saying] or a warning . . .
> *Is it that black parents think that white boys are going to get [the black kids] into trouble or what?*
> I think it's the trouble aspect. 'Cos a lot of white boys who are . . . not no good, but, erm, get in trouble in any case, about seventeen, eighteen that's when they start house-breakin'. They don't really do street crimes as that, muggin, it's house-breakin' and shops and that's when they start doin'. The parents, black parents, see it and know it and they say to your kid, 'Don't do it.' And then you might go there, do it wiv 'em and get caught and *they* get a little fine and you get a big fine, or time.

My direct contact with the parents of my informants was, for the most part, negligible. What I learned of parental attitudes came through interviews with the adolescents, and could not usually be corroborated in any way by observation, as could the peer group interactions. Because of this limitation it was difficult for me to build any real picture of the role of parental influence on the racial attitudes of children. Certainly there were those white adolescents who were not at all given to expressions of racism, who reported to me that their parents were extremely hostile to black people. It was more common, however, at least in interview subjects from Area A, for youngsters with many black friends and a critical view of local adolescent racism, to have parents who actually expressed very positive attitudes towards black people. David was a case in point.

Throughout his secondary schooling David had black friends both in and out of school. By the fourth year, most of his school mates were black and a number of these friends he also saw out of school, so that out of school about half of his friends were white and half black. A year later, towards the end of his fifth year, all but one of his out-of school friends were white, although he still had the same black friends in school. His out-of-school white friends also had black friends, and one was very much into black music and fashion. David himself liked 'heavy metal rock' and did not really like reggae and soul music.

His father, a lorry driver, had 'loads of' black friends himself, according to David, including one in particular who would come to the house from time to time and cook the family Caribbean food as a treat. He told me that his father and mother were vociferously opposed to the National Front and that, as a family, he, his parents and his sister all had the same atttitudes on race and racism: they disliked racism intensely and enjoyed the company of black friends. David's parents appear to have been unusual even for the parents of those in my already biased sample. The combination of outspoken opposition to racialist politics and *themselves* having black friends who regularly visited the house meant that David's parents succeeded in providing their children with a degree of resistance to some of the most common forms of racism.

Although many of my white informants who had black friends and who expressed to me their opposition to racism reported that their parents 'were not prejudiced' and 'got on all right with black people', the simple *absence* of the expression of racist attitudes in the home was never sufficient to provide adolescents with any resistance to racism. One example to deter simple equations was that of Matthew, another white boy with a close inter-racial friendship that went back to his junior school days. Matthew expressed his opposition to the forms of racism of which he was aware, and had maintained close friendships with several black boys throughout secondary school and into his sixth form. He was amongst those (as was David above) who preferred to keep a low profile when race was discussed between his white school acquaintances; but, despite his reluctance to make his views public, he was persistently critical of adolescent racism in his interviews with me. According to Matthew, his parents had 'good' racial attitudes, and always welcomed his black friends to the house. Matthew's brother, younger by a year and a half, was a skinhead, often expressed racialist views – although not in front of Matthew's black friends – and at one stage had seriously considered joining the British Movement. He maintained his skinhead style and the appropriate racial attitudes throughout the two-year period over which I interviewed Matthew. Examples of this kind indicate that without very positive guidance from parents, additionally supported by strong social contacts with black people, the simple lack of expression of racist attitudes by parents can guarantee nothing about the attitudes of their children.

Even under 'ideal' circumstances, inter-racial friendships can be increasingly remote after about the age of fifteen. David, for example, followed the pattern described by other informants above: when he left school he came to see very little of his black friends and this appears to have been primarily due to a kind of cultural drift that occurred at that time:

> Delroy and his mates. I haven't seen them for ages. See, I can't be bothered to go and see them 'cos when they're going down the Harlow they say 'come along' but if I go down there I don't like it. It's not that I've got anything against it. It's just that I don't like what they like . . . If they go to a blues – it's their music, it's packed, the atmosphere and all that . . . I went to one, and they really accepted me, you know. I've never seen them and they go, 'All right?' But then you get the occasional one. I'm not sayin' that because they're black, you get that at white parties too. It's not just that, it's the music, the atmosphere and I think I could be rather doing something else. But if Kevin [a close black friend] came round my house and I put my records on, he'd think 'crap'. We're totally different but still friends. We accept each other as we are.

What emerges from the longitudinal studies of inter-racial friendships in Area A is the extent to which such friendships are overshadowed and marginalised by the racism prevailing in a variety of forms in the local adolescent community. This appears to have been the case despite the fact that friendships of this kind commonly occur in peer group locations that are beyond the immediate ambit of the extended networks found amongst boys. Within this social terrain, the primary response of whites with black friends to the locally dominant forms of adolescent racism is either an avoidance of any confrontation with it – an avoidance possibly related to the ideological vacuum surrounding inter-racial friendships – or the adoption of the 'cultural option' – the embracing of black stylistics in the provision of a wider social dimension to friendships. As has become evident, this latter option is itself a contradictory response, in so far as it provokes hostility from some blacks concerned about the external insulation of the semiotic codes of race and ethnicity. Inter-racial friendships in Area A, therefore, appear only to limit the *degree of diffusion* emanating from the networks within which certain racist attitudes and practices are relayed. In no way do they challenge and contest racism, because the associational basis of inter-racial friendships is not complemented by parallel ideological and cultural continuities. While racist ideological practices are promulgated persistently within the local white adolescent population, alternative accounts are severely restricted once they move beyond the black community itself.

I have been concerned here less with recounting for their own sake the individual biographies of whites subsequent upon particular inter-racial friendships than with exploring the social and cultural conditions in which young people participate during an important span of adolescence. In summary, my research in Area A suggests with regard to social organisational features that:

(*a*) One important source of racism in the adolescent community is the racism which is enacted, boosted and relayed within the larger networks of adolescent association.

(*b*) The attitudes and practices so relayed are diffusely spread out from these networks into the surrounding social terrain. This process is just one amongst many by which racism is transmitted to adolescents.

(*c*) The extent to which any individual gives expression to racist attitudes and engages in other forms of racist practice is partially dependent on the nature of his/her primary peer group and its relation to larger extended peer group networks.

(*d*) Inter-racial friendships limit the social basis upon which some forms of racism are relayed and diffused within the local adolescent community, but do not provide an order that significantly contests the prevalence of racism locally.

The above points concerning the organisational bases of ideological relays are true for other ideological features besides those directly relating to race. However, in the articulation of certain forms of racism with certain notions of masculinity, the existence of extensive boys' social networks, bonded by an exchange structure of services and information, is highly pertinent. This is borne out by the notably lower levels of expressed racism evident amongst girls. These features also tie the specific forms of ideological transmission to specific class locations. Different modes of transmission and different expressions of racism are likely to be evident in different class locations. However, as will be seen when Area B is considered, intra-class cultures can differ widely, and class taken on its own is only of qualified relevance when variations in the forms of racism are considered. This is of significance to any examination of the social contexts within which racism is interrupted and contested.

2

Inter-racial friendship in Area B

The most significant respects in which Area B differed from Area A were the more or less uniform poverty of the area, and the much larger scale of Afro-Caribbean settlement. These factors also influenced inter-racial friendship. The first of these factors meant that the forms which racism would be likely to take would be those elaborated around a white working-class community closure, underpinned by high unemployment and the insecurities of unskilled labour, in the twilight of a long and steady economic decline. Within the adult social world this option had, to an extent, been realised, and had given rise to some strikingly high levels of voting for the National Front throughout the decade preceding the start of my research, even though Labour Party support remained fundamentally unshakable. The second factor, however, functioned contradictorily, for, despite such reactive expressions of racism, as the black population had increased steadily throughout the 1960s and 1970s, black community groups, churches, clubs and shops had come to impress themselves firmly on the local scene, and the older, long-established, exclusively white working-class social networks became eroded to some extent by white out-migration, and overlaid by black social networks. Thus the social landscape within which my young white informants had grown up was one in which black people and black cultures were not, as in Area A, a scattered and socially marginal component, but a significant and undeniable part.

Also absent was any identifiable white lower middle class within which the more 'genteel' forms of racism might be articulated, and where 'respectability' and 'a white neighbourhood' could be equated with improved social status. While both working-class and middle-class factions were present in Area A, and racial attitudes derived from those

66

bases became articulated amongst the overwhelmingly white adolescent population there, only the working class was strongly represented in Area B, and that was recontextualised by the racial composition which had developed in the area.

There were no 'white districts' within Area B by the 1970s, even though some estates and some streets were more white than others. This inevitably gave rise to a social context for adolescent inter-racial friendships that was very different to that found in Area A. While a minority of older whites might still give vent to their racial antipathies in their voting habits, the majority of whites had settled down to the realities of living in a multi-racial neighbourhood. For young whites, any hostilities that might have been felt towards the black population were qualified by the knowledge that, at street level, the balance of power was rather different from what it was elsewhere. In Area A, the prevailing adolescent white attitudes over race provided the backdrop to black/white friendships; in Area B, the attitudes of black adolescents and *their* concepts of race relations were the single most important 'ideological' feature. It is valuable, therefore, to examine closely some of the positions found amongst young blacks before looking at those friendships themselves. In Area B, unsurprisingly, a very different set of attitudes was evident. The issues were not simply inversions of those expressed by white adolescents in Area A, but were centrally concerned with questions deriving from the issue of racism itself, and with its expression not just in local interactions but in society at large. Everyday experiences were, in fact, very commonly seen as grounded in a wider context. While there was considerable variation amongst black adolescents in responses to the forms of racism which they encountered and observed, around the actual location of racism itself and in the belief that a connection existed between the minutiae of daily experience and the wider sociopolitical context, a great deal of consensus was apparent. Not only did I find many black adolescents who expressed ideas *about* racism, but this also seemed to engender in many an ability to relate the individual, personal dimensions of social experience to some notion of the social system as a whole. In this sense their awareness of racism was highly 'politicising', without imposing *specific* solutions or responses.

It was rare for young blacks, in their accounts of the forms of racism which affected them most acutely, to address themselves to the racism of the extremist right-wing groups such as the National Front. Appalling as the activities and doctrines of such groups were felt to be, and however much encounters with groups of this kind cause real distress, such manifestations of racist extremism were regarded and treated as far less routine and pervasive than the forms of racism encountered in everyday interactions, or observable in the media, or encountered in relations with institutions of various kinds. It was evident that while the activities of racist political groups could be regarded as the vicious and dangerous but essentially limited and 'lunatic' antics of a minority, the most basic, powerful and painful forms of racism were those embedded in daily life, and which had become so 'normalised' that they were invisible as such to a majority of white people. The connections between this level of racism and the more sociologically evident facts of racial disadvantage in areas such as education, employment, housing and relations with the police, were forcefully expressed by many of the black adolescents I interviewed.

The area of greatest concern with regard to racism was, inevitably, employment, although the high degree of youth unemployment nationally and locally appeared to render the even higher rates of black youth unemployment less of an issue than the actual *quality* of employment generally available to blacks, and the limited representation of blacks in the upper rungs of occupational ladders. Black youth unemployment, and the role of racism in job recruitment, certainly featured in my informants' reflections on racism, but many were even more acutely concerned with the wider structural implications of black exclusion from advancement to the better paid and more desirable occupations.

This awareness has sometimes been represented by sociological observers in the narrow terms of the putative 'generation gap' between black parents and their children. The lack of willingness by black British school leavers to accept the low-paid work taken by their parents' generation has been sometimes emphasised (Pryce 1979) at the expense of the more fundamental critique of white society which this emphasis masks. Certainly the generational contrast was often explicitly made by young blacks but, in my sample, expressions of this kind had more to do with hopes, and with the construction of a dignified approach to racism in employment, than with any lack of respect for the older generations, who were usually seen as having done their best in very different historical and economic circumstances. As one seventeen-year-old black girl put it:

> Most of them [black parents] came over in the fifties, didn't they, when they was just brought over to do all the shit jobs and all that sort of thing. And now we won't accept it. We want to be part of this society. We were born here. It's our country. You know, and they come over from Jamaica and were born there and this isn't their true country is it? And they just accepted what they had to but now these days we're fighting for our rights, aren't we? We're not just going to do all the dirty work. Why should we?

What this desire to be fully 'part of this society' is thwarted by was the real focus of such generational contrasts amongst the young people I interviewed. Indeed, a *continuity* with the experience of older black people was emphasised by many, as is evident in the following extract from an interview with a fifteen-year-old boy who was born in London:

> The thing I wonder is, what did they want us over here for? To do their dirty job an' all this, but once they see black people who have got the determination to get higher they don't like that. They go 'Oh, that black nigger's gettin' out of hand. We don't want them here. He's takin' all our jobs away.' You know, soon as we try to better our lives they want to down-grade it again.

Comments on the scarcity of black teachers, lawyers, doctors and other professional groups were very frequently expressed. Indeed, this scepticism about real promotional prospects for blacks even found expression in a group discussion of the desirability of having black policemen. One contributor commented:

> I think it would help if more black policemen went in but it wouldn't be doin' *them* any good. They'd just be kept at the bottom anyway. They wouldn't be made the Deputy, or the top one, *never*. They'd probably shoot 'im if he became the top policeman.

Racism as a force in society was rarely taken to be merely the aggregation of 'prejudiced attitudes' on the part of some white people, and such expressions of the structural dimensions of racism as the above were not uncommon.

The policies of the Conservative Government of the day were very often cited as exacerbating these structural features and, perhaps inevitably for a premier with a highly personalised style of leadership, Margaret Thatcher was regularly singled out as blameworthy for consolidating the social relations which were seen as perpetuating racial oppression:

> I mean like Margaret Thatcher now she's only helping high-class people. And you can't really say there's a lot of black people who are high-class. So therefore she's really workin' into giving *white* people a better kind of living. Whereas mainly the black people are working-class or even not working-class they're lower than that.

I asked the sixteen-year-old girl who made this comment if she thought that the Labour Party would be a party for black people to vote for. She replied:

> I think for black *and* white. I mean there's still a few whites that are in the deep end as well as we are. So I think they're just to help the working-class people, whereas *she* wants to make the white people who are rich even richer.

In housing, too, the policies of the day were felt to perpetuate disadvantage, and the run-down areas in which many black people live were also frequently mentioned:

> If the Government was prepared to spend a little money to make their country what they want it to be then I don't think there'd be so much trouble but they're always forever dumping black people in the worst houses you can find.

Not all the youngsters I interviewed were as convinced of the usefulness of the Labour Party to black people, although those expressing a preference for it over other parties constituted a clear majority. However, the equation made here between structural disadvantage and racism was a constantly repeated theme.

Supportive of and consequent upon such disadvantage, the stereotypes of black people which flourish amongst whites gave rise to an inventory of personal experiences which bore witness to their impact on, and perpetuation in, the 'small change' of daily interaction. This ideological aspect of racism was fed by several specific events occurring at the national level during the fieldwork period. Specifically with regard to young people, both the disturbances in Bristol, Brixton, Toxteth and elsewhere and, later, the release of statistics by the Metropolitan Police, purporting to reflect street crimes perpetrated by black youngsters, contributed to the popular image of black youth as dangerous and criminal. The relationship between the 'law and order debate', 'black youth' and the economic crisis has been subjected to considerable analysis (Hall *et al.* 1978; Centre for Contemporary Cultural Studies 1982) and will not be touched on here. The local effects of these events, however, were keenly felt by the black adolescents I interviewed, who found themselves positioned by popular discourses which they had no power to avoid in their daily lives. The following extracts from interviews with one black adolescent typify the impotence and frustration experienced by youngsters who found themselves the objects of powerful white stereotypes:

> I was walkin' down [the] High Street one time, right, and there was this old woman in front of me and I walked into her,

right, and moved out. And the woman went – [making a
sudden clutching movement] Grab her bag underneath her
arm, right. She made me feel as if I was a criminal and I
wanted to really go up and cuss her off, you know. It's just
that she's an old woman, guy, and she really made me feel bad
inside.

Or again:

I, I understand the rioting and things like that but I don't
condone it because it makes it worse for black people like me
who are trying to try, who are really trying hard because I'm in
a job and the day after [the riots] I went into work I felt
shamed but I had to walk with my head high because if you
hang your head you're just making them feel you're as bad as
the ones that actually done it.
Did anyone say anything?
Yea, there was comments and there was an argument in work
with some black girl and they said, 'Oh, better shut up, she
might start riotin'' and you know, normal little jokes like that.
The only white person that can really understand a black
person is if they've been in contact with black people for quite
a while, otherwise they just see you as stubborn and
aggressive.

The positioning of black people in this way is, of course, not new, and
even the particular forms it assumes are often reworkings of older
themes. The stereotypical association of blacks with unemployment has a
long history, and one not based on any economic understanding or
personal sympathy. This same informant explained:

My colour seems to be a big issue nowadays.
In what ways?
Well, you read . . . What I've experienced also . . . not only at
work but certain things like a little kid, a little white kid I 'ad
an argument with round my way. I said to him, 'Put that stick
down' – 'Cos he was knocking this car and I knew the bloke
whose car it was, right. So he goes to me, 'You got a job?' . . .
Just out of . . . And I was wondering, 'You come out with
this . . .' And when you read the papers, unemployment,
blacks, this an' that, it just makes you more conscious of what
you are . . .

Underlying many such accounts was a sense of incredulity and outrage at
how the terms by which social 'normality' is constructed are, as they saw

it, manipulated and controlled by white interests. Many young blacks felt themselves to be objectified and positioned by whites in a way that is underwritten by power relations. Any challenge to these relations by blacks are ruled out by appeals to a social 'normality' which whites define. Such an analysis is by no means beyond expression in everyday language, and was often present in shadowy form behind many group discussions. One of its most clear articulations, however, was the following statement by a fifteen-year-old boy, who began by making a connection between the commonly expressed white opinion that 'all blacks look alike', and the objectification which is written into white definitions of social normality. The language he uses is far from academic, yet the connections he makes are certainly not confused:

> Another thing I don't like is this attitude of the white of, 'All blacks look alike'. Many people seem to reckon all blacks look alike and I find that wrong 'cos I know for certain if there's a group of white people there I wouldn't say they all look alike. It's as if to say they're classing us as a *thing* and this an' that. And to me I don't like that at all. If I start to class white people as a *thing* what kind of looks would I get throughout life? See, I'd go out as a hypocrite. As for white people in a way they *don't* do they? They don't show it. They can act how they like. In a way, if they think 'black is this an' that', people say that's *normal*, but for a black person, if he sees white as this an' that [people say] 'what's up with him?' You know what I mean? In a way we can't win. And from the beginning of history you could say that black people have life bad, innit, and up till today when black people [are] sayin' this an' that people say, 'Oh, there he goes again.' White man come run our lives for us, innit, and when we say we don't want him to run our life they think, 'Ha! *It* . . . What does *it*, or that *thing* think it's doin'?' You know what I mean? It's disgraceful.

The linkages made here between the different forms of racism, and the insights into social mechanism displayed in this account, are not un-typical of the kind of analyses which young black people often displayed in reflections on their situation. While discontinuities and disagreements abound with regard to the appropriate forms of *response* to racism, most of the young people I interviewed were in no doubt about the nature and location of racism itself.

The background to this understanding lay as much in the cultural as in the social developments of the past decade and a half. Black youth culture itself has been a medium by which many young people have come to interpret and question their experience. In this connection, Rastafari has probably made the single most important contribution to young people's conception of the *systematic* nature of racism, even though, as some writers have argued (Troyna 1977), adherents to Rastafarian religious beliefs may be separate from those who have incorporated elements of Rasta blazonry into an essentially secular stylistics. Notably through reggae lyrics, Rastafari has offered an historical and social overview of racial oppression which has been taken up into black youth culture and, by that means, has become available as an analytic resource to large numbers of young black people. It is this dimension to Rastafari in Britain which gives it its special place in the history of contemporary black British struggles, regardless of debates over 'true' and 'false' Rastas.

Rastafari has by no means been the only such analytical resource. The ideas and practices of, amongst others, an ecumenical range of black American activists and political thinkers, from Martin Luther King to Angela Davis, George Jackson and Malcolm X, have also had their direct and indirect impact on the racial consciousness of black British youth. In recent years, however, no other articulation – secular or religious – of the social, economic and 'spiritual' conditions of domination within which the black communities exist has achieved such widespread appeal or become so profoundly encoded within black youth cultural forms.

The impact of Rastafari on youth culture was especially powerful in the late 1970s; but its steady decline in visibility since the early 1980s has reminded observers that youth culture is itself an independent and flexible agency. The culture, which was for Rasta consciousness a popularising vehicle, was also traversed by other strands, other modalities of perception and being, which, while not contradicting the Rasta analysis of oppression, seemed to offer more pragmatically interpretable solutions, and spoke more clearly to the stark desire of youth to combat prevailing correlations of blackness and low status by a vivid display of stylistic excellence through the iconography of material success. The message in this strand of black youth culture was less suggestive of revolutionary change and more of success within 'the system' – albeit a system to be 'played' with only a street-wise and strategic belief in its value. If one of the secular messages within the worldly wing of Rasta analysis was that racism needed capitalism, behind the option described here was the *hope* that capitalism did not need racism.

Such a stance almost inevitably involves a rejection of the symbolic means by which Rastafari expresses its critical distance from 'Babylonian' society. As one boy put it:

> Now most people go in for expensive clothes. [The Rastas]
> reject all fashion but people nowadays they just say, when you
> go out on a date you like to look nice. You know what I
> mean? Like if you see a friend there, right, and you dress like
> a Rasta, they're gonna laugh after you. Say, 'How can you
> come to a party dressed like that? You must be a real tramp.'

Furthermore, many young blacks took a literal view of the little they
knew of the Rastafarian faith, and rejected what they took to be its
explicit dogmas, like the divinity of Haile Selassie or the 'return to
Africa'. However, I did not find such a rejection of Rasta solutions
accompanied by an equivalent rejection of the Rasta account of the
history of black domination or of the underlying principle of black unity.
What black youth culture did with regard to Rastafari was to select what
it found meaningful, and to integrate that message of resistance into the
blazonry of urban anti-racist struggles – cultural, political and economic.
The dialogue between the politics of dissolution versus appropriation,
between revolution and reform, has long been present in black cultural
and political responses to conditions; its appearance, enacted at the
cultural level in the late 1970s and early 1980s, and glimpsed by some in
the dichotomies of reggae/soul, Jamaica/America, was but an unresolved
part of a deeper, more everyday concern with survival and future.
Differences of gender, age, class location, parental provenance and so on
also contributed to make the lives and views of young black people as
directly non-equatable with 'black youth culture' in general as they were
distant from the monolithic stereotypes of 'black youth' that impinged on
them, 'right, left and centre'. Nevertheless, the stereotypes of both of
these over-convenient generalisations were often part of what they
positioned themselves in relation to, even when they were outlining their
most pragmatic philosophies of daily survival. I did not find that
involvement with any aspect of 'black youth culture' could be correlated
with any belief or lack of it in the possibility of personal success within
'the system'. The variations on these points were as wide as could be
imagined, and the 'positioning' I mentioned was most often through a
language which well understood the fine print of cultural misrepresenta-
tion and the shadow-like tenacity with which it adheres to the words and
actions of young black people.

Much of the impact of Rasta analysis was registered at the cultural
level in encoded forms operating below the level of articulated ideas. At
the level of explicit 'opinion', as was seen above, the ideas of young
people may even seem to contradict such encoded social messages. More
complexly, however, what occurred most often was that individual

informants positioned themselves in relation both to the oppositional politics through which racism was analysed *and* to the popular stereo-types of 'young blacks' that emerged especially from media narration. Thus it was often the case, for example, that girls presented and saw themselves in contrastive relation to the image of the aggressive, lawless *male* that had become stereotypical in media and other accounts of 'black youth', as much as to the actual young black males whom they knew. Girls' self-presentation was often characterised by a desire to distance themselves from what they called the 'negative attitude' of 'most boys'. The following are typical of the kind of statements girls made about boys, especially in group discussions:

> 'All black boys think of is blues, weed and sex.'
> 'Some black boys ain't got no ambition.'
> 'Girls have more ambition.'
> 'Probably the next generation of girls coming up now are going to have better jobs than boys.'

As well as distancing girls from the popular stereotypes, these views may reflect the results of stronger parental control for girls, and may also be something of a restatement of the traditional view of Caribbean women as the familial achievers (Prescod-Roberts and Steele 1980). They do not represent, however, any acceptance of the status quo as far as racism is concerned. Neither do they imply a necessary denigration of the alter-native critique proposed by Rastafari, even if they were inclined towards a rejection of what were taken to be glib misuses of Rasta beliefs by boys – a tendency which was sharply criticised by some of the girls I interviewed, quick to notice any inauthenticity in boys' cultural strategies:

> Rastas don't eat pork, right? but the boys here [at this school] just for the sake of it say, 'I don't eat pork', 'Mi na wan' de pork' – bacon and sausages, say, they won't eat it. I think they're really immature. They make me sick.

Despite a respect for 'true Rastas', however, the determination to beat the racism of 'the system' by succeeding through 'the system' itself was the most commonly articulated response to racism expressed by the girls I interviewed:

> If you're a conscientious person you just wanna try harder to prove something to not only yourself but *people*, that you're one who doesn't want the normal thing for black people.

However, the ambiguities of being 'the exception to the rule', in the eyes of those who accept the stereotypes, did not escape this sixteen-year-old girl:

> I am proving to myself and my family, but not only to me but to all the people that know me, white people that know me or people that have insulted me in time, to see me doing something good, say, 'Oh, she tried!' But a black person that makes it in any case, they say, 'Oh, she's different. She's different to the normal set of black people.'

Many boys were often just as pessimistic about the possibility of radical social change, and regarded black revolutionary politics as a thing of the past when it came to examining the available responses to racism. The following extract is from an interview with a seventeen-year-old black boy who had been unemployed since leaving school:

> *Do you ever hear much revolutionary-type politics now?*
> No not really. That was years ago, innit, when Black Power was out an' everybody was standin' up for their rights, an' all that. Everybody was a revolutionary.
> *It sounds like you're talking as though it's all over now . . . the battle's all over.*
> It ain't all over but it isn't so strong as it used to be because people just lost interest. All they're thinkin' about now is makin' their money an' all this, buyin' clothes, buy a house, buy a car, get married an' all that. They're just thinkin' about *life*. They ain't really thinkin' about society. All they're interested in is where the next money is comin' in, an' all this, an' you have to make payments on the mortgage, an' pay rent, buy food, clothes . . .

Such practicality was contained in the desire to be 'part of this society', and was more typical of what was expressed than any rejection of the idea of personal career that simplistic readings of 'black youth culture' might suggest.

Where the critique of racism *did* transect personal philosophies was more often at the level of immediate community involvements. The ground for such involvements was the actual sense of community and locality itself, which for the black adolescents of Area B was inevitably far stronger than for the dispersed adolescents of Area A. As one young informant expressed it:

> What I like about my street is that all the black kids and a few of the white kids are together. If there's any trouble we're all

out there together. And the thing is that we all feel that we're
part of . . . If anybody troubles one we're ready to fight for
that person. We're all together. This boy's mum got beat up
by this white guy. We was all out there together, you know, to
get the man and that's, kind of, unity.

Or again:

Every black person that moves in [to our estate] we make a
point of letting them know that we're the gang, the clan, and
they can join us. If they've got kids we just let them know.

It was this same sense of local loyalties that led young people who were so
inclined to associate themselves with specific black campaigns, such as
those related to the aftermath of the Deptford Fire and the community
action surrounding the death of Colin Roach in police custody. An
involvement in organised black adult campaigns was, in other words,
predicated both on the shared perception of racism and on the sense of a
black community of interests which was given added meaning by the
demographic and cultural presence which black people had established.

The sense of community and of black community interests which
operated through this medium was the real context within which the
culturally *encoded* messages of black political struggle resonated. Importantly for black/white relations in the area, it formed the basis of black
adolescent hegemony in Area B, just as certain forms of racist ideology
functioned to bolster the local power of adolescent whites in Area A.

II

Although large black acquaintance networks existed, the patterns of
adolescent social organisation in Area B did not correspond with those of
Area A. While many black boys claimed, when questioned, that they
could get up 'a little posse [gang]' if the need arose, those who had ever
done so were insignificantly few, and the scale was nothing like that
which I found to be true for Area A. Furthermore, although stylish dress
was important, style-group differences were *not*, and no divisions of this
kind emerged as the basis for any inter-group conflicts. Fighting between
posses – which in any case tended to be primary peer group affairs rather
than between agglomerations of linked peer groups – were rare. It was
reported to me occasionally that the area might be visited by a large
number of adolescents from another distant location seeking reprisal for
some occurrence involving one of their number, but such events were
treated as having special historical interest, rather than as being part of
the normal flux of social intercourse. Fights were sometimes also

reported to occur between groups of girls, and girls' gangs, although uncommon, *did* exist. These were generally simply 'hang-out' groups, although they could be a force for boys to reckon with, as one boy indicated to me when he told me of 'a whole heap of girls [who] go around together': 'One was fighting [with a boy] and all the girls joined in, bust the boy's arse.'

During the early part of my fieldwork I found some all-black and some racially mixed gangs of boys who were collectively involved in theft. These gangs had names, 'The Ghettomen', 'The X street Gang' etc., and were engaged primarily in street crime and occasional burglary. White adolescent crime in the area was not organised on a gang basis, according to my white informants, and mainly involved house-breaking and shop theft. It was regarded as a fairly normal activity for those between fourteen and eighteen. The larger black criminal gangs were broken up during the early stages of my fieldwork, and I subsequently discovered no large gangs organised around crime, fighting, youth cultural style or any other such principle.

The real basis of black adolescent alliances was simply friendship and neighbourhood proximity, as it is for most adolescents, and as it certainly was for most of the white adolescents of Area A. However, the black *acquaintance networks* of both boys and girls were generally very extensive, and were promoted to some extent by wide socially function- ing kinship networks. This, of course, actually paralleled the original structure of the white community in the area, which was also strongly bonded by kinship. Amongst the contemporary black population, this contributed to community coherence, and to the kind of adolescent social contacts that naturally occurred in school, college and youth club attendance. Other activities, such as the following of professional or local amateur 'sounds' by some, also contributed a further source of cohesion amongst adolescents through specifically black cultural inputs.

Although in Area B all-black primary peer groups were as common as all-white primary peer groups, racially mixed groups, in a catholic variety of combinations, were also completely normal, and most of the all-black and all-white groups I encountered even had satellite members who were not of the same race as the core members. This was a natural conse- quence of the area's being a racially mixed, lower-working-class neigh- bourhood with strong community traditions; and while a tendency to same-race primary groupings was a clearly discernible feature, racial mixing, established at an early age in junior school and in estate playgrounds, carried on into adolescence and continually qualified and eroded hard-and-fast racial divisions.

This had a profound effect on the white adolescent population.

Despite strenuous enquiry, I found absolutely no evidence of the kind of extensive, all-white peer group networks that I found amongst boys in Area A, either on the basis of youth cultural style, or on the basis of inter-group alliances organised around the reciprocation of help in fighting; and most small all-white friendship groups contained adolescents who also had at least some black friends. In an area whose reputation for street fighting, children's and adolescent gangs, and ancient ties and feuds went back in unbroken tradition to the nineteenth century, the absence of this agency of white working-class cultural reproduction was highly significant with regard to contemporary adolescent racial attitudes and practices.

In many ways the kinship networks of the black community and the scope of black adolescent association had, over twenty years, come to replace and supplement the old white local patterns. Thus there could be no racially exclusive associational basis upon which white adolescent territoriality and racial antipathy might be founded, as it was in Area A. Furthermore, the 'cultural space' associated with the district could not be perceived by young whites as transected by conflicting interests that demanded defensive action, because black culture, and specifically black youth culture, was by now incontrovertibly woven into the local social fabric. Indeed, while the sense of pride in the reputation of the district lived on, it was actually taken up into a transformed 'community spirit', which included both black and white and was not disrupted by any clear differences of economic class, either between or within the black and white local populations. Such remnants of the old white lower-working-class racial exclusivity that did re-surface in the younger generation of whites were severely restricted both by an emergent ideology of multi-racial community and by the sheer numerical strength of black youth. White adolescents who did nurture strong racial antipathies were actually incapable of setting the youth cultural tone of the neighbourhood by symbolic or any other means, if that involved the kind of appeals to 'white ethnicity' that skinhead style, as the clearest example, automatically implied. This lack of any wide and efficient associational basis for exclusively white adolescent groupings meant that the isolated few who chose to embrace skinhead style could not indulge in the kind of political activity that characterised the skinheads of Area A, nor even organise themselves into gangs on the basis of their style preference, because the social and political meanings associated with that style made them immediately the most vulnerable of targets. Those adolescents wishing to adopt skinhead style could only do so as the exponents of a passing fad, and not as the real or 'imaginary' representatives of white proletarian culture. As one black boy reported to me:

> There's only a few skinheads round here but they only do it
> for fashion. 'Cos like, if something else came out tomorrow
> morning you'd see them start growing their hair again. But
> they're alright, 'cos they know [that] where they live down X
> Street they can't really do nothin'. 'Cos everybody knows
> where they live, an' that, an' they'd all burn down their houses
> or kill 'em or something.

The underlying dominance relations which here locally precluded
skinhead youth culture from assuming any organisational basis is also
what, more generally, ultimately safeguarded and underwrote all contacts between black and white adolescents. In Area A, both 'proletarian'
and lower-middle-class 'respectable' racist attitudes and ideologies were
mapped onto other features of male peer group and inter-peer group
practices, so that not only were antipathies *intensified* but racism actually
became embodied in group practices. In Area B, where any significant
lower middle-class input was absent, and the only class-grounded vehicle
for racism was lower-working-class, the underlying power relations
between adolescents at street level *interrupted* any process of ideological
embodiment in social forms with respect to adolescent racism. Whatever
racist ideas and hostilities might be attributed to young whites, these
remained immobilised at the level of the individual and the primary peer
group, and were unable to extend into inter-group practices. As another
black commented to me:

> I'm not joking, the white boys are really good. In a way you
> could say that they're good because they know we can batter
> them, so they ain't got no choice. And you know they never
> get out of line, and if they never get out of line, it's alright
> then.

This does not imply that individual whites were intimidated into
friendship with blacks. White and black friends fell out with each other
just as much and just as little as did any other combination. What it did
mean, however, was that the underlying potential of group relations was
already resolved in favour of the black adolescent community, and it was
the knowledge of this that provided the ground upon which friendships
were constructed. The necessity for friendly relations was written into
the power structure at street level, and became submerged and taken up
into white 'common sense' as a 'fact of life'. What for white parents may
have been an *economic* necessity to remain in the district was translated
into a necessity at the level of social interaction for the young. Thus it was
that, in response to my questions concerning why black and white

youngsters appeared to get on so harmoniously, I was repeatedly told by whites that it made no sense to behave in any other way: 'White people get on with blacks [around here]. You have to.' This statement, and the following quotation from a fourteen-year-old white boy, are typical of the comments I received from young whites on this question:

> We just get on. You 'aven't got much choice. If you're livin' in the same country then you've got to go to the same school. It ain't no good if you ain't gonna get on with no-one. You'd just be in trouble all the time so you've got to mix wiv 'em, be friends, an' you don't really get much trouble an' that.

The imperative that 'you have to get on' was, in fact, rarely explicitly presented in terms of street *power*. More often, the power dimension was submerged beneath a more general expression of belief in the basic sensibleness of 'getting on' for its own sake:

> If you live with them you've got to put up with them, and if they live with you they've got to put up with you. That's how it goes. They've got to put up with you and you've got to put up with them so you might as well live with it. You've gotta. That's how it goes. That's no joke. In my street, I'll tell you, there's more blacks in my street than there is whites, see. And they've got to live with the whites and you've got to live with the blacks so you've gotta, sort o' like, *join* them and they've got to join you. D'you know what I mean? That's the way it goes.

The racial mixing characteristic of this area became a matter of simple fact, unquestioned because, for these youngsters, it had never been any other way:

> Round my way there's all black kids and white kids, like. 'Cos, like, they've all mixed-in all their lives. You know what I mean? It's *always* been blacks wiv whites.

The hegemonic authority of the black adolescent community, expressed numerically and culturally, guaranteed and underwrote basic relations, and permitted white youngsters to develop, where they chose to do so, close friendships with blacks which were free of the kind of white peer group interference so common in Area A. While some groups of white friends might occasionally express hostility to blacks in the security of their small circle, peer group pressure on whites designed to discourage black/white contacts would have been totally unrealistic in a setting in which most white youngsters had at least some black friends and many had more black friends than white. One white informant, asked about the racial attitudes of his two best friends, who were white, replied characteristically: 'They don't mind 'em. They've got just as many coloured friends as what I've got 'cos they've come from the same surroundings as what I 'ave.'

At the same time, the possibility of *ambiguous* attitudes over these matters was philosophically accepted by both black and white inform- ants. It seemed to be taken for granted that, in same-race interactions, general antipathy to the out-group might from time to time be expressed. However, both the necessity for good relations and the simple power of friendship was taken to be of more fundamental significance:

> I suppose when the blacks are together on their own they
> probably say, 'White cunts', fings like that, you know. But I
> bet probably you meet one of your mates in the street an' that:
> 'alright?' – like that, 'alright?'. And they probably think, 'I
> ain't seen 'im for a long time. It's good to see 'im again.' But
> probably an hour before he was tellin' 'is mates 'e hates white
> cunts or somethin' like that, you know.

Black youngsters too did not assume that white kids were entirely free of racist attitudes. They simply applied a behaviouristic pragmatism, in the knowledge that, even if white kids did have such ideas, they could not act on them.

In fact, however, the demographic and class features of Area B meant that the ideological mechanisms relevant to racism were very different from those in Area A. The ideological relays that extended from peer group to peer group did not function to promote racism at all but, on the contrary, actually promoted the social ideas of the black adolescent community – which included implicit and explicit critiques of racist practices and attitudes – because black adolescents constituted an important and often dominant part of those networks. White ado- lescents, while by no means free from the influence of racist perspectives, were additionally provided with this alternative and opposing ideological input directly from the black community itself. Thus it was both possible and common for white youngsters to (*a*) have close black friends, (*b*) express strong anti-racist opinions, and yet (*c*) from time to time use racist language – but not in the company of black people – tell racist jokes, and even (in certain contexts) express antipathy to blacks in general. Transected as these youngsters' lives were by differing and sometimes contradictory ideological strands and by contradictory social practices, it was inevitable that different aspects should have been brought to the fore by different interactive situations.

The combination of these contradictory elements and practices differed from person to person, and even within individuals from time to time. The notion of fixed, one-dimensional 'attitudes', by which degrees of racism might be measured, would be quite unhelpful in attempting to understand adolescent race relations in this context. While living in a social environment of this kind and having black friends did not guarantee that racist attitudes would necessarily be excluded, it did ensure (*a*) that racism would not become mobilised as a socially active force at the level of adolescent group association, and (*b*) that alternatives to prevailing racist accounts of social relations were also powerfully present. Such a socially active resource, based on both class and locality, promoted the ideological and cultural terms within which young whites lived out their often contradictory lives. In many ways, it also provided the ground for the genuinely strong white anti-racism which was evident in many of the young white people I interviewed and had dealings with in the course of my participant observation. This opposition to racism was derived neither from white liberal nor from white leftist political sources but directly from the black community, and was imbibed through local social relations.

The contrast between black/white relations in Area B and Area A was sometimes alluded to by those of my informants who were aware of it, when attempting to make clear to me the nature of local loyalties and community coherence in Area B. One black boy who lived in Area B but who had school friends from both areas told me:

> My best friend, you could almost say, is Peter [a white boy from Area B]. When you're talkin' to him you could be blue, pink ... He don't think white. But those from [Area A] and that kinda area ... The way Geoff [a white school friend from Area A] carried on! He kinda change, innit. He just change over night. He start paintin' black as black and white as white, whereas Peter, he doesn't – well, maybe he does but I've never heard him do that. And what it is, down [where we live] if a white person do a favour for a black person he's friends for life. You know what I mean? But in [Area A] it seems a bit shaky.

Loyalties to the area, which included an awareness of a reputation for community cohesion as well as for street toughness, surfaced in many of the interviews I conducted. In attempting to explain how this sense of local community brought black and white together, one white boy reported:

> 'Cos the coloured and the whites ... It's not like, em ... a place where, say, you're livin' there an' a black bloke lives

next door. You see 'im. You think, 'You black bastard' and 'e thinks, 'You white cunt'. It's not one of them. It's er, you come out: 'Alright?' Even if you don't *know* 'em: 'Alright?' Everyone combines with each other.

For working-class *male* adolescents, this kind of unity is often best symbolised by the ability to combine in the physical defence of the district from outside 'attack'. So it was with a certain pride that this same boy told me:

> Once they said Greenwich and Lewisham was coming down to do [our district]. You had all the blacks [and] all the whites waiting in the High Street, sitting on the pavements, waiting' for 'em. And they never come. They knew they'd die that's why.

Although such putative macho esprit de corps was rarely put into practice, its mythology is significant in indicating how loyalties to a district can merge into an ideology of community itself, and can symbol- ise forms of coherence evident at other levels.

  For such young whites, whose familial contacts with the area often stretched back over generations, growing up with black families around them was all they had ever known and so, unlike their parents' gener- ation, a multi-racial neighbourhood constituted their most intimate experience of social life. In whatever ways adult whites accommodated the multi-racial composition of the district, a gap undoubtedly existed between the white generations with respect to their actual social experi- ence. One thirteen-year-old black boy remarked: 'For some of the younger generation [of whites] growing up with black kids is a way of life, but the old people, since they ain't grown up with us, like, they don't understand really.' Most of the white youngsters I interviewed reported that their parents got on 'alright' and some 'very well' with black people. Some, however, plainly registered differences in racial attitudes between themselves and their parents. One informant, for example, complained:

> My old man, he can be reading the paper and it'll have on the front page 'White Man Kills Black Man'. He won't say nothin' about that. On the middle page it could have, 'Black Man Rapes White Woman' – he'll start going on and on: 'Silly black bastards, doin' this!' He'll go on and on and on, my old man. He makes me sick.

Although the longitudinal study showed that the intimacy of association between black and white gradually declined after school-leaving age (a point that will be returned to below), there is no doubt that the patterns of association in childhood and adolescence contributed greatly to the erosion of racial attitudes that may have been prompted within white families or imbibed from other sources within or outside the community.

The most significant difference between Area A and Area B with regard to adolescent race relations was the absence in Area B of peer group pressure on whites who developed friendships with black young-sters, and the absence of any inter-peer group relay for racism. Further-more, not only was there no associational basis for such a relay, but the far-right political groups whose ideas gained some currency amongst groups of young people in Area A had no discernible influence on the young whites of Area B. Together, the absence of these features and the presence of local community traditions meant that the 'ideological vacuum' which surrounded black/white friendships in Area A was not apparent in Area B. Whites with close black friends were not called on to justify, defend or keep quiet about their friendships and it was those who kept themselves aloof from inter-racial contacts who were anomalous.

Local trends in friendship patterns inevitably varied to some extent within the area, depending on the racial composition of the immediate neighbourhood, white youngsters living in estates, or on streets where there were fewer black families, often having fewer black friends than those elsewhere. However, such variations did not alter the overall character of the area, nor qualify the contribution of black culture to life in the neighbourhood.

David, a white boy, was born in Area B. His family lived in a block of council flats where a little more than half the families were black, and he had attended the local junior school, where the majority of the other children were black. He had always had both black and white friends in and out of school, and from an early age he would play in racially mixed groups. By the time he went to secondary school, the majority of his out-of-school friends were black, and he had two especially close friends, one of whom was black, the other white. At the secondary school he attended, the majority of the pupils were white and about a quarter were from Afro-Caribbean homes. He was extremely popular at school with both blacks and whites, although he had one especially close friendship with a white boy in his own year.

He had two brothers who were nine and ten years older than him, and one brother who was six years younger. By any standards his parents were poor: his father, with no occupational skills, was often out of work, and his mother suffered from an illness which made it impossible for her to work. His older brothers apparently contributed substantially to the family income until they married and left home.

My interviews with him began when he was fifteen. Like many other adolescents from Area B, he treated inter-racial friendship as a completely normal feature of life. There were black neighbourhood acquaintances whom he liked and disliked, and, unlike most adolescents from Area A, he never converted dislike for particular black youngsters into expressions of dislike for blacks in general. Indeed, he was completely free from placing any racial interpretation on the behaviour of the black youngsters he knew.

He had no direct contact with street racism, and expressed vehement dislike not only for the political racism of far-right groups but also for such things as racism in employment, the harrassment of young blacks by the police, and what he saw as the white bias of the local and national press. During one early interview he explained:

> I'll tell you why so many white people don't like blacks. It's because [of what] they read in the paper. [. . .] As they get to read it they hate blacks more and more. It's white people who print the papers anyway.

He consistently expressed criticisms of the police with regard to race relations; and when I asked him if any groups like the National Front were at all active in his neighbourhood, he said that they were not, adding:

> I'll tell you who are the National Front in [my neighbourhood]: The Old Bill. They're the ones who are the National Front round our way. They hate coloureds. They really hate 'em, like.

He saw police stereotyping as one aspect of this:

> You get a muggin' an' say a coloured kid gets caught doin' the muggin', they say, 'right, black people mug' and then all the muggin' goes down to blacks.

but he also regarded the police as more generally prejudiced against black people. As evidence of this he gave an account of a National Front march which had attempted to go through his neighbourhood. He told of how both black and white local people had fought with the Front marchers and with the police. I also had other accounts of this locally famous battle from young blacks in the district, who confirmed that blacks and whites fought together against the marchers. It was an exceptional event, but notable for being a clear expression of multi-racial neighbourhood unity. David was in the thick of the fighting, and described the police role in the following terms:

> They were using the toilets as police stations to keep the
> people in. I went down there. I was shitting myself. The Old
> Bill, yeah, they was using the toilets and I'll tell you what,
> every single person they took down the toilets was black. Tell
> you what, this is the truth, I've seen this wiv my *own* eyes.
> Three white geezers were beatin' the cunt out of a black bloke
> who must 'ave been about fifty. These geezers must 'ave been
> about eighteen, twenny. 'E's about fifty. They were kickin' 'im
> to death. The Old Bill come over, pushed the blokes away.
> What did 'e do? Nicked the black bloke for causin' trouble.
> The black bloke's nearly screamin' on the deck. That's what
> makes me feel sick things like that. It's just not right.

It was very common for white youngsters with close familiarity with the
black community to recount occasions on which they had been struck by
police prejudice. It was apparent from David's accounts throughout the
years I interviewed him that his direct experience with the police
consistently contributed to his negative view of them.

He had a strong sense of local black/white unity, however, particularly
with regard to the adolescent population, and speculated (probably on
the basis of his experience of the National Front march):

> If Enoch Powell came into [our neighbourhood] for a day, 'e
> wouldn't get out of 'ere alive. No way would 'e get out of 'ere
> alive.

adding:

> Tell you what I'd like. He's got three married daughters and a
> son. I'd laugh if one of his daughters married a black bloke.
> That would shoot 'im right up the kilt!

His basic friendships remained unaltered throughout his last year of
secondary school, although his two closest out-of-school friends, being a
year older than him, had both left their schools. The white friend, John,
had got a job in a factory and Terry, the black friend, had not managed to
get a job. David himself left school with no qualifications a few months
before he was legally entitled to. Through a relative, he got a job with a
painting and decorating firm, where he worked for about a year. During
this time Terry and John both started 'going steady' with girl friends.
Terry's girlfriend became pregnant, and once the baby was born David
saw Terry only very occasionally. John, too, went out less often, and
David also came to see less of him.

David would drink, on a couple of nights a week, at a pub where one of
his older brothers worked on a part-time basis. The pub was mainly

frequented by white people, and thus, when a group of the younger regulars, including David, started up a football team, it was an all-white team. Some of the members of this team came to be David's regular 'hang-out' group, and by the time of my final interview with him, when he was eighteen years old, he no longer had any close black friends, although he still regarded his large circle of black acquaintances as his friends: 'I've still got as many [black] friends, I just don't see 'em so much.' He also started going out with a girl on a regular basis when he was seventeen and this too, he told me, had changed how much time he actually spent with *any* of his male friends:

> Me coloured friends, I don't hardly see 'em at all. Most of me close friends are white now. Since I've been goin' out wiv [my girl friend] it's a bit different now, you know. I just pop out wiv me mates once a weekend or twice a weekend.
> *Is it that you don't see your coloured mates at all or what?*
> I don't really, 'cos I'll tell you what I've found. As you get older an' you start wantin' to go out for a drink, 'cos not many coloureds drink that much do they? I s'pose if they did go in the pubs the same as we do I s'pose I'd be just as friendly wiv 'em as what I've always been.

It seemed to be a convergence of cultural factors that had altered the basic associational patterns of his life since he was sixteen; and although a black friend of some of his football team mates had become a regular drinking partner, and he now also worked with a black friend in a new job he had acquired in a warehouse, the prevailing trend was that he had come to associate more with whites, and led a more settled, less 'street'-orientated life, with engagement to his girlfriend undoubtedly on the horizon.

His fundamental attitudes over race had remained unchanged throughout the three years that I interviewed him, even though his late teens were clearly bringing about changes in his social life. Whatever changes of attitude may or may not have occurred later on, he expressed just as much opposition to racism at eighteen as he had at fifteen.

Like David, Barney was born in Area B but lived in a part of the district where there were rather more whites than blacks. His father ran a second-hand shop, and his mother worked as a supervisor in an office-cleaning firm. Out of school he had three close friends who were black, and four or five white friends who lived near to him and also attended his school. As well as these white school friends, he had one very close black school friend, with whom he spent much of his time during the fourth year. This, he told me, was similar to his experience in junior school, where he had also had one especially close black friend.

At the age of fourteen, about a quarter of Barney's out of school friends were black, and the majority were white. A year later, in his fifth year of secondary school, this was still the case. Several evenings each week, he would go to a racially mixed youth club on an estate near to his house, and he would hang out with both black and white friends there. Unlike David, who never displayed any real ambiguity about race, Barney and his white friends clearly fell into the category of youngsters whose social experience and attitudes were contradictory, although the influence of racial antipathy was obviously kept low by the mixed friendship networks which they inhabited. Displaying considerably less awareness of racism than David ever did, he told me, 'I never say things about coloureds . . . Well, I *sometimes* do when I'm mucking about but I don't really mean it.' The same ambiguity came out when he was describing the racial attitudes of his white friends:

> They like 'em and they don't like 'em, if you know what I mean. Like, they say things about 'em and the next minute they're talkin' with 'em and friends with 'em. It's stupid really.

His own attitude also combined real friendship with pragmatism and some ambiguity. At nearly sixteen he told me:

> You've gotta live with 'em ain't you, so you might as well start now. I don't mind 'em. They're alright. It's only the few I don't like, like the thievin' ones. You know what I mean. But some of *them* are alright. There's this one black kid round my way, name's Colin, right. 'E thieves an' this, right, but 'e's still an *ace* kid. 'E's alright. 'E's a right nice kid 'e is. 'E'd do anythin' for you.

Unlike David, Barney did not move from having a number of close black friends to having any articulated critique of racist practices, although he did express the view that blacks found it much more difficult than whites to find work and, like most young people in Area B, regarded far-right political groups with contempt.

During his fifth year of school he saw less of Ray, his close black school friend, because Ray had taken to hanging around more with a group of black boys. Ray and Barney nevertheless still considered themselves to be good friends. When he left school, however, and started work in the cleaning firm for which his mother worked, Barney rarely saw Ray again except by chance. He continued to use the youth club, although less frequently, and would play pool and table tennis with his black and white friends there. On the final occasion on which I interviewed him, he told me that he still had about the same ratio of black and white friends that he had always had, and did not foresee any immediate change.

While both David and Barney had close black friends throughout junior and secondary school, and neither of them would entertain the kind of attitudes which are most commonly taken to characterise racism, the differences between them are instructive. In Barney's case, his immediate small group of white friends clearly *did* occasionally make derogatory remarks about blacks in general, as he himself admits to doing, though 'not seriously'. Such verbalising probably could not be said to constitute 'racial hostility', and there was no other way in which this white friendship group did anything that might be construed as 'racist behaviour'. Nevertheless it is clear from Barney's references to 'the thieving ones' as a subcategory of black adolescents rather than as a subcategory of adolescents in general, that the publicity given to black crime had made its impact on him.

David had managed to avoid much white 'common knowledge' of this kind insinuating itself in his thinking, and he was consequently comparatively free from having such paradoxes to deal with. Because he actually thought critically about racism, he had taken his distance from the popular parlance over race. Examples of white 'misinformation' stood out very starkly for him, and he displayed no difficulty in saying directly and simply what he felt was true on the basis of his own social experience, without reference to any national consensus.

Barney's family were materially much better off than David's, and David had had more black friends than Barney during pre-adolescence and adolescence. These factors may have been influential. Furthermore, the poverty of David's family may have worked against any personal investment in the values and ideologies of which the legitimating notions of racism often form a part. However, variations between adolescents in very similar circumstances to those of both David and Barney are such as to render predictions based on individual biographies of this kind very unreliable. What *is* more certain is that, whatever the causes of differential susceptibility to implicit racist conceptualisations, the presence of alternative accounts generated from within the black community itself, underwritten by close social contacts and, more simply, by black adolescent street power at the local level, provided a context in which some whites could come to perceive the position of black people in a way that more closely corresponded to how black youngsters themselves perceived it.

The element of 'street power', so important with regard to adolescent peer group relations and so significant in limiting the embodiment of racist ideas in racist practices, indicates that the outcome of the social contest between racist and anti-racist ideas more generally is likely to be ultimately dependent upon the structure of actual power relations. Such, at least, is one lesson that might be learned from inter-racial adolescent relations. It is obvious that 'inter-racial friendship' alone cannot secure the more fundamental changes that are necessary for the eradication of racism, even if it may contribute to the erosion of some of its effectiveness in particular localities.

Not only was friendship underwritten by power relations, but the ideological and cultural continuities which were so obviously *absent* from the social context of inter-racial friendship in Area A were available supports in Area B. This difference was brought home especially forcefully when I began working with a group of youngsters in a racially mixed youth club in the heart of Area B. Race and racism were difficult topics to begin discussing directly with whites from Area B, because the terms within which race is usually discussed were not regarded by them as constituting an issue in their daily lives. Furthermore, for them, usually the only *whites* who introduced the subject of race were older people expressing racist views. Thus when I first began talking to a group of five or six thirteen to fifteen-year-olds about black/white friendship, I was immediately suspected of coming into this category, and was forcefully challenged by a girl of thirteen with 'You're not a racist are you?', and by others with similarly direct questions. There were no black youngsters present, yet these young whites only agreed to talk to me when they were satisfied that I was 'not a racist'. This kind of reaction was the reverse of my experience in youth clubs in Area A, where the first assumption was always that I shared with my informants their hostility to blacks and Asians, and that this was just as it should be.

Although this kind of articulated anti-racism was not present amongst all the young whites I interviewed and observed, it certainly formed a significant part of the local ideological landscape within which inter-racial friendships were situated and was taken up equally by girls and boys. Although girls did not customarily conceive of local loyalties in the macho terms that boys sometimes used, they just as frequently insisted that they 'had to get on' with black people, and that in their neighbourhood black and white youngsters 'get on well' and 'mixed in' with each other.

Most of the inter-racial friendships of white girls were with individuals of the same sex, a pattern repeated in the case of boys. White girls with black boyfriends were almost as rare as white boys with black girlfriends. Unlike Area A, inter-racial amatory relationships in Area B were uncommon. This was supported by community pressures on both sides. Black girls told me how they would never go out with a white boy, that they would feel ashamed, and that their families would not like it at all. One girl explained that white boys were far too scruffy for her tastes, adding: 'a stylish white man isn't white, he's black'. She also commented that she wouldn't go out with a black man who had been out with many white girls, because black men got 'bad ways' from being allowed to be selfish and to abuse white girls' affection. One black boy reported that he had been accustomed to think that going out with a white girl was 'a crime' from a 'black point of view'. Being accused of being a 'banna-check' – a person who has over-close relations with whites – was, for him a particularly compelling criticism.

White boys were also, usually, in principle against black boys going out with white girls. One boy commented crisply, 'Whenever I see a black [man] with a white girl I think that's wrong. They both should be shot. Stick to your own colour and keep it that way.' However, the extreme concern over this issue which characterised white male attitudes in Area A was not evident amongst white males in Area B. Common racist themes still intruded themselves usually from older generations – 'My dad says that the only reason white girls go out wiv coloured blokes is they've got bigger pricks' – but such troubled thinking was uncommon, and white boys could be equally capable of appearing quite unthreatened by black boys. One white boy, talking about his youth club, told me:

> There was a [black boy] there called John and all the girls
> were talkin' to him. My [white] mate says 'Why are they all
> talkin' to him?' I said, 'Well, coloured people have got nice
> personalities towards girls – white girls and coloured girls –
> and that's most probably why they're always talkin' to him.'

The very low incidence of black/white boyfriend/girlfriend relations, however, obviously kept the issue itself from having much force in local relations or from extending into other racial issues. What was, in fact, a major source of tension within the adolescent population of Area A was of no importance in Area B.

The *development* of consciousness over racial matters and their relation to everyday black/white interactions was, perhaps, the most important feature of the way in which the available anti-racist attitudes were conveyed to young whites. The often encoded social messages relayed within the adolescent community developed in interactions throughout childhood. Where opposition to racism, and a sensitivity to what (for black people) was deemed to constitute racism, was learned, it was learned gradually rather than rapidly, and was often less than articulate. It was through interactive negotiations with friends and acquaintances over a long period of time that sensitivity to the issues was developed, rather than by any sudden exposure to a social or political programme of ideas wherein racism was seen to be false or morally wrong.

In terms of adolescent inter-racial relationships, Area B was extremely relaxed, and as a promoter of 'peaceful race relations' between adolescents, the structures provided by inter-racial friendships were important contributors. However, as with many such friendships in Area A, here too there was a clear tendency for friendships within racial groups to be sustained after the age of about sixteen, whilst those *between* the racial groups tended gradually to fade after that age. Leisure-time contacts became less frequent, and the kind of 'cultural drift' which pulled at inter-racial friendships also commonly affected friendships in Area B. But while in Area A this divergence was also often accompanied by a move towards explicit racist attitudes, here this was not the case for the youngsters whom I interviewed into their late teens, nor was there any evidence of it occurring more generally. Whatever social factors affected the formation of racial attitudes after that age, certainly none that could be traced to features of adolescent association appeared to be influential.

Despite the importance of inter-racial association, however, it is less the peer group's value for 'community relations' per se that is ultimately of social significance than its role as the agency of cultural transmission, translation and contest.

What inter-racial friendship permitted at the ideological level was an increase in the variety of positions that might be taken up within the white adolescent population. That is to say, while association, in the form of friendship, provided one basis of ideological relay, and at the same time the actual numerical and associational dominance of young blacks provided the necessary power axis, more positions than those which were merely reproductions of racist ideologies could be generated. It was the interactive relationship between black and white ideological positions that gave the adolescent population its identity as a 'community', despite its divisions. Socially circumscribed racist perspectives existed side by side with critical anti-racist ones, each to be brought into prominence or cast into the background by specific interactional variables. It was this range of ideological 'lects' that distinguished Area B from Area A, where the ideological 'lect' of a genuinely working-class white anti-racism found few speakers and fewer listeners.

III

I have focused so far on *explicit* attitudes with regard to race, and have attempted to indicate the complex of young people's practices and ideas before moving to an introduction of the aspects of cultural relations which are explored in detail in the remainder of this book, and within which ideological themes – where they are present – are most usually refracted and diffused. It is these cultural aspects, perhaps even more than the 'purely' attitudinal ones, that provide the language through which implicit social concepts become expressed. Here the 'lects' of urban culture are often less starkly differentiated than the contradictory ideological strands of white adolescent 'opinion'. It is largely through the cultural domain that group memberships are claimed, contested and evaluated. Notions of social relationships are enacted rather than spoken, encoded rather than articulated.

As an element of this cultural arena, the impact of black youth culture on young whites functioned at two levels, one of which – the deliberate adoption of black cultural markers by whites – was also noted in the discussion of adolescent relations in Area A. The indirect validation of specific aspects of black culture through the commercial entertainment industry actually contributed to the prestige which black youth was able to generate for itself within particular localities. White youngsters attracted to this extent by black youth culture were sometimes implicated in the articulation of black political perspectives, but this was more an *effect* than a cause. What was of primary concern appeared to be the desire to participate in the 'prestige' attaching itself to black youth, and, indeed, by the very act of imitation such young whites were themselves simultaneously contributing to and demonstrating that prestige.

At the other level, black youth culture of a less obvious kind also made itself felt – the barely conscious spread to local white adolescents of cultural ephemera and distinctive modes of interaction generated within the black adolescent community. On the surface of cultural life, this spread was effected by the simple prevalence of black youth cultural forms in the life of the district.

In most of the youth clubs, and in the street life of the district, black youth culture – and especially black music – was dominant. Reggae, soul, jazz-funk and occasional socca echoed from youth club disco speakers or from the 'ghetto blasters' – the high-volume radio and tape-deck units that were laboriously carried by young blacks and whites. The smart styles of dress, within the limits of adolescent utility, were predominantly the black styles for both boys and girls. For a time it was the 'Farah' slacks, 'Cecil Gee' pullovers, moccasins and gold chains for boys, and for girls, box-pleated skirts, black or burgundy high leather boots, or slightly frayed blue jeans with a raised crease. The styles evolved continually, many becoming gradually taken over by whites, ultimately spreading outwards even as far as to the all-white suburbs and beyond. Some of these fashions, such as the wearing of 'old colonel' hats, were directly appropriated from the white upper classes. Others, like the adoption of costly suede and woollen cardigans and gold chains, were simply cultural expansions into pre-established 'expensive' styles. Such things, when worn by whites, could not be taken as stolen 'markers of ethnicity' unless the combinations were particularly blatant. Although young blacks were usually well aware of the black origins of the fashions as they came and went, only in specific circumstances were some features treated as charged with meanings of this kind. Much of the unselfconscious surface of black youth style was, in other words, merely a currency, even if details of it might become elevated to a more 'ethnic' status under certain interactive conditions.

In this socially uncharged domain of youth culture, differences between black and white youngsters might still be expressed, but were of a different order to those relating to boundary-maintenance issues. One young white boy with many black friends explained, for example, about his 'only' area of reservation about certain young blacks:

> The fing that gets me about some coloureds, some coloureds like dressing in really smart clothes and if you tread on their shoes they get annoyed about it. Well, I pay a lot of money for my shoes but I don't get annoyed if people tread on my shoes or say, 'You trod on my shoes. I'm gonna bang you', an' that. But they get so annoyed...

However, this kind of expression is very different from that found in Area A, where whites were particularly vigilant about 'encroaching' black youth style and, amongst boys, any garment to be bought was screened for its use amongst blacks.

The influence of black youth culture was also registered amongst white youth in other ways. Especially amongst boys, styles of masculine behaviour were transmitted to the white boys from the black, so that, at levels of culture deeper than simply those of fashion and style, an impact was made on white adolescents through other social and cultural codes. In replying to a question about what kinds of ideas or attitudes he had picked up from having black friends, one sixteen-year-old white boy answered:

> Well ... if I was goin' into a fight an' all, they say I shouldn't be scared. Go there to fight, an' if I lose I lose. Just go back a nex day and get 'em. Where if I [hadn't known black boys] I s'pose I'd ... if I was gettin' beaten I'd just run. And er, sort o' like, when you're chattin' up girls, don't be shy wiv 'em, an' that. Like, they just go straight up to 'em an' that, so I do

them things. But the main thing I picked up is how to control a
sound system properly. And one of 'em who works in a
record shop he tells me to listen to the tune of the music and
not the words, really, just the tune . . .

This is something of a 'ready-mix' recipe for black adolescent masculinity, and is indicative of an aspect of cultural transmission that may have
been supportive of – though by no means conflatable with – more socially
pointed aspects.

The 'low-level' effects of black youth culture on whites remained one
simple expression of contact, the underlying determinants of which
perhaps only come into view where specific cultural items or configur-
ations of items become bestowed with a significance *beyond* themselves,
through interaction or deliberate choice. By whatever processes cultural
materials – hair styles, dress, speech, musical affiliations – become
charged with social and political meanings, the existence of such
'marked' items *can* place black/white interactions very starkly in the
realm of ideological contest. Whatever its local outcome, and however
invisible it may be to the actors themselves, what is being 'spoken'
constitutes the very material of social struggle in culture through which
interactants may, however obliquely, learn something of the submerged
meanings which shape their lives.

It is here, in other words, away from the realm of explicit social
'attitudes' and ideas, that young whites may become instructed in the
issues surrounding racism and black/white relations; here that young
whites move towards or away from a form of introduction to social life
that is different from that which familial or other forms of 'socialisation'
may offer.

Those who moved from the ethnically unstressed but decidedly
black-inflected 'bottom line' of local youth culture, and were knowingly
attracted to the declarative black modes, inevitably entered a more
dangerous and contested arena. Some, especially in their early teens,
adopted black style as completely as they could. Like the cultural hybrids
of Area A, they attempted to 'become black' in musical loyalties, dress
and speech. Despite the fact that black adolescents in Area B were more
confident and hence, if anything, less vigilant about white cultural
incursions than the isolated blacks of Area A, pressure from the
immediate black adolescent community certainly worked against such
transformations, and white boys and girls indulging themselves in the
attempt to 'pass' culturally were, again, heavily reliant on the support of
a few close black friends.

What proved an obstacle to their attempt was not the use of black style per se, or the enthusiastic following of black music, but the apparent appropriation of those specific aspects of the culture that were charged with sociopolitical meaning – such as Rasta blazonry – combined with the very public display of their white 'blackness'. Whites identifying with black culture to this extent and in this way often provoked critical and sometimes very hostile responses, not only from young blacks protective of the cultural/political boundaries, but also from other whites, on the grounds *not* that they had 'sold out' to the 'opposition', as was frequently said in Area A, but that they had lost their integrity as white 'individuals'. Such criticisms and effective hostility usually restricted the most blatant white incursions into 'blackness' to those in their early teens, although a few survived up to school-leaving age and even beyond.

Despite this, in the usually unspoken negotiations with black friends and acquaintances surrounding such moves, the lessons which had not been learned at the level of articulated opinions at least had the possibility of being ingested in encoded form at the level of culture.

The context of this informal pedagogic activity also has its own contradictory aspects, however. The process whereby the innovations of black youth culture feed into the commercial world of entertainment, and are appropriated for use at levels far removed from inner-city street corners, is not without its paradoxes, even though this same process may also indirectly reflect back on the local prestige of young blacks. The transformations that take place within the commercial sector do not unambiguously work in the interests of black people, and the equation of blacks with entertainment that is reinforced through this channel may serve a more sinister function in positioning blacks in ways that contradict deeper concerns with political and economic struggles. The 'coincidence' of the rise of minstrelsy in nineteenth-century American popular entertainment with the serious challenge presented by the Abolitionist Movement – first pointed out by Le Roi Jones (1966: 83–4) – should, perhaps, be borne in mind in this context, even though at that time a genuine black culture remained invisible to most whites to an extent that is not true today. The modern British street-corner 'whites in blackface' are, of course, now by-products of a rather different conjuncture; but *some* of the elements of the old equation remain unchanged, and must seriously qualify and limit the value that may be placed on any popular validation of black youth culture.

Furthermore, even where cultural contacts within which ideological themes are processed *do* provide a site of alternative social learning for young whites, what is learned is likely to be subject to a limitation of scope which may, for example, leave untouched principled formulations incorporating the effect of racism on Asian or other non-white communities, even while perceptions of the deeper significance of Afro-Caribbean boundary maintenance are sharpened. Thus, although black culture may be drawn upon by young blacks as a politically strategic resource in certain forms of interaction, the informal pedagogic value of this activity with regard to the inculcation of any broader understanding of racism in young whites is probably very low when it moves beyond the specific terms of black/white relations. This question of the relation of black and white attitudes to Asian and other minorities is treated more fully in Chapter 6, below.

The differences between Areas A and B were more stark with respect to explicit attitudes and forms of association than they were with respect to such cultural themes. The class divisions within Area A, where differences in the forms of racism were also expressed, were not substantially present in Area B. While both areas contained a white lower working class, areal differences between the white adolescent members of that class fraction were moderated by local demographic and historical features. In particular, the community loyalties which had been to some extent preserved by the lateness and partial nature of urban renewal programmes, coupled with the scale of black settlement, constituted in Area B a different social context to black/white adolescent relations from that found in Area A, with its early postwar renewal and its small, highly dispersed and socially differentiated black population. These differences, when expressed through adolescent associational forms, provided a very different social terrain within which particular inter-racial friendships might be situated and through which explicit concepts of race and race relations were relayed.

In contrast to this clear areal differentiation, the issues regarding *cultural* relations were much the same in both areas, the differences here residing more in the strength of the issues than in the issues themselves. In this sense the cultural questions were over-arching, and although the shared middle ground between black and white was far broader in Area B than in Area A, in both areas the basic questions posed within black/white friendships that were dealt with at the cultural level were often very similar, and are likely to be pertinent to adolescent race relations elsewhere. For this reason, the following chapters are given over to an examination of the cultural issues which emerged from the research in both areas.

The process of social development through inter-racial contacts occurred most significantly through the cultural languages that were available to, and engendered by, young people. Such cultural codes transpose struggles over power into struggles within signification and, as will be seen, were capable of registering a variety of voices and positions, as well as dealing with some of the material paradoxes of racism and inter-racial friendships.

Adolescence is a period of apprenticeship in social semiosis, in which coarse images of social life are innocently related to a fecund community of signs. Here, before adulthood obscures them, emergent structures are sometimes caught reflected in the signifying practices of adolescent life. In the contrastive semiotic of inter-racial friendship, this was particularly evident. Thus, the informal pedagogic practices through which whites were able to assume the critical postures of anti-racism were largely conducted through these terms, and as exposure to them decreased, so too did the possibilities of social learning that inhered in the process.

It is here that the importance of the cultural drifting apart of black and white youngsters, remarked on above, resides. The racial division of social and economic life ultimately exerts its pressure so that the 'cultural drift' itself intervenes to terminate the productive dialogue of youth. As the frames of interaction become more 'adult', and the structural realities of race edge even more firmly into the spaces between black and white youth, the languages of contact thin to nothing, leaving only the dominant tongues through which to speak. The ground of that 'productive dialogue of youth' is, therefore, in need of special attention. It is to an examination of these issues that I now turn, beginning with the language of black youth culture itself.

3

The language of black youth culture

Black youth culture in the United Kingdom has been neither static nor uniform since its distinctive emergence in the 1960s. Developments have been generated both from within the adolescent population and as a result of influences from the Caribbean and North America; and although the strands most closely associated with Rastafari have been those which have attracted most attention from sociological and other commentators (Cashmore 1979; Hebdige 1976; 1979; Troyna 1977; Garrison 1979) and from the media, 'the culture' has in fact developed as a complex of independent but inter-related aspects. The Rasta strand was for a while simply the most spectacular, and certainly one of the most articulate, while never necessarily being the most widespread. In the 1970s the prevailing Jamaican 'rude boy' culture gave way to Rasta influence *and* to the 'stylers', whose interest in appearance could not be identified with Rasta other-worldliness. Later, 'soul boy' fashion provided another development along a similar 'worldly' trajectory. Throughout, the twin influences of black America and Jamaica have been apparent, and by the mid-1980s the influence of North American soul/disco and New York dance, as well as other black American youth 'crazes', has actually come to rival the more community-rooted Caribbean elements.

The balance between Jamaican and North American cultural orientations was at a pivotal point during my fieldwork period. In the very early 1980s, the strongest input was clearly still Jamaican, and was closely associated with reggae music. At the same time, the American influence was effected through black American soul music. Soul, it was often said, was a black musical form but one equated with black and white social mixing, while reggae was a music essentially for black people. A key concept in black youth culture at that time, and one also closely linked to 'dub' reggae (see below), was the concept of 'dread', derived originally

100

from the Rastafarian religion, where it is a term of esteem. Amongst Rastafarians, 'dread' continues to have this meaning, but amongst many young people it came to be used with cultural rather than religious overtones. To be truly 'dread' in this cultural sense was to be especially worthy of respect as an initiate of a black Jamaican cultural mystery, the indicators of which were a commitment to reggae music, the employment of creole and an assiduously maintained separation from intercourse with white people. It represented a strong statement of cultural separatism, and a deliberate avoidance of contamination by white values. This 'ideal' definition was in practice hedged in by other strands in the developing culture, but it was for a while influential. As one boy told me, 'If you're dread you're supposed to stick with black girls, stick with your own colour and go for your own tune, and that's it, right? And soul [music], soul is for white *and* black so if you go for soul you can't really say you're dread, can you?' The concept of 'dread' became much less central by the early 1980s, when the word also carried a more general meaning simply equated with 'good', and in this sense it has persisted. For generations growing into the culture, the concept remains an ideological resource, but one submerged beneath the surface of cultural life and open to distortions.

Like the American concept of 'soul', that analogous quality which is said to inform soul music and many other aspects of black American life (Hannerz 1969), the religious origins of 'dread' permit a redefinition in individualistic rather than in black community terms. To be amongst the 'elect' can be interpreted as an inner state, a condition of individuation rather than membership. One female informant, significantly with a black father and a white mother, claimed that, regardless of musical affiliations or colour, 'dread' was a condition of *being*: 'I think dread is how you are within', she said. This was not a common view, but for this informant it clearly offered one solution to the contradictions she experienced in the concept's ethnic/racial specificity, and permitted the possibility of individual 'salvation' without reference to group boundaries. This option clearly displays the potential for ideological reinterpretation possessed by religious formulations.

During the 1970s, the creole of black youth came to be referred to as 'dread talk'. Although this nomenclature has itself changed, and despite the subsequent variations that have emerged within black British youth culture, the Caribbean-based creole, or 'patois' as it is often called, has continued to be an important feature, resonating as a marker of race and ethnicity throughout all the forms that the culture has taken. Indeed, the creole of young blacks itself appears to have changed as the number of young blacks born in Britain has increased; and its relation to Caribbean creoles has also been mediated by British urban speech and by the expressive needs formed around the changing experiences of urban youth.

Despite the wider social stigmatisation of creole, the distinctive language of black youth culture is in fact a 'prestige' variety amongst many young people. This is consonant with Suzanne Romaine's assertion that, 'during the adolescent years the use of socially stigmatized [speech] forms is at a maximum' (Romaine 1984: 104). The development of generational languages and dialects – especially where an ethnic and race dimension is also present – has been internationally reported in many urban settings. Suttles' account of black 'jive talk' in Chicago (Suttles 1968: 65), Labov's (1972b) sociolinguistic studies of 'Black English Vernacular' (which he locates particularly in the nine to eighteen age-range), and other North American studies such as those by Kochman (1972), Smith (1972), Mitchell-Kernan (1972) and Folb (1980), have well documented the language of young black North Americans. Such 'youth languages' manage to establish themselves as prestige varieties in generationally specific social contexts. Escure, reporting on linguistic variation and 'ethnic interaction' in Belize (Escure 1979: 114) claims:

> Among young people . . . both Creoles and Caribs, Creole constitutes a fashionable *lingua franca*: 'taaking raas' is as prestigious as American disco music and blue-tinted 'shades' (sunglasses) but borrows some lexical items from Black English – phrases like 'Dig?', 'Check it out!' for example.

Hancock (1976: 168), discussing lexical expansion in West African Krio, asserts: 'For some younger creoles their language is regarded as a badge of ethnicity; with the current American-influenced assertion of Black awareness Krio is sometimes identified in a positive way with "soul talk", a kind of English uniquely black.'

Such prestige youth languages are not restricted to black youth. The report by Ramirez (1974) on the use of a Chicano dialect of Spanish by adolescents in the south west of the United States and E. B. Ryan's (1979) evidence concerning Mexican American non-standard English are both examples of non-black generational 'prestige' speech forms. In Canada a generational language called 'Chiac', in which French and English are mixed together, has been reported amongst adolescents in the Atlantic provinces (Blanc 1982), and a similar example is 'Taal', the 'mixed' language of black South African adolescents (Jansen 1984). (See also Schwarz and Merten 1967; Cheshire 1982; Romaine 1984.)

The creole languages employed by some black English adolescents vary from Dominican and St Lucian French-based creoles to Guyanese,

'Bajan' – the creole of Barbados – and those of other Caribbean islands. These, however, are the creoles learned within families and small communities. The number of British-born speakers of these creoles appears to be small, and none of these actually constitutes the generational prestige variety used by black British youth. Here the influential creole is Jamaican, which has been described in detail by Le Page and De Camp (1960); Cassidy and Le Page (1967; 1980); Cassidy (1961); Bailey (1966); and DeCamp (1971), although caution is needed. First, it is important to distinguish between the creole spoken by people who were brought up in Jamaica, and the creole employed *alongside English* by an unknown number of young blacks born and raised in England. The only extensive study of Jamaican creole used in this country by people born Jamaican is by John Wells (1973) and is restricted to pronunciation. No full survey of the speech of young blacks born in this country of Caribbean parentage has as yet been undertaken, but some evidence is available in the fullest account to appear to date, David Sutcliffe's 'British Black English' (1982), and more concisely in Sutcliffe 1984. Other accounts may be found in Edwards 1979; Sebba 1983*a*; 1983*b*; 1984.

Estimates of the extent to which young British-born blacks employ creole differ widely. Sutcliffe (1978) claimed that some 95% of black children speak some creole, while Rosen and Burgess, in their survey of the speech of London school children (1980), put it as low as 10–20%, and less than 4% for 'a full Caribbean creole'. However, there are problems here with what might be taken as the criteria for creole use. Are these criteria, for example, to include a wide range of creole features used frequently, or the intermittent use of some creole features on some occasions? Clear-cut divisions are difficult to draw where some grammatical, lexical and phonological features appear often in the speech of some young blacks, others not at all. It is an extension of the problem of defining any creole speech community. Labov, in response to Le Page's theoretical proposals for the interpretation of Belize vernacular, has indicated that there is an absolute difference to be drawn with regard to the presence or absence of 'systematicity' in a speaker's *partial knowledge* of creole forms (Labov 1980; 384), while Le Page, wishing to provide a model capable of accounting for movement across a number of 'languages', finds such a definition unhelpful (Le Page 1975*a*; 1975*b*). For the purpose of this description it *is* necessary to draw some broad informal distinctions, despite the debate within linguistics, based on my own data and on the work of those who have written on the subject of Caribbean-based creoles in Britain.

Whatever the relationship of the creoles used by young blacks born in this country to the creoles of black British people born and raised in the Caribbean, it is apparent that *some* young blacks can employ both an indigenous dialect of English – London vernacular or Yorkshire, say – and a dialect closely related to Jamaican creole which has been termed 'British Jamaican Creole' or, specifically in relation to London speech, 'London Jamaican'. Some can also employ another creole, e.g. the French-based creole of St Lucia, as well as the generational prestige 'British' or 'London' and an 'indigenous' dialect. It is also the case that the young black users of these dialects switch from one to another at certain times and in certain contexts which for the moment await full investigation. (Some discussion of code choice among young blacks is to be found in Sutcliffe 1982: 147–9; Sebba 1983*a*; and Sebba and Wootton 1984.)

At the same time, the *English* spoken by many young blacks often contains a number of lexical items and occasional grammatical features found most commonly in Jamaican creole and London Jamaican, although when these appear transposed into English they usually lose the characteristic features of Jamaican pronunciation. Sebba (1983*a*) argues that this London English, with its highly variable creole influences, constitutes a distinct variety, which he has called 'Black London English'. He sees this as distinct from both London Jamaican Creole and London English. Sutcliffe (1984), working with some data from several English towns including London, also distinguishes what he calls 'British Black English' – this creole-influenced English – from other Englishes, although, unlike Sebba, he sees a continuum existing between this variety and what he calls 'British Jamaican Creole'. Because it is not the case that *all* adolescent black Londoners speak a variety of English that shows the impact of creole forms, and because no research has been completed which might establish how many adolescent black Londoners speak such a dialect, it seems over-inclusive to label this variety – if distinctive variety it is – 'Black'. Furthermore, as the speech of some young whites in London also displays some creole-derived features, there would seem good grounds for simply referring to 'London English' and in specific instances examining the nature and levels of creole penetration. Further linguistic research may clarify these matters; but the creole-influenced speech of adolescent Londoners will not be treated here as a distinct variety of London English.

London Jamaican Creole is more clearly definable, although even here problems are apparent. Several linguists have affirmed that the most common creole forms used by young blacks born in Great Britain are distinctively Jamaican rather than Barbadian, Guyanese etc. Even when a youngster's parents do not themselves come from Jamaica and do not speak Jamaican creole, that youngster – if he or she uses creole at all – is most likely to use a creole which shows close phonological, grammatical and lexical relationships with Jamaican (Edwards 1979; Sutcliffe 1982; 1984; Le Page 1981; Sebba 1983*a*; 1983*b*). This appears to be because, as Jamaicans constituted the largest Caribbean immigrant group in Great Britain, and as Jamaican culture has had a powerful impact on young British blacks, it is the Jamaican-based creole that has become the dominant and distinctively prestigious language of black youth culture. The gathering of sufficient reliable data, however, has lagged behind interest in this field. The extent to which British creole can be simply equated with Jamaican has been questioned by Craig (1983); and at the same time, the degree to which creole speech is employed uninterrupted by non-creole English has also been raised as an issue by Sebba (1983*a*; 1983*b*) and by Rosen and Burgess (1980). It is certainly the case that many black adolescent Londoners do not habitually employ any full or fluent creole, even though they may on occasion use creole forms with a strong Jamaican pronunciation sporadically interjected into their normal English speech. It is also the case that some, although probably only a minority, are able to conduct extensive conversations in creole. Nevertheless, there has been little research that might give better definition to these issues.

From my own observation and interviews it appears that demographic factors are influential. In the areas of densest black settlement the lateral supports for creole use are inevitably greater. It was certainly true that the two areas in which I conducted research amongst adolescents differed in this respect. In Area A there were many black youngsters who knew and used very little creole. Indeed, it was common for black adolescents from both lower-middle-class and working-class homes in the area not to use creole at all. In Area B the use of creole was substantially greater amongst adolescents, and was also supported more strongly by continuities with the adult population. Even in junior school, children in Area B were far more likely to hear creole used by their peers than were the junior school children of Area A, and this is likely to have had an influence on the ease with which they may later have moved towards London Jamaican.

On the other hand, moderating parental influence also operated in both areas. Many black parents equate creole use with economic failure. They positively discourage their children from using creole forms, in the belief that it will interfere with their mastery of school English and, ultimately, lessen their chances of getting a job. Although this was reported to me by youngsters from both areas, in Area A this parental disapproval was further supported by the greater relative isolation of black peer groups; and it was apparent that, until attending secondary school and meeting more black children, many black youngsters had heard comparatively little creole except, to varying degrees, in the home. School became, in fact, a major site of creole use and acquisition.

> At home I'm not allowed to talk in patois because my mum won't allow it because she says that I was born in this country and I ought to speak in this language. But when I'm at school, if I'm arguing, right, it just comes out. But I do really enjoy talkin' like that, or when we're talkin' about boys or something like that.
>
> (fifteen-year-old girl)

Although this parental discouraging of creole use was common, it was unevenly applied. Many parents discouraged children of both sexes from using creole, but where a discrepancy did exist, it was more usually in favour of greater leniency for boys. Fathers appear to have been especially implicated in this bias. I was told by some of my male informants how their fathers would not mind their using creole in the home but that their mothers would not allow it. I did not encounter any examples where the reverse was true. One girl reported: 'When my brothers and dad are talking to one another I don't bother to listen because some of it I can't understand. And when mum comes in they just stop.' Because the peer group and not the family is the site of most creole use amongst young blacks, these parental restrictions were often of limited effect. Where, as in Area A, they coincided with less dense black peer group networks, however, it seemed to contribute both to less creole being used by youngsters in general and to girls knowing and using less creole than boys.

Even in areas of dense Afro-Caribbean settlement, like Area B, there is considerable variation in the extent to which young blacks use creole; but because of the equation of black cultural identity with creole speech, many are loth to admit when their command of the language is poor. One fifteen-year-old black girl told me:

> Somebody black was speakin' to me, right, and they was speakin' Jamaican and honestly I didn't understand a word. And a white friend aks me, they go, 'What did she say?' and I couldn't turn round and say, 'I don't know'. I just went, like you know ... [making a dismissive gesture with her hand] I didn't understand a *word*! 'Cos my mum doesn't speak it. She's totally against that.

At the same time this informant's brother, older than her by two years, did use a smattering of creole words and expressions with his male peer group, none of whom had any fluency in creole but all of whom moved into Jamaican pronunciation at times.

However limited or extensive the use of creole might be, its *symbolic* importance is very apparent, and many youngsters will claim to speak 'patois', 'dread talk' or 'bad' (all, at different times, common terms for creole) even when their command of it is negligible. Thus the self-report surveys of creole use (Sutcliffe 1978; 1982; Palmer 1981) have been especially vulnerable to distortion through over-reporting. At an age when social relationships may begin to register broad social and political issues, group identity itself gets taken up into language use and language attitudes. Where creole use is equated with black group identity, youngsters often feel the need to display some facility with socially marked creole forms. As one sixteen-year-old boy reported to me:

> I feel black and I'm proud of it, to speak like that. That's why
> when I talk it, I feel better than when I'm talking like now.
> You know what I mean? . . . When I speak more dread I feel
> more lively and more aware. In a way I feel more happier.
> *Do you reckon you speak it more now than you used to?*
> Yes. *Much* more. 'Cos, sounds funny but, I just kind of feel
> that as a black I should speak it and I feel that now if I'm . . .
> Say I'm walking the street and a black man goes to me,
> 'Dread, d'you have the time?' if I turn round and say, 'No,
> Sorry I haven't got the time', I'm gonna sound funny. So I go,
> 'No, man mi na got de time. Sorry Dread.' That's the way it is.
> And sometimes you just look at someone and you know
> you've got to speak it. You'd feel a right idiot if you went up
> to a Rasta and said, 'Excuse me have you got the time?' He's
> gonna think, 'No, man, you na black.' That's it. So you have
> to speak [their? your?] own language. An' say you go to a
> blues an all this, you see them smoking up weed an' that,
> when they talk to you you have to talk like them. You know
> what I mean? You've gotta feel like you're one of them.

For many speakers, creole tokens and formulaic expressions are embedded in their normal London English to mark and represent the group language in certain contexts. Such a nominal use of creole markers appears to establish itself especially through pronunciation. Thus, even where command of the grammatical features of creole is insecure, utterances may be clearly marked and distinguished from their London English by a move towards Jamaican phonology. In such cases, single

items located within stretches of London English appear to suffice to
meet the cultural requirements of particular situations. Indeed – and
perhaps because of this minimal marking procedure – pronunciation is
consistently employed as the linguistic means par excellence by which
black youth-cultural group identity is expressed and is even employed
when, out of either ignorance or choice, lexical and grammatical features
are not used in the same way.

The switching that occurs between London English – even between the
creole-influenced London English of some young blacks – and a clearly
marked creole is likely to be amenable to systematic analysis, for
regularities are readily apparent. Both topic and function appear to
trigger switches. Informants were often broadly accurate about their own
switching practices. The following statements by two informants in
conversation with me were echoed many times by other informants. I
had asked, 'At what times do you talk patois most?' The first informant
replied, 'You use it when you're angry and when you're in a good mood
and joking about.' His friend added, 'But when you're taking things
seriously you sorta tend to speak in English.' Although the range of
occasions on which switching occurs is in fact far wider than this type of
formulation suggests, and furthermore even the functions of creole
indicated in such statements were internally differentiated, in general
outline these statements are accurate. What inevitably vitiates such
accounts – which usually implicitly refer to peer group interactions – is
when interlocuters vary in their relation to the speaker. Here a whole
range of strategic impulses emerge to interact with topic as a motivating
force. Here, too, the social semiotic dimension edges into the issue, and
the association of creole with specific social stances and positions comes
into play. For example, beside other associations, connecting creole with
(*a*) lower-class life and (*b*) conflict, especially with the police, was
common for many of the young blacks I interviewed and these connections also emerged in their accounts of what shaped their use of creole
when the interlocutors were not of their own peer group. One boy
reported: 'When I'm speakin' to an adult [a black adult] and I don't really
know the adult, I speak English 'cos it shows respect, but you come out
with Jamaican it shows disrespect.' Others reported:

A: If you meet an older [black] person who looks a bit cruff [scruffy],
   you'ld still speak to him in English but if he looks a bit cruff
   ... an' he says, 'Wa 'appen, son. Wa gwaan', an' all dem tings
   der, an' you start to speak to him in English, then you just
   break into the Jamaican habit – patois – then you become
   more friends, like.

B: Yeah. *Patois is sort of a relationship*, an' when you meet someone you don't really just come out speakin' like that – only when you have a problem-ting wiv a person. That's when you'll speak it, 'cos it sounds a way of aggression to them.

(my emphasis)

Here both associations are explicitly expressed and related to actual interactive practices which are readily observable in the use of creole in everyday settings.

The association of creole with aggression – that is to say, the idea that in certain contexts the use of creole is treated as appropriate for the expression of aggression, and that outside of such contexts, therefore, it is capable of being misinterpreted – is indicated especially in the realm of pronunciation and style of delivery. Arguments often trigger an excursion into the deeper forms of Jamaican pronunciation. An inability by one of the parties to match this pronunciation can be disadvantageous, although what is involved is not confined to accent itself. The two boys quoted above demonstrated how a switch to creole involved both different lexis *and* a change of accent and tone. The sound was especially credited with efficacy in conveying aggression:

B: If I really wanna talk, if someone's annoyin' me, you know, I could just go, 'So wa 'appen, man, we 'ave fe walk I-an-I, man. Fe I-man never do not'n, na check wi' dem fibes der, ya know, na deal inna dem sing tings der,' like that. See, I sorta change my tone of voice as well.

A: It gets lower, see, so it sounds a bit dangerous.

The equation of danger and toughness with the creole speech of youth actually provides it with further strategic uses. Situations, for example, in which relations with authorities are involved – such as certain contacts with the police, as alluded to above, or in conflicts with teachers (Gilroy and Lawrence 1986) or with youth workers (Brandt 1984), may foster the use of creole largely because of its association with strong and dauntless assertiveness. Where the race/power dimension is also present, this connotation may be further supplemented by a concept of black *group* identity, so that the power of individual assertiveness may be translated into an assertiveness concerning group (i.e. race) relations. Here there is a convergence of the cultural/political significance of creole – where creole is treated as standing in a metonymic relation to a concept of black cultural/political identity – and one of the individualistic functions which a switch of creole is capable of performing.

This is only one of a range of strategic switching practices evident amongst black adolescents; but it is clearly important to any discussion of the political dimension of creole use. As in several other respects with regard to the immediate history of black youth culture, the influence of Rastafari in elaborating the connections between creole and political relations has been unmistakable. Because the Rastafarians have their own conceptually inflected variety of Caribbean creole (Pollard 1983), the penetration of Rasta terms into the creole of black adolescents confers a further political/cultural dimension, over and above that earned through the position of their creole as a class, race and generational language within a specific set of power relations. This is possible in part because Rastafarian-inflected creole is itself regarded as the language of a cultural elect, from which basis challenges to white domination are generated. One young informant regarded 'Rasta language' as demarcating a socially prestigious group which was a source of strength and a force for good in the cause of black culture. His concept of Rasta, and its signalling of social differentiation by linguistic means, is unusually explicit:

> The whole thing of Dread and Rastafari is sort of upper-class ... different. That's the whole point of it. People, like the first-class people, they have a different way of speakin' from the workin' an' the middle class, innit. And, you know, this is a class, *Rasta* is a class as well. It's different but they don't use words like ... like all those toffee words. They use their *own* words.

The convergence of features which give the use of creole in certain contexts a political function have, to date, received little analytical attention. Although the political aspect of creole language use has been touched upon by several writers (Garrison 1979; Gilroy and Lawrence 1986), this feature is frequently claimed as a non-variable attribute of *all* creole use by young blacks. Such assertions, however, are too general to differentiate between uses of creole which are explicitly political and others which are not. As such they are, perhaps, only of polemical significance. What is certainly relevant, however, is that, because claims to creole language use can be indicated at one level merely by a few token lexical items, and even by phonological means alone, as a political strategy it is open to any black youngster, and not simply to those whose facility with creole is well developed.

It is also worth noting that the prevailing ideology of linguistic stratification expressed through the equation of creole with low social status – a feature in keeping with popular white stereotypes of Caribbean creoles – is actually itself re-employed in the service of the politically *oppositional* use of creole. If, in contrast to the prevailing evaluation, actual linguistic practices express an underlying motivation which is contrary to expressed 'attitudes', then these can be regarded as containing a linguistically enacted and implicit folk taxonomy of social relations. In the case of the political use of creole in certain contexts, both the folk taxonomy of social relations enacted in creole use and the prevailing ideology concerning the relative status of creole are brought into focus and recontextualised. Indeed, much of the force of politically strategic creole use would be lost if its ranking were *not* low within the prevailing evaluation of social dialects. There is, therefore, an interesting *interaction*, which is easily overlooked, between the levels of social meaning attached to creole use.

The most common switches into creole that may be casually observed to occur within peer groups are prompted either by the topic or by the type of interaction. Greetings, departures, highly charged enthusiastic talk, as well as arguments and aggression, are all common triggers. Sutcliffe's account of switches to creole in situations where disagreements occur – his data were drawn from school playground interactions (Sutcliffe 1982: 55–6, 147–9) – certainly coincides with my own casual observations in schools, youth clubs and the street. I would add, however, that any context in which a form of rivalry exists, or is produced by the interaction, increases the chance of creole being employed by one or more of the interactants to signal toughness, superiority or annoyance. Such uses of creole by black youngsters were mirrored by the white adolescent creole users whose speech I recorded and subjected to analysis (these are discussed in detail in Chapters 4 and 5). I suspect that a similar study of the use of creole by black adolescents would discover a mode of usage akin to that described for white creole users below, and referred to there as the 'competitive mode'. This also relates, of course, to the characterisation of creole speech – or rather the creole of young British-born blacks – as 'aggressive' and 'dangerous'. In such uses, as in all strategic uses, the *contrast* with English is an important feature in itself. It is, in other words, the act of switching which conveys at least as much information about the state of the interaction as the nature of the codes employed.

Just as competitive situations can motivate switching, so too, can topics alluding to competition. Talk *about* fighting, for example, can produce texts in which creole is switched to for short phrases, or where the impact of creole phonology impresses itself suddenly upon a narrative. The same is true of accounts of sporting events. Indeed, anything which embraces questions of prestige and personal excellence – either by way of a celebration or a lament – can, when referred to in narration, increase the chances that creole will be used in certain passages or at certain moments by way of stress. John Gumperz, in his studies of conversational code-switching, found a similar 'enacting' feature in the Spanish/English switching of Chicano professionals (Gumperz 1982: 81). Although both of these types of situation seem to apply more obviously to male rivalries, and the above observations *may* apply more to boys than to girls, in my experience they are certainly not restricted to boys. As with many other aspects of this field, this question requires much more research.

Other topics which commonly increase the likelihood of code-switching include relations with the opposite sex – whether boasting, admiring or recommending is involved – and popular music. Because black music is an extremely significant aspect of black youth culture, its importance for black cultural identity, as interpreted by adolescents, is extremely high. Common topics of conversation amongst adolescents were the relative merits of different commercial 'sound systems' and – especially when the building of sound systems by groups of youngsters was at its most popular – boasting about the 'weight' of volume and bass possessed by the amateur systems, and proclaiming the inferiority of local rival sounds. Much of this type of talk – possibly because it combined both a competitive and a 'black cultural' component – was commonly conducted in a language shot through with switches between English and creole. Indeed, the whole topic of black music, being important both for its own sake *and* as a symbol of one type of black cultural excellence, was intricately bound up with the status of creole speech amongst young people. Many of the words and phrases which came to be taken up into the creole of black youngsters were adopted from popular reggae records. Furthermore, as 'toasting' (see p. 115 below) was always done in creole, reggae music was quintessentially the music of creole, and its rhythms were directly equated with the rhythms of creole speech – a fact which black poets from Lynton Kwesi Johnson onwards were also able to use in their verse. It is not surprising, therefore, that black music as a topic of conversation should itself be one of the factors tending to prompt switches into creole.

These observations, however, only give a clue to some of the most common motivations for switching, and are therefore mainly reflective of the practices of those whose use of creole is limited in function and scope. This naturally masks a great deal of differentiation within the contexts I have mentioned, and within the many contexts not covered by these most obvious of areas. Some of the work of examining code-switching with proper rigour has been begun by Sebba (Sebba 1983*a*; Sebba and Wootton 1984), and this area of research is likely to prove one of the most rewarding approaches to the use of creole by young blacks. This is because, as those British-born adolescents whose facility with creole enables them to conduct extended and sustained speech in creole without recourse to English are few in number, and are likely to become fewer still with succeeding generations, the principle use of creole forms will inevitably reside in such practices. It may be, however, that definitions of 'code' and 'switching' will need to be re-examined. Most commonly, the notion of 'code-switching' is based upon a concept of two or more fixed and discrete linguistic systems, between which speakers alternate either randomly (Labov 1971) or in ways that show meaningful patterning (Gumperz 1982). The theory of language developed by Le Page (1985), however, which interprets a speaker's positioning within 'linguistic space' as constituted by numerous linguistically expressed 'acts of identity', and which avoids strict definitions of purely linguistic boundaries in favour of a phenomenological approach, may prove to be of greater accuracy and flexibility in dealing with the very fluid linguistic situation which obtains amongst some black adolescents.

Certainly, any approach which could reflect the diversity of practices amongst black youth would be an advance. The linguistic situation is both varied and changing. The black youth culture of the 1960s had a creole that was learned and developed in the Caribbean. It was not, as London Jamaican is today, a language engendered within British urban life. By the late 1970s the language of black youth was substantially different from that of the earlier 'rude boys'. By the end of the 1980s it is likely to be as different again. But even if what passes for 'talking patois' amongst black youngsters is now more often the code-switching variety referred to above, its symbolic significance is not dependent on linguistic definitions.

However close or distant the creole of young black Londoners may be in relation to the full creoles found amongst some individuals of the parents' and grandparents' generations, it is a language that is certainly enjoyed by the youngsters who choose to use it, according to those I interviewed. The notion that its use made youngsters feel 'more lively, more aware', expressed by one of the informants quoted above, was echoed many times; and it became clear that it was felt to involve a creative dimension lacking in other available types of language. Especially, creole was apparently felt to provide a vehicle for a more colourful mode of expression than is associated with London English. One sixteen-year-old black boy explained the nature of creole in terms of its expressive vigour:

> All you do is you spice up the words a bit. You don't just say a little word. You kinda say, 'Move! Move ya rass for me!' And what you do, you put a bit of action in it and you spice it up

and, you know, that's the way you make it sound a bit more better.

This at least, was how he *understood* creolisation, even if he was unconscious of the source of his linguistic 'spices'.

In keeping with this expressive aspect, a number of informants claimed to have invented words which others took up, and could also name acquaintances who had invented words, or who had taken familiar words and modified them in ways that had also become widely adopted. One informant claimed to have adopted the word 'gritty' as a synonym for 'girl'. He and his friends said that they habitually used this word, and that after several months of doing so they heard the same word used in the same way at a party in North London. From this they deduced that their coinage had spread to groups of people who were quite unconnected with them. Certainly I was often told that 'new terms come along all the time', and there appeared to be a fairly high level of lexical inventiveness amongst young blacks within the ambit of their London Jamaican. Also, some Caribbean words, I was told, learned from the parents' generation, underwent a change of meaning when used amongst young black Londoners. 'Legobees' was one such example. In the Caribbean it is generally applied to someone who is always going out to parties and 'living it up'. Amongst the younger generation of black Londoners, however, it became exclusively applied to promiscuous girls – by both boys *and* girls.

Whatever the sources of vocabulary in London Jamaican, the constant influx of new vocabulary kept the language within the young black community and rendered it difficult for outsiders to understand. At the same time, young blacks who were not themselves part of the networks wherein the language was especially alive also tended to be excluded by it, and again demography and social class were important factors influencing the circulation of new items. It was thus possible for *black* youngsters to be excluded by London Jamaican creole in the same way as most whites. What had a special value within strategies of ethnic/racial boundary marking was capable of actually alienating some black youngsters who could not see themselves within the culturally elaborated definitions of 'black youth' – even if they might, on occasion, have been able to 'pass' for membership with a few exclamatory fragments of creole.

Despite such sites of discontinuity, the use of patois was the single most persistent feature which bound together the disparate strands of black youth culture. At the heart of the cultural complex, it was the oral dimension which provided the medium of coherence and, within this, 'toasting' – although unequivocally on the reggae side of the equation –

was of special importance, combining creole language, reggae music and a spontaneous expressiveness, which allowed whoever was sufficiently confident or well-connected to take up the microphone and improvise verbally for as long as he or she could, across the simultaneously manipulated channels of recorded sound.

'Toasting' should not be confused with the classic black narrative 'toasts' of urban America such as 'Signifying Monkey', 'Stackolee' and 'Shine' (Abrahams 1963). Although these toasts have occasionally been put to music (for example, Cab Calloway's 'Jungle King' (1948), or the collection of raps and toasts recorded under the title 'Snatch and the Poontangs'), North American toasting is essentially a *recited* narrative form. It is likely, however, that the word was adopted by Jamaican disc jockeys from this source.

The toasting referred to here is *the* oral art form of reggae music. From the late 1960s onwards, when Duke Reid, Sir Coxsone, King Tubby and other sound-system men began popularising reggae, and disc jockeys would 'talkover' the records, thus combining recorded and live sounds, it has rarely been the musicians or singers who were the 'stars' of reggae music, but rather the disc jockeys and record producers. Growing out of 'talkover', toasting proper began with accomplished performers such as U-Roy, Al Capone and Big Youth. Toasting was at first performed over the B side of records – the 'dub version' – which contained primarily the instrumental rhythm tracks of the A side, with perhaps fragments of the vocal or instrumental 'top line' also sparsely present. The disc jockey's vocal line would comprise an intoned chant, often employing only three or four pitches, while the words themselves were a carefully paced flow of often formulaic expressions, now doggerel, now social and political comment – images of urban life – mixed in with pure vocal sound and rhymes which skirted the borders of meaning.

As the 1970s saw reggae grow in popularity, and while a few musicians, notably Bob Marley, brought reggae an international audience, for Jamaicans and other West Indans in or out of the Caribbean, the real protagonists of reggae remained such disc jockeys as I-Roy, Dillinger, Trinity, Papa Kojak and, by the early 1980s, the albino toaster Yellow Man. Producers from early on released records on which the toasters performed over recordings which, themselves, may have served on several previous releases; and numerous records were released of great (and not so great) toasting performances. Inevitably, Rastafarian themes influenced the content of toasting, although with the later toasters, especially Yellow Man, themes of urban struggle and metaphors of social and religious transcendence gave way to more hedonistic themes, and to scatological versions of nursery rhymes.

Jamaican style sound-system men and the whole culture of dub and toasting naturally became replicated in Britain, with its own major sounds such as Sofrano B, Frontline International, Jah Shaka and Saxon. Many minor sounds also aspired to professional status, and there was a great spawning of amateur sounds as young blacks attempted the expensive business of building up the equipment of amplifiers, pre-amps, record decks and giant 'boxes' – loudspeakers – necessary before they could begin to seek party or club engagements, or hire a hall themselves and confidently charge for entry. Despite the difficulties, small groups of youngsters would gradually build up such systems, give their sound a name and, when they could, 'play out'. Toasting would be performed by one or more of the members of the group, depending on who best had the skills. At parties and small clubs, not only would the sound-owners themselves toast, but known and competent members of the audience would also take over the microphone for a few records, the aim especially being to brighten up the party or contribute to the mood of the occasion – in the common phrase, to 'nice up the dance'.

Fragments of popular song, formulae with pedigrees that stretch back to the beginnings of reggae and beyond, and newly minted phrases are combined in toasting around themes sometimes suggested by the track title, sometimes not. Toasting shares the compositional principles of most oral art, from the epic poems of the Baltic states to the blues of the Mississippi delta. That is to say, a language of formulae – phrases, standardised couplets etc. – becomes established as a *shared* resource for performers. While individuals may innovate within, as well as contribute to and shape, these collectively held resources, the notion of the individual performer/composer is different from that of the literary culture (Lord 1958), and the relationship of any performance to the toasting culture of which it is a part is far less of an individualistic one. Although a relatively new oral art form, toasting very rapidly established its core 'vocabulary' of themes, vocal gestures, syntactic devices and verbal formulae, and these have continued to be explored by numerous performers, professional and 'folk', in both commercial and non-commercial, 'party' situations. It is especially strange that, whilst being so well known within the world of popular black music, this major urban form of oral folk art should have been largely ignored in academic discussions of 'verbal skills in West Indians' (Edwards 1979: 40), commentators concentrating on the more quaint traditional forms, such as Anansi stories (Sutcliffe 1982: 35–57, 159–68), for which young urban blacks have shown very little enthusiasm, and of which they have probably far less knowledge than the commentators 'reporting' on them. Despite its lack of recognition from academic circles, however, toasting, like its North American counterpart 'rapping' – which has a much longer tradition – has been the major modern oral art form of black youth.

The following extracts from a toast performed by a disc jockey in a club displays some of the features evident in toasts encouraging people to join in with the dancing. Fragments of narrative content describing the dancers, the sexual undertones of the occasion, and a celebration of black unity provide the thematic materials, which are expressed through couplets and other rhyming and syntactic figures improvised over the recorded music, with snatches of the recorded lyrics (not transcribed here) occasionally allowed to punctuate the live toast:

> (*spoken*: Here me now, star)
> Some o' dem a-bouncin' over dere.
> Some o' dem a-bouncin' over dere.
> Mi seh out-a in-your-yard an-a inna disya dance.
> Come out-a in-your-yard an-a inna disya dance.
> 'Cos which a-one o' dem ya seh your bruvver?
> 'Cos which a-one o' dem ya seh your bruvver?
> Inna ya yard you jus' a-watch T.V.
> Inna ya yard you jus' a-watch T.V.
> [***] de late night movies [***] de late night movies.
>
> (*spoken*: Here me now)
> Seh inna disya dance seh you smoke ganja 'ard,
> Leave [***] an' simply go abroad
> So out-a in-your-yard an-a inna disya dance . . .
> A-which a-one o' dem ya seh ya brevver?
> Well gal I seh, a-which a-one o' dem a-seh ya brevver?
> 'Cos you-wi are a-popsin' a de dancin' corner.
> You-wi a-check out de high headquater,
> De high headquater of a naasti rocker.
> True wi jus' a-popsin a wi corner
> but a-right a-now wi jus' a-popsin' a wi corner.
> True wi make out later wi stronger dan iron
> A likle after dat dey wan' a-stokin' pon knee.
> I say go inna corner an' pray pon your knee.
> Go bend pon your knee an' go pray to Jah
> Your almighty God livin' an' rightful ruler
> 'Cos den we popsin' in de corner.
> Ba-da-mek-up, ba-then wi popsin inna corner . . .
> But I really am-a-sure dey com fe stick it all togedder
> But I really am a-sure dey com fe ram it all togedder
> But it really am a-true dey com to love all togedder

But a-mek I tell you somep'n, com wi love-a one anodder
Say lovin' one anodder you got to love you black brodder.
Love your black brudder got to love your black sister.
Love your black sister you got to love your black muma.
Den love your black muma got to love your black pupa.
'Cos your pupa is your pupa. Your muma is your muma.
Brudder is you brudder an' your sister is your sister.
Got to love-a one anodder, yeah!
You got to love-a one anodder . . .

Often such toasts will include a boasting element in which the disc jockey will celebrate his own skills at the 'controls':

Long-long time mi na 'old disya mike inna Brixton.
Long-long time mi na 'old disya mike inna Brixton.
Mi com fe ram it up-a bing bong bing bong!
Mi com fe mash it up-a!
Mi com fe love it up-a!
Ram it Mr Operator!
Do it Mr Operator!
Rock it Mr Operator!
I say you greater dan ever!

Other sequences will be structured around well known nursery rhymes:

I say one a-two, you be buckle fe you shoe.
'Cos three a-four, you be come to mi door.
Go five, six, you got to run com quick.
Go eight, nine, you got to feel so fine.
Den ten, eleven, with rock it togedder.
A likle after dat wi like a-bird of a fedder.

Besides such 'party' performances, toasting also treats more serious themes, as is evident in the following fragment addressing itself to the difficulties of the marginal, hustling way of life:

Struggle! But a-dey continue right a-now.
Some a-struggle. Ay!
Some o' dem a-struggle
But a-dey continue right a-now.
Some a-struggle.
Bung-dung biddle-ee, biddle-ee dee.
Some a-struggle.
Eya! Mi said eh, some upon de 'erb jus' a-tief what people
    earn.
Some upon de 'erb jus a-tief what people burn.

Some pon de earth jus' a sell-up de 'erb.
Dat's a-struggle, but a-dey continue right a-now
An' dat's a-struggle.
Bung-dung drrrrrrrrrrrrrrrr, bung-dung.
Dat's a struggle ...
A big struggle ...
(*spoken*: Yeah! Ya hear dat, styler star!)

As in the extracts above, nonsense words and trills are often used to punctuate the flow of words and stress the rhythms of the underlying music, however serious the theme. Youngsters may readily pick up such rhythmic devices, but the demands of keeping up a constant flow of words for long stretches is rather more exacting, and requires a great deal of practice before a public performance can be risked. I asked one sixteen-year-old boy who, together with his friends, had built up a sound system, at what age he had started toasting. He replied:

When I started goin' to parties. When I was about twelve, somethin' like that. Started hearin' some good records an' when they came to the middle, like a disco fortyfive, an' you jes' hear strickly bass line, I jes' start gettin' in the mood. You know what I mean. I've got to make somethin' up for it 'cos it sounds kinda borin' to me jes sittin' there listnin' to 'dvv, dvv, dvv', so I get in de rhydim of it.

Inevitably, however, the toasting done by young adolescents tends to be rather directly derivative, leaning not just on the broad language of toasting but on specific toasting performances of the better known and commercially recorded toasters. The following toast was performed by a fifteen-year-old schoolboy in his school lunch-break to a small group of friends. While it includes references to his own sound – Ambassador – and some other embellishments and structuring of his own, it is much derived from the toasting of the Jamaican Rasta toaster Prince Far I. Pacific Rasta themes were often used by this young toaster, whose boasts even parodied the language of Christian religion in spoken comments such as 'Man cannot live by bass alone but by faith in Ambassador'. Despite the plagiarism, this lengthy toast, with its description of a dream-like journey of culture-hero Natty Dread into the land of milk and honey, far away from the police who hunted him in the city, is a coherent performance which keeps close to the underlying religious and political spirit of the theme.

Seh you seh wi born inna Africa.
Seh you seh de Dread is a righteous man.
Seh Natty Dread never trouble no-one

Because mi born in eart'
A-christen inna fire.
De Dread inna valley
Seh de dread is a lion.
De talk o' de lion a de righteous sound,
So dat de general sound.
Seh a dis is my country,
A Natty Dread country.
And den wi live inna country.
We live on a-bounty, a righteous country . . .
An den wi walk wid each other in de valley,
And den a-fear no evil, no.
An den wi smoke-up mi I-tal, de friendly vital. [. . .]

So Natty Dread is a righteous man
Till you said 'im live inna Babylon
An den you take out de root
Natty speak-up de trut'
Bout de righteous dreadlocks.
Go Natty Dread inna valley jes' a-burn up de weed.
De wicked in de town jes' a-lookin' for de weed
So Natty chuck down your weed cos dat ain't my scene.
But de river was shallow an' de river was high.
De milk an' honey on de other side.
I seh de river was shallow an de river was deep.
I jump in de river mi go take a likle peep.
I seh dey fallen asleep, ohol!
Yeah! Natty Dread, dem a-sleep, yeah . . .
Go-yeah, seh I went up de mountain
A do a likle scoutin'
A-drink from de fountain, ya!
An' den I take out de [***]
Den I said I burn up mi I-tal weed . . .
De righteous sound say wi gadder roun'.
I said de righteous sound says wi gadder roun'
Cos Ambassador Sound is a general.
I seh Ambassador a master . . .
A righteous country.
Go nah, Natty Dread country,
Yeah mi born inna Babylon
An den mi [***] lion
An den wi take it to de valley

Till you seh you play where de water go, (*spoken*: Wash you!)
(*pause*)
(*spoken*: Dis wi call, 'Chapter Two', strickly Rasta, yeah.)

De righteous man is de general man, yeah!
Mi said mi run out de Prodigal Son out o' Babylon.
Mi run out de Prodigal Son o' Babylon
Mi lick mi face wid mi heavy arm . . .
Mi read my bible . . .
I read my bible . . .
I seh I check out de bible
Out inna Babylon.
(*spoken*: One time, tell you)
Seh mi pour out mi I-tal curry
An' den mi go deh in de dreadlocks valley.
Seh de Natty Dread an' de wall
Natty Dread na fall
Seh fe run' for fall
Mi said de bwoys down town jes' a-gadder roun'.
Ambassador Sound jes' a go-deh righteous sound.
Jes' a-lay some jump an' bass.
Jes' a go deh in de I-tal place
An' den wi go deh wid de [**] sound
Let wi 'ave some fun, yeah,
Ya said de Babylon a-run
Mi go dere by de [**] town.
Mi go check sister Brown
Natty Dread is no clown.
An den mi go deh up de I-tal valley
And den mi root in de valley.
[. . .]
Natty deh-an deh-an!
Natty den-an deh-an!
Natty deh-an deh-an,
Na let go!
Natty go deh, go deh!
Natty go deh, go deh!
Natty go deh in de I-tal town.
An' den wi went down town fe go check sister Joyce
An wi rappin', on de roadside
Till ya seh wi wait in de park
Ya seh wi wait till de night turn dark

Mi climb up de beanstalk.
Tell ya seh I Jack an' de beanstalk
Watch, oh!

[...]
Oh den mi go deh an de bankin'
Natty Dread jes' top rankin'.
De Dread is ranker
Yeah, seh I said de Dread is ranker.
An de Babylon a-skanker.
De Dread is de rankin'
[...]
De Dread is a-rankin'.
De righteous sound jes' a-humble
Because the wicked dem a-stumble.
I seh de sun come down an' de eart' get hot
De eart' was like a meltin' pot ... (*spoken*: watcha!)
De righteous seh ...
Seh de righteous sound jes' a-gadder roun', roun' roun' ...

This young toaster was building up his own sound, together with a small group of friends, and aimed to 'play out' at parties and dances, but some youngsters would simply invent toasting routines and perform them to each other 'just for fun', without music, on odd occasions, perhaps seeing such casual performances as rehearsals for when they might actually perform 'on mike'. Two fourteen-year-old boys who were wearing radio microphones for me during their school lunch-break for quite another purpose were prompted at one point, probably by the presence of the microphone, into a dual toasting routine, which combined elements which they later claimed to have invented themselves with fragments derived from professional toasters Yellow Man and Papa Toyan. Even these plagiarised elements were rehabilitated by a reorganisation of the material and by the insertion of their own names – David and Rodney – into the toast. Thus Rodney chanted:

I seh wi sharp but wi smart
But wi know 'ow fe talk.
Papa Davey make de cripple-dem walk.
I seh mi sharp an' mi smart
But wi know 'ow fe talk
Papa Rodney make de blind dem see.
I make de blind dem see.
A bam ba bee

I make de fadda see
A young gal sleepin' by de mornin' side.

Or again, together:

RODNEY: All young gals dem a-mad over me, a-mad over me.
DAVID: But Papa David inna different style-ay!
Com fe nice-op de dance o style-ay!
RODNEY: Not because my complexion
A-show mi 'ave ambition . . .
When dey see me pon de road dem a-call after me.
Some o' dem a-say mi should-a inna cemetry!

And amongst such exchanges, familiar sound-system boasts were also included: 'Dis combination make you feel like a bird in a tree!'

Many black youngsters know a large number of toasting lyrics, as well as inventing their own rhymes and sequences; and there is evidence that a rich corpus of urban oral verse exists amongst them. This area would undoubtedly reward the researches of any urban folklorist.

Toasting is overwhelmingly a male activity, but there are some extremely good female toasters too. Boys are often grudging in admitting that girls can toast, and tend to view it as a male preserve. Occasionally, all-female sounds, such as one called 'Rebel Princess', flourish for a while, but many boys seem almost affronted by the idea of female toasters. One boy justified this view on the grounds that girls' voices did not possess the necessary quality for toasting:

> Some girls can toast but, put it this way, it depends on how their voice sounds when they're on the microphone because some girls will sound like they're singing Lovers' Rock [a particularly romantic type of reggae] when they're toasting, ya see. An' other girls sound like they're just a little boy, a little boy pon de mike.

Another boy told me:

> You see girls, they've got a soff voice, right? Most boys an' men they got a rough voice. [. . .] You have to have to have a rough voice for toastin'. If they're singin' or somethin' that's OK but not toastin'. Toastin' sounds too rough. You know what I mean? And the girls that do toast are them *rough* sorta girls.

This male view of female toasters was, however, strenuously opposed by girls I talked to. One girl insisted, 'I don't toast myself but I know girls that do an' it don't mean it's mannish or nothin'. That's rubbish.' I certainly heard some extremely good female toasters who were also well respected; but there was no doubt that males dominated both commercial and non-commercial toasting.

Since the onset of the decline in the popularity of reggae during the first half of the 1980s, the practice of toasting has also diminished somewhat. Economic factors also affected the nature of parties. One young boy told me how his own sound system was once popular with people who lived local to him: '[We were going to advertise but] we had so many people to play out [to] already. We was playin' up an' down our street, like you know, as people were 'avin' parties here and there an' askin' us to play [. . .] It was mostly friends. We did it for fun, like.' Circumstances, however, had changed and such neighbourhood sounds were vanishing, leaving only the well known commercial sounds:

> These days people don't have as many parties like they used to
> before. And really they seem to be buyin' good stereo
> equipment for their house, like. So when they want a party or
> something they've got the hi fi equipment there already. So
> that's how sounds really die out. But apart from that, sounds
> don't really die out to me, because there's clubs round here
> [. . .], you know an' you can go there an' listen to Saxon or
> Shaka or somethin'.

Furthermore, the New York influence on black youth culture in Britain involved a transition to vernacular *dance* forms such as 'body poppin'' and 'breakdancing' rather at the expense of the oral forms with their Jamaican roots. The combination of these factors has led to a dilution of the oral reggae culture. Despite this, the toasting tradition continues to enrich the language of black youth.

Together with the social practices which inevitably grew up around the small-scale collective ownership of sound equipment by groups of friends – the local followings which sounds attracted, the parties which flourished around them, the free open-air 'play-outs' held in some districts (members of Ambassador sound and its closest followers even had their own 'Ambassador' football team!) – sounds provided an armature within black youth culture, and informed it simultaneously with an associational and symbolic integrity. Despite the variety of styles of music played by different sounds, their importance in giving definition to the ethnicity of black British/Afro-Caribbean youth during an important period of demographic development cannot be overstated.

Furthermore, the relevance of sounds to the promotion of creole as *the* language of black youth – however unevenly that language may have been employed in practice – is also significant when looking towards the multi-racial social context of the culture. The culture generated many of its own 'markers of ethnicity', which were taken up into the political arena of inter-racial relations and which informed the character of black/white contacts. The 'prestige language' which was established as the culture's unique voice, and which could modulate into the oppositional tones and 'registers of resistance', had both an inward and an outward aspect. It is here, especially, at the interface of black/white cultural/political relations, that the significance of London Jamaican Creole can be observed in its *interactive* dynamic.

If the inward-directed aspect of black youth culture was concerned with solidarity and group coherence, its outward-looking face was both expressing and affecting the local interactive order of economically and institutionally structured social relationships. The public symbolic forms through which social relationships were expressed by the culture in fact contained the possibility of transforming the local interactive order from one determined by social relations in the wider adult society to one which reflected the alternative definitions and ideologies generated from within the black communities. The potential for such transformations could only occur at the cultural and ideological levels, and there only partially and imperfectly. Nevertheless, what was played out at the cultural level in terms of black/white 'contact' is both significant and instructive. It is here, therefore, that black/white speech *relations* are important, for it is here that the local interactive order is explored, and here that solutions are sought to problems posed at deeper levels.

The relationship between the black 'prestige language' and the speech of white adolescents in contact areas, examined in the following chapters, itself bears the impress of these issues. Studies of 'languages in contact', however, rarely move beyond the bland 'ecological' frameworks which have dominated sociolinguistics; and it would be especially neglectful of important social, economic and political dimensions to examine black/white adolescent speech relations in isolation from the contested social terrain which gives them their specific meaning and resonance. At the same time, it would be mistaken to approach the facts of linguistic interaction with preconceptions about the way in which the specific social context of black/white adolescent relationships in the 1980s may manifest itself at the cultural level. Here it is only in distorted and refracted form that underlying relations are exposed in the daily casual speech habits and linguistic explorations of urban adolescents; but it is here that the 'productive dialogue of youth' alluded to in the last chapter may be seen in some of its sharpest definition.

4

Creole forms in white adolescent speech

London vernacular speech has developed out of numerous influences, which include the historical migrations of people from the countryside, as well as from other metropolitan centres, bringing their own regional and class dialects. They include also the specialised jargon of street traders, costermongers, market workers and so on, the influence of Cockney rhyming slang, the words and tones of Romany and Yiddish and the idioms of Irish immigrants. The vernacular is, indeed, an amalgam of elements incorporated from many different tongues; and it is unlikely that any of them occurred without social adjustments, conflicts, tensions and accommodations between and within the groups and peoples caught up in the process of change. Indeed, the living vernacular is something of a forest floor, on which may be traced the spoor left behind after the obscure drama of conflicts and couplings between social groups and classes has passed by in the dark.

The immigration of people from the Caribbean and other parts of the 'New Commonwealth' has proved one of the most recent additions to this process; and it is not surprising, therefore, that these languages and dialects should, like those of other peoples before them, not only thrive independently in their own right but also make their impact on the language their speakers share with other Londoners. Unlike many of the changes of the past, however, in these more recent events we are able to observe a sociolinguistic process as it is occurring.

With specific regard to the Caribbean input, the employment of creole forms by the black British children and grandchildren of immigrants, described in the last chapter, has been an important factor, as has the prestige of black British youth culture itself. Not only are *these* children users of both the indigenous language and, in many cases, creole but, through their association with white children in the local neighbourhoods and schools, their speech has come to have an impact on the new

126

generations of white Londoners, especially in areas of relatively dense black population.

The phenomenon of white creole use is very much a minority activity. Nevertheless, in recent years it has come to be noted by teachers and youth workers (Rosen and Burgess 1980; Girdwood *et al.* 1982), and is of special interest with regard to questions of race relations, touching as it does on an important element in racial/ethnic group identity. It also raises several questions. Given the symbolic significance of creole to many young blacks, how has it been possible for some young whites to negotiate for themselves the right to employ it with their black friends? By what process of social adjustment or ideological contextualisation has even the partial acquisition of creole by whites taken place, and what have been its consequences for, or influences upon, the forms of racism also evident and enacted in relations between white and black adolescents?

In beginning to answer some of these questions, it is necessary to look in detail at the interactive contexts of white creole use, and to examine exactly what social meanings are involved in particular cases. In this chapter I shall merely start by examining first the ways in which, at the very lowest level, creole influences were evident in the recordings I made of the speech of white children in interaction *with other white children*. Here, in the contexts of use in which the presence of black children do not influence either the language employed or the co-ordinates of interaction, it is possible to trace both the unmarked influence of creole on the vernacular and the blatant and conscious employment of creole by whites freed from the constraints which usually necessitate negotiation in the presence of blacks. The more complex area of white-with-black creole use will be described in Chapter 5.

As was observed in Chapter 3, the London English of many young blacks shows influences from Caribbean creole. These include grammatical, phonological and lexical features, although there appears to be little uniformity in what features are adopted and there is much variation between speakers. Specifically with regard to lexis, it is common for items to be anglicised in their pronunciation in the process of their incorporation in London English; and this process has significance for any description of the use of creole by *white* adolescents because, through the contact of whites with their black peers, some of these anglicised creole items have entered the vocabulary of white adolescents in some areas of London and are employed by them *unmarked with regard to ethnicity*. The use of such items by whites must, therefore, be distinguished from the use of creole forms which *are* marked for ethnicity, and which constitute what Brown and Levinson have called 'emic markers', i.e. markers 'where [social] information associated with the relevant speech variable is available to participants' (Brown and Levinson 1979: 326). As will be seen, however, the distinction between creole features which may be regarded as 'emic markers' and those which may not is difficult to draw independently of the immediate context of interaction, and can only be derived from the practices of particular interactants. This is because creole-derived items which have been taken up into the local vernacular of one group of white adolescents and which are *not* so marked (and are not regarded as being so marked by the black peers of such white adolescents) may, in another nearby locality and another group of interactants, plainly function as 'emic'. However, the extent to which creole-derived items are integrated into any 'local vernacular' and employed in ethnically unmarked ways is (as will be seen) a constantly changing and negotiated quantity. (It should be borne in mind that the strongest influence from creole on white adolescent speech occurs in localities of dense black population, where school and neighbourhood contact between black and white adolescents is greatest. Most of the recordings of speech from which the following data are drawn were made in Area B. Similar data are likely to be obtained only from demographically similar areas.)

The major original source of lexification in Jamaican creole was, of course, English. Hence, the borrowing of words from Jamaican creole can only mean the transposition of items used in distinctive ways in Jamaican creole, or derived from one of its other sources of lexification, and different from items exactly shared with the indigenous dialects of English. Locating items within the Jamaican creole lexicon is made possible by reference to Cassidy and Le Page's *Dictionary of Jamaican English* (1967), and to Cassidy 1961. Some items which form part of London Jamaican are not found in either of these works, and here the glossary to Sutcliffe 1982 has proved useful in establishing their provenance. There are, however, a few items to which I will make reference which do not appear in any of these works but which are nevertheless well established in London Jamaican. In such cases I have had to rely on my own records of black usage in South London. Some of these items have been incorporated into London Jamaican from American and English sources, or very recently from Jamaica. They are usually peculiar to the younger generation.

No exact description of the degree of penetration of creole into South London local vernacular, either directly through London Jamaican or via the London English of black adolescents, is possible, because many creole elements unmarked for ethnicity in one group of adolescents *are* so marked in another, and it is only unmarked forms which we are identifying as the multi-racial local vernacular. What can be described, however, are the processes by which some creole words have been taken up unevenly into local speech, and some of the indications that certain of these variable features may be stabilising, to the extent of being more widely and evenly absorbed.

In the schools recordings made in Area B, some thirty distinctly creole lexical items were recorded, scattered in the speech of white adolescents. In most cases, the use of such words occurred rarely. In a few cases, the use of creole-derived words became part of a shortlived fad, and occurred frequently. In some cases it was clear from the contexts of utterance that the ethnic origins of certain words *were* known to speakers, while in others the ethnic origins were unknown. This was in keeping with Weinreich's observation that, 'loanwords are in many cases not recognizable as such to the unilingual' (1966: 56).

The items found and recorded were:

bahty (n)	buttocks
bamba (n)	female pudenda
bambaclaht (n)	sanitary towel
cha/cho	exclamation of annoyance
chip (v)	to take one's leave
cruff (n)	a scruffy person
dread (adj)	of high respect in Rastafarian religion; excellent
facety (adj)	cheeky
go deh!/there	exclamation of encouragement
guy (n)	term of address
hard (adj)	excellent
innit	interrogative tag
Irie (adj)	of high esteem; excellent
mash-up (v)	to break; also many metaphorical uses, e.g. to be ill or drunk
murder/ation	general purpose exclamation
rass (n)	buttocks
renk (adj)	cheeky
ress (v)	stop, cease
sad (adj)	pathetic
shame (v)	to shame or be shamed, and (n) state of disgrace
soff (adj)	weak, ineffective
stylin' (v)	showing good style
star (n)	close friend
sweet (adj)	pleasing
tarra/tid	exclamation of annoyance/amazement

tief (v)	to steal; (n) a thief
wa'appen	friendly greeting
wicked (adj)	excellent
wickedness (n)	mischief

In addition to these the expression 'crucial' was also found, another term of strong admiration like 'excellent' which seems to have been calqued directly by the London English of black adolescents, and the mixed form 'wretch-claht', combining the insult 'wretch' from English with the Jamaican word 'claht' (cloth), commonly combined in Jamaican insults with other words such as 'bamba' and 'pussy'. A reverse combination, where an English vernacular word was suffixed to a Jamaican word, was 'cruffbag', where 'cruff' provided the Jamaican insult, and 'bag' indicated in English the gender of the recipient of the insult – female. Such hybrid forms are evidence of a linguistic inventiveness being brought to bear on the basic 'given' components of the available dialects. A large number of such hybrid forms enjoy a very brief existence; others have stabilised and passed into wider use.

Many of the recorded items had been casually observed during the period of participant observation. Quantitative analysis of lexical evidence is notoriously difficult and is probably inappropriate, due to the relative infrequency with which most words are used (Laver and Trudgill 1979: 26). However, certain of the items listed above did occur in a significantly higher number of cases than others, uttered by a significantly larger number of recorded speakers. These were 'go there', 'innit', 'hard', 'shame', 'wicked', and 'rass', and their patterns of use as items frequently employed quite unmarked for ethnicity, correspond with my casual observation of local vernacular. However, low occurrences in the schools' recordings could not be taken as indicative of non-inclusion in the local vernacular, as written control tests were able to show. In one girls' school, a written test was run to ascertain the extent to which white pupils were familiar with the meaning of certain selected creole items. These items were chosen on the basis of evidence gained from casual observation in local youth clubs. They were 'facety', 'skank' – meaning to dance and to steal or act fraudulently – and 'mash-up'. Note that 'skank' does not appear at all in the recordings of spontaneous speech.

A total of 47 white English girls participated in a group consisting of most of the fourth year, including girls of Afro-Caribbean, Asian, Turkish and African parentage. The group total was 78. Of the 47 white English girls, the following numbers accurately supplied the meaning of those words:

'facety'	37	(78%)
'skank'	29	(61%)
'mash-up'	26	(55%)

Of those numbers the following claimed to use the words themselves:

'facety'	14	(29%)
'skank'	5	(10%)
'mash-up'	7	(14%)

The evidence with regard to 'facety', the word showing the highest scores for both knowledge and self-reported use, can be compared with evidence on the same word gained from a limited test which was applied in another school situated in Area A. In that test, applied to 81 white pupils of both sexes, 40 correctly supplied the meaning of the word (49%) while 15 (18%) claimed to use it themselves. The lower scores for both knowledge and reported use, compared with those of the other school, is almost certainly related to the differences of school location, as there were no significant differences in the two gender groups from the mixed school.

A further element in the test was that pupils were given examples of the origin of certain vernacular expressions and then asked to identify the origin, if they thought they knew it, of several items, including the three creole items listed above. Many did not manage to identify the origin of any of the creole words; but several of the white pupils mis-identified the place of origin of creole words as South London, or the East End – the one-time source of so much white working-class linguistic innovation. It is worth noting that several of the pupils of Afro-Caribbean parentage also mis-identified the place of origin of some items as South London, whilst correctly identifying others as Jamaican.

Although the self-reporting of use is of limited value, the evidence it produced did correspond with my casual observation of the use of 'facety' by white pupils, and with a small amount of unsystematic interviewing of 10 pupils regarding their use of this word. Evidence concerning their knowledge of the meaning of those words is more methodologically reliable, however, and does at least suggest, especially as the origins of these words were mis-ascribed to local or East End vernacular, that these items were, for some, both well known and unmarked for ethnicity. Assuming that the same is likely to be true for other items, the high incidence of 'go there' (but not 'go deh!'), 'innit', 'shame', 'hard', 'murder', 'rass', and 'wicked', suggests that these too may be regarded by many as purely local phenomena – or at least that they operate like 'facety' unmarked for ethnicity, and may be said therefore to have made the move from creole into the local vernacular, probably via the London English of black adolescents. Of the above words, 'innit' has become particularly well established over the past few years. Its distinctiveness from the common English usage, which is found in such phrases as 'it's a nice day, innit', resides in the fact that the 'it' morpheme does not refer back to a previous 'it' but to any general state, as in 'we had a lovely time, innit', and 'she's really nice that girl, innit'. Of all the items to penetrate white speech from the Caribbean, this is the most stable and most widely used amongst adolescents and amongst older people.

The same naturalisation process is true for 'tief' (/ti:f/), although for very specific reasons. 'Tief' (n) in Jamaican means the same as 'thief' in Standard English, but Jamaican does not have the 'th' phoneme within its phonological system, hence /ti:f/. At the same time, in cockney rhyming slang a 'thief' is a 'tea-leaf', and this expression is subject to a contraction rendering it also as 'teaf', homophonous with Jamaican 'tief', and having the same meaning whilst having a quite different etymology. Thus it is impossible to say in any instance which /ti:f/ is being used. It is probably best to say that /ti:f/ in South London vernacular is supported from two independent sources simultaneously. The same applies to 'aks', the Jamaican variant of 'asks', a few scattered examples of which occur in the recordings of *white* speech. However, 'aks' again has other supporting sources as well as Jamaican, and is therefore impossible to place as an item specifically derived from creole.

In some cases, where an overlap of English and Jamaican dialect features occur, it is only the *frequency* of occurrence that can be said to belong distinctively to one or the other. Such is certainly the case with one feature of Jamaican described by Cassidy (1961: 68) in the following terms:

> Jamaicans particularly like to tag adverbial particles on to verbs. The favourites are *up* and *off*: 'Ketch up him hen', 'Kiss up de gal dem', 'Puss pose off eena book', 'Anancy baptise off all of dem', 'Him nyam dem off clean', and, with the new verb *to foreign* (to make something seem foreign):

> Den me sey me want fe learn it to,
> Me haffe buckle dung,
> Screw up me mout and roll me y'eye,
> An foreign up me tongue.

Such a use of 'adverbial particles' is not unknown in English dialects, but its strong presence in the English of black adolescents, where expressions such as 'I'm gonna nice-up the sound' etc. are common, would seem to indicate that this is the source of similar expressions found amongst the white adolescents I recorded. Amongst such examples were: 'I'll just safe-up me neck' (when the speaker wished to make safe the microphone attached just below the neck of his shirt), 'you love her off in your bed', 'they stab him up', 'burn-up me hand' (in cards), while 'shame him up' combines this feature with the creole-derived lexical item 'shame'.

A similar ambiguity obtains in the case of the item 'one', used as an emphatic. Sutcliffe gives the example 'is one piece a ting gwaan' ('it all happened!', literally, 'is one piece of thing went on') (1982: 189). English, again, also uses 'one' as an emphatic. It is found commonly in sentences such as 'one hell of a fast car'. However, examples occurring in my data, such as 'one brilliant film', do seem to suggest strong support from a creole source.

It is also relevant to mention here what is to the best of my knowledge a very recent idiomatic innovation, and one which appears to have been developed within the London English of black adolescents but derived from a Caribbean source. It is widely found amongst both black and white working-class adolescents in South London, but is much more common amongst blacks. It involves using the expression 'you know what I mean' in such a way that it is approximately equivalent to 'I agree' or 'that's right'. Thus if A says, 'she's a silly girl', B may comment, 'you know what I mean'. I recorded numerous examples of this idiom from both black and white adolescents. Many white adolescents also use 'that's what I mean' in the same way, although the use of this seemingly related idiom is not so widespread amongst young blacks. A vivid example of the boundaries of idiomatic use was provided by an occasion on which a white 'alternative' radical comedian was attacking the government's record on unemployment with considerable wit at a South London cabaret. A young black member of the audience was moved to shout out encouragingly, 'You know what I mean!', in the same way as some Americans (initially black Americans) used 'Right on!' during the 1960s and 1970s. The comedian, unaware of the idiom and feeling threatened, mistook the intent of the heckler for one of derision and, sadly, turned on him too!

The investigation of the phonological influence of creole on white adolescent working-class speech has not as yet been undertaken by any linguist. However, I did record a number of features which I anticipate might prove useful points of departure for any such future study. In particular, I noted a number of cases in which white adolescents used a certain apparently creole-influenced vowel sound consistently on the same two words. These words were 'come' and 'fuck', both of which were realised by a few speakers quite unselfconsciously as /kɔm/, and /fɔk/, as they would be in creole pronunciation. Similarly, the word 'boy', when used as a tag in sentences such as 'get out of the way, boy!', did have a tendency to be realised somewhere in the direction of the Jamaican pronunciation, 'bwai' (although not fully so) by some white speakers. Other features of this kind were the heavy emphasis and voicing with initial consonants in such words as '*m*ove!' (a characteristic Jamaican command), '*n*ice', '*w*alloped' and '*l*ate'. It is a tendency I have consistently noted in the speech of black adolescents. Similarly, the very emphatic use of glottal stops, especially before initial vowels, found in the speech of black adolescents, is also found in the speech of some white adolescents.

Prosodic and intonational features, too, seem to tie some utterance styles of white adolescents to those of black adolescents. The clearest example is the intonation pattern characteristically used by black adolescents with the tag phrase 'you know'. A common black adolescent intonation of this phrase comprises three notes, one on 'you' and two on 'know', thus:

'you know'

I have collected a number of examples from both black and white speakers, and there is good reason to believe that this particular pattern (though obviously not the same expression when used with other intonation patterns) has been adopted by some white adolescents from their black peers. This intonational pattern should not be confused with the very different but equally distinct pattern found on the same phrase in London Jamaican. This latter intonation pattern has been described in detail by Local *et al.* (1983).

Another feature which has been absorbed to some extent is the dental click, which is an abbreviated form of the tooth-sucking which is used throughout the Caribbean as a sign of disapproval and scorn. While tooth-sucking is widely used by black adolescents, a highly abbreviated form is also used, realised at the start of utterances expressing annoyance or disapproval, and followed so rapidly by the initial sound of the word that the aural effect is similar to that of the dental click of the Khoi-san and Nguni languages of southern Africa. This abbreviated tooth-sucking has also been adopted to a large extent by white adolescents in contact areas. Indeed, if the 'dental click' were treated as an item in its own right, it would rank on a frequency count along with 'innit' and 'go there' as amongst those most frequently occurring.

It is evident from the examples above that there has been some penetration of creole into the local vernacular shared by black and white adolescents, and that many creole-derived features are unrecognised as such by many speakers. However, the presence of creole features in the multi-racial local dialect is a significantly different socio-linguistic fact from the deliberate and conscious use of creole forms by whites, either in interaction with each other or with their black peers, and it is to this conscious use of creole that I now turn.

Perhaps the best known use of creole by whites, certainly as far as most black people are concerned, is its employment as an instrument of derision. Here, at its crudest, English words are used with an accent that sets out to be a gross parody of 'black' speech. However, snatches of authentic creole are also sometimes acquired by whites who specifically use them with racist intent. As was seen in earlier chapters, white adolescents in some areas often go through a phase of having black friends, only to change later as the influence of white peer networks intervenes. Hence some white adolescents with strong explicit racist inclinations may have a fair degree of lexical knowledge acquired in their early teens which can be used for racist purposes. The derisive use of creole forms can both occur between whites and also be directed openly to blacks. Indeed, it is the use of creole in derisive ways, and even just the possibility of its use to serve those ends, that sensitises some blacks to *any* uses of creole by whites.

It has also been reported to me by a number of black informants that some white policemen in areas with relatively large black populations occasionally use odd items of creole in their interactions with blacks. The fact that such use usually involves Jamaican obscenities, the full weight of which is not realised by these policemen, means that even without the explicit desire to offend – which does often appear to be present – the result is usually blatantly racist. The hidden assumption in such use is that any black member of the public will be a creole speaker, and that any creole speaker will customarily employ obscenities. However, I have no evidence on the use of creole forms in racist derision specifically between white policemen or policewomen when blacks are not present. More will be said on racism and language in later chapters. Here my main concern is to outline those uses of creole by whites with other whites which are *not* consciously racist.

At the very simplest level, the conscious use of creole by whites takes two basic forms. The first consists of the employment of direct quotations from the most public surface of black culture as it is presented in the popular entertainment industry. These quotations, intermittently peppering the speech of some young whites, include catch-phrases from black television shows, and fragments of reggae and other lyrics closely associated with black culture. In these, the accents of (usually) Jamaican speech are attempted and employed in a similar way to that in which 'funny voices' and other exotic materials are incorporated into the playful speech of many young people, to decorate and enliven utterances and exchanges between peers.

At one level, language is here being used purely as a source of amusement. However, there is a certain coherence and consistency obtaining in many of the examples of this activity which I recorded. They seem especially to be employed by adolescents who are attracted to black culture, or at least by those forms of black culture which are articulated in the public realm of mass entertainment. Secondly, such use of quotation appears to be situated within a very broad spectrum of similar cultural incorporations from other realms of signification which many children and adolescents employ, and which seem to function as a kind of sketching in of cultural markers, situating speakers both for themselves and for their peers.

'Markers of identity' is too strong a term to be applied here, but certainly adolescents often do seem to create in language, as they do in dress, some of the cultural terms through which they wish to present and see themselves. The use of quotation represents little more than a flirtation with the public surface of black culture, but in its employment the culture is evoked and established as bearing some unspecific relation to the speaker.

The second form which the conscious use of creole takes at this primary level is in the employment of terms of abuse. Terms of abuse, often obscene, occur frequently in the verbal play of adolescents in inner-city areas. Many white adolescents have incorporated the terms of abuse they have learned from black children into their own abuse lexicon, as black children have learned from them, and often this has taken place to the extent that, as was seen above, some items have become detached from any ethnic specificity and their origins lost to their users. Nevertheless many terms remain firmly associated with black speech and are used consciously, often with London Jamaican accents, by whites.

Although the use of creole abuse terms is frequently to be found in the speech of those white adolescents who also employ quotations in the manner described above, the function of such terms is somewhat different from those uses, for it expresses both a cultural self-contextualising and a *positioning* through the rivalries of verbal and other forms of play. Its reference is not simply that of cultural position but of personal position, with the emphasis on individual competitive relations. The use of creole terms of abuse between whites occurs, as do most terms of abuse, in real and ritualised rivalries. In both, it is the assertion of self over other that is stressed and functional within the interaction. In such use, a narrow set of cultural associations of creole are evoked, specifically those relating to forms of individual dominance associated with toughness and street rivalries. Such associations are likely to be (*a*) those most available to whites not privy to the functionally less limited uses of creole, as displayed, for example, in normal everyday family conversation or in its growing literary employment, and (*b*) those which map most readily onto the requirements of quick-fire competitive interactions.

These two modes of creole use – one signalling a certain representation of a generalised black culture, the other providing a kind of culturally associative warrant specifically for individualistic competitiveness – also emerge significantly in many of the more complex forms of white-to-white *and* white-to-black creole use. In the generalised cultural mode, where a sometimes merely fleeting reference is set up to the contiguous black culture, a cultural identity is toyed with through the interplay of cultural referents. This generalised cultural mode is substantially different from, but sometimes found in association with, the competitive mode, in which specific street 'roles' associated with dialect are acted out. In this second mode, the language with which those roles are associated is used, because of that association, to stress competitive relations. This kind of strategy – the employment of language culturally associated with positions of command – is of course very common in many different forms and contexts of discourse. The economic conditions in which black people have been historically placed in post-slavery societies, and particularly in urban contexts, have contributed to the emergence of a strand of – usually male – survival strategies and ideologies, traceable in many urban black cultures, encompassing a combination of toughness and quick wits potentially employed in the service of individual survival. The association of this street code with lower-class life and language has led to the establishment of the lower-class forms of black language as a resource for suggesting those very qualities and the 'roles' associated with them. Such associations have been observed repeatedly in the Americas (Abrahams 1963; Kochman 1972; Folb 1980), and they are to some extent also apparent in British urban contexts. As was seen in Chapter 3, the use of creole has exactly this reference for many young blacks, who associate the language with a distinctly oppositional street culture. It is for these reasons that, amongst some white adolescents, creole has come to be employed in a range of real and playful competitive situations.

The usefulness of creole in individualistic play rivalries becomes particularly apparent in ritualised contexts, where the ability to 'slag down' an opponent with an apparently inexhaustible stream of formulaic or (more rarely) spontaneously minted abuse is particularly prized, especially amongst boys. In such games a command of creole can be a powerful asset, combining both a whole supplementary range of terms with the advantage of a possible opaqueness of meaning for the confusion of the recipient. Games involving ritualised abuse are very well known, of course, in many cultures and have always been common amongst British school children (Opie and Opie 1959). It is, nevertheless, interesting to see how recently expanded linguistic resources may be taken up into this activity. One fifteen-year-old white informant described the advantage he had over a white friend when the medium of abuse was London Jamaican:

> Say he says to me, he calls me, a 'rassclaht', and then I say
> something in the dialect really funny, he'll go, 'All right. You
> got me there', like. Later on a bit he'll try and beat me. He
> normally always beats me when it's English [as opposed to
> London Jamaican]. He always beats me 'cos he knows a lot of
> words [i.e. abuse terms].

I have no evidence, however, of the extension of this kind of ritualised abuse into anything more structured than is described here. I also know of no ritual forms amongst black adolescents similar to those described in Dollard 1939; Abrahams 1962; Kochman 1970; 1975; 1977; 1983; Labov 1972*b*.

The most common expression of individualistic rather than cultural relationships are to be found with games, whether of the more or less spontaneously created playground type, involving chasing and friendly fighting, or within the more formally structured games such as cards or dominoes, played by youngsters during lunch periods and other breaks in the school day, or in games like table tennis and pool, played in youth clubs in the evenings. By having ultimate positions of loser/winner, and graduated positions in relation to these, during the various stages of a game, and in some cases by having formal offices within the game – dealer, bidder, banker and so on – with appropriate vocabularies of play, e.g. 'deal', 'cut', 'raise', 'twist', 'fold', a structure is provided within which statuses relative to the game can be claimed or challenged by players. A player who is consistently losing may be derided by a fellow player; winners can be accused of having luck rather than skill, or may assert their superiority over the others by boasting. These status claims and challenges can be effected by explicit comment – 'I'm the greatest!', 'your luck's about to run out' etc. – or may be enacted by the use of markers which inflect the vocabulary of play with statuses established in relation to those markers externally to the game – in other words, by the importation of status-related cultural referents. It is not surprising, given the association of creole with a range of 'street' skills, that it too should be occasionally taken up into such games by white adolescents to perform exactly this function, whilst at the same time bestowing an associative aura of street machismo on the game itself. Exclamations following success or failures are amongst the utterances most commonly incorporating London Jamaican lexis and pronunciation. Within the structured relationships of play, it is also frequently employed as a way of avoiding the loss of face threatened by the flow of minor advances and setbacks within a game.

Particularly useful in this respect is the tooth-sucking, mentioned above, which is employed by many blacks broadly to indicate disapproval. Its uses are various, expressing as it does both annoyance – usually at other people, but sometimes simply at bad luck – and/or disdain. Its ambivalence is especially useful in games, where it may assert the self in disdain of other players *and* simultaneously express annoyance at 'external' factors. Tooth-sucking has proved to be one of the most infectious importations into white adolescent street culture. It is particularly this defiant assertive quality, epitomised in tooth-sucking, that fits some common assertive functions of London Jamaican for its role in white adolescent competitive situations. Thus, for example, in a game of pontoon between white fourth-year schoolboys in their lunch period, a player with two cards in his hand asked the dealer for a third. The dealer slammed the next card on the table with the command, 'Bust, you shit!' The player picked up the card, looked at it and found that it did indeed, take him over twenty-one. 'Boss-op!' he exclaimed, using the London Jamaican form, and enacting the aggrieved but undaunted brand of macho style he had learned from the black boys.

The same player, on another occasion, celebrated his luck borrowing from the same set of cultural referents in the following more cheerful exchange:

DEALER: Put yer money in! Put yer money in! [said to all the players]
PLAYER: John's putting mine in. I'm owed money.
[the dealer deals]
PLAYERS: [picking up his cards and looking at them] A Jah Card!

Jah is a Rastafarian term of the highest respect. Like the term *dread*, however, it has also been taken up into a purely secularised sphere of reference to indicate a more general commendation of excellence. Although its use here is, at one level, a simple exclamation, it also performs the function of bolstering the player's morale, and indicates to the other players that he is now in a superior position.

Although luck intervenes significantly to mediate status claims in games such as pontoon, the more skill is needed, the more personalised become the remarks. The following exchange took place halfway into a hand of knock-out whist. Players A and B (both white) had been inattentive, and B had mistaken the trump suit for diamonds. (Tooth-sucking is indicated by the sign /.)

A: What is it?
B: Diamonds, man.
A: Might as well take it while the going's good, innit.
B: You might as well, but if you've got a heart you've got to lay it though.
A: Haven't got a heart.
B: Well that's all right then, innit.
A: Why not. [He lays his card and assumes he has won the hand, despite the fact that there is another player left to lay.]
C: Oy! that's cheatin'. I'm playin' spades. What you talkin' about?
B: Didn't you choose diamonds?
C: Oh *no* man!
A: /, Now he's gonna take it.
B: /, Let 'im take it, *big bahtyman*! /.
A: Shit! He's got an ace of spades and . . .
B: I'm out of this.

Here the London Jamaican insult, 'big bahtyman', i.e. homosexual, gains in force from the masculine tone set for the game through the occasional use of 'man'. Here, of course, its utterance is the product of chagrin at having been seen to be careless *and* at being about to lose the hand. A and B's embarrassment at their mutual lack of attention to the game is also channelled into further expressions of disgust at losing, in the form of three instances of tooth-sucking in quick succession. The ambiguity of tooth-sucking, expressing both annoyance and disdain for others, is here quarried for all it is worth, with A employing the first tooth-suck, and B taking it up immediately and then further combining it with the insult 'big bahtyman', directed at the winner. The use of tooth-sucking, often combined with creole insults, is also very common in pool, where bad play or mis-cueing can similarly produce a temporary embarrassment in need of rapid alleviation – if the player is to save face. The non-strategic use of 'innit', in A's second utterance in the sequence, is a further indication of the proximity of black linguistic forms in the immediate school culture.

The placement of such scattered and fragmentary creole elements, displaying competitive positionality through culturally 'imported' stresses, merges at times with the collective enterprise of placing the game itself within an imaginary arena of dramatised masculine 'low life'. Here imaginary social identities, implemented with the occasional use of creole, are assumed purely within the temporary bounds of the game, and are often played out by adolescents exclusively within that context.

At one remove from these creole uses in formal game-structures – yet functionally continuous with them – is the use of creole in non-game contexts which nevertheless possess a real or playful competitive component, or at the least provide the elements of conflict or disagreement. The inflections of competitive identities employed at stress points within games, whilst not exclusively the province of males, are certainly underwritten by an ideology of the masculine. However, the same orientation can be equally carried over into exchanges between white girls employing these forms. As with boys, this may take place both within and outside of formal games. The following examples of the functional extension of the competitive mode beyond the game context are taken from a series of conversations between two white girls during their school lunch periods. The two girls frequently addressed each other as *man*, as do many girls. One used fragments of creole occasionally with her black friends; the other used them consistently to her white friend in a kind of playful toughness within the mild forms of banter in which they engaged, as can be seen in the following exchange:

A: I got these fags here. Where shall I put them?
B: In yer pocket.
A: They might fall out. Wanna carry 'em?
B: No thanks, 's all right.
A: I don't care. I'll carry them.
B: Well then, man, what are you askin' for, you silly crun?
A: For me, you ol' bag!
B: [Sucking her teeth loudly] Fucking *rass! Rass bamba!*

Here a series of utterances merges, at turn 6, into a playful exchange of insults initiated by girl B, who does not want to take responsibility for the cigarettes which they will both soon be smoking. She moves from the defensive 'No thanks, 's all right' into the offensive 'you silly crun', which produces the returned insult, 'you ol' bag'. B then terminates the exchange with her far-from-mild final insult employing London Jamaican forms. While remaining within the bounds of friendly and playful banter, with little really at stake, creole is evidently being strategically employed to suppress, by verbal force, any further discussion of this disagreement. Within this low-key conflict, it has functioned to ratify the imposition of one speaker's will over the other. As in the game contexts described above, a competitive positioning in relation to the ulterior objective has been achieved by the strategic importation of creole items.

Occasionally, in other exchanges, speaker B would also use creole pronunciation, where the lexis was not itself so marked, when dissenting from an opinion or suggestion made to her:

A: Let's get the register on the way back, eh?
B: *Fock aaf!*
A: Just a thought.

The use of creole inflections to signal emphatic dissent was widespread amongst white adolescents, and must be taken as a further aspect of the individualistic/competitive function which London Jamaican frequently serves.

In contrast to the competitive forms of creole use described above, the *cultural* mode, glimpsed at the simplest level in the use of quotation, becomes evident where no strategic purpose with regard to the immediate discursive relationship between the interactants is served. In such cases, the motivation for creole use appears to reside in the creation of a fictive social identity, albeit very temporarily established, for the differentiation of the self. Here markers are employed, 'which are deliberately projected by a speaker in order to lay claim to characteristics of identity which are not actually his' (Laver and Trudgill 1979: 26) but which nevertheless indicate something of the cultural terms within which the speaker wishes to be seen. Many adolescents try out a range of such self-presentational markers, and the spectrum of youth-cultural styles of dress provide them, in that area of signification, with contrasting sets upon which to draw (Hall and Jefferson 1976; Hebdige 1979). As was seen in earlier chapters, this could involve white adolescents in drawing on black youth-cultural styles, although not without difficulty, in the same way as they might draw upon styles predominantly associated with white youth. This same endeavour is also evident in linguistic behaviour in the use of creole by whites, and is substantially different from the discursively strategic uses described above, which do not necessarily imply any wider cultural self-identification. This is not to say, however, that speakers who employ creole for one of these functions may not also employ it for the other, and in some cases these two functions *may* overlap.

The following piece of dialogue was recorded from the speech of the same two girls who featured in the last examples. The positional rivalries are absent, but girl B again employs an item of creole, this time exclusively as a kind of cultural diacritic, accenting her style of self-presentation. Unlike the male-influenced competitive mode seen above, here she presents herself, as does girl A, in an almost stereotypically female role, commenting sardonically on a girl they had just passed in the street in the company of a boy who was not her regular boyfriend:

A: Oh yes! 'Young Love', eh?
B: What would Gary think?
A: Know what I mean.
B: *Tarra!*
A: Well it's her bit on the side, innit, Christopher.

Note here both the Jamaican exclamation, 'Tarra!', which contains scandalised undertones, and which is a conscious importation into her speech in the service of a stylistic differentiation of self, and girl A's use of the (originally black) agreement marker, 'Know what I mean', which had become well established in the local multi-racial vernacular and was clearly *not* used in any way related to stylistic self-differentiation. Throughout all of the recording sessions, girl B employed quotations from black shows and records very frequently, and also used the creole greeting 'wa'appen' occasionally to her friends. Unlike girl A, who at times did use creole interactively with her black friends, girl B consistently chose to present herself to her white friends through implicit references to black culture.

The desire to establish differences between the self and the white peer group through the use of such cultural markers is more pronounced in some adolescents than in others. For those whites in a position to do so, being closely involved with black friends and black culture sometimes provides a useful source of individuation that can be mobilised within their relationship to their white peers, as one boy, reflecting on his early teens, explained to me:

> I was the sort of person who liked to stand out, and being able to speak patois seemed as a form of being able to stand out. And they was all white kids at school. Because I went round with black kids I was different. They was all the ones saying you can't walk down Brixton, you know what I mean. Whereas I was the one could say I go round with 'em.

The desire for individuation can, of course, be served by a variety of means. The fact that association with black culture is chosen can, however, have rather different consequences from those which might follow from other choices. As was seen in Chapters 1 and 2, this initial act of stylistic choice *can* – especially if it is supported by close association with black friends – lead to a keen awareness of the white racism which is explicitly attacked in many reggae lyrics and implicitly opposed at several levels of black culture. Furthermore, by placing the adolescent in a culturally ambiguous position, this initially simple choice can enmesh him or her in a number of problems concerning black/white relations, the solution of which can be socially extremely educative.

Just as the use of creole in limited competitive ways does not necessarily imply any wider cultural identification, so an identification with black youth culture does not *inevitably* lead to any ideological questioning of white racial attitudes. This much was observed in Chapter 1, where temporary influences from black peers on young whites were described. Nevertheless, in many cases this process of social questioning is initiated through such stylistic choices, for within black youth culture the inter-penetration of culture and ideology is particularly evident, and is often dynamically activated within the white adolescent biographies that come to be transected by it.

Where a move is made into this cultural arena, a complex social semiotic is called into play which is not necessarily involved in the competitive mode of game and game-like contexts. Adolescents who are recognised by their peers as having made such a move, *themselves* become a kind of Janus-like cultural sign whose white-directed face may actually assist in the promotion of the status of black youth culture amongst white youth. At the linguistic level, such agents are often responsible for the spread of creole words to groups of white adolescents who themselves have no direct contact with blacks, thus promoting a kind of linguistic nimbus extending, with decreasing strength, into the white adolescent community.

The conscious and emphatic use of creole by white adolescents – to any degree above that of simple expletive – does depend, however, on their actually having black friends who employ it, and on their being au fait with black youth culture. Given this condition, their employment of creole with other whites becomes a kind of cultural showcase, whether the mode within which they perform is purely cultural or whether it embraces strategic functions *within* that mode.

The following example is taken from the speech of a boy who was considerably further along the path of identification with black culture than girl B in the examples above. He had a large number of black friends, with whom he used creole to some extent. Here, however, he is in the company of two white girls only. The recording site was a fish and chip shop which had installed a number of electronic games. Young people regularly 'hung out' in the shop, which was situated at a busy crossroads and so provided a good spot to watch out for friends passing in the street. Barry had been playing 'Space Invaders' whilst waiting for his black friend, Frazer, but had then stopped. One of the girls offered to play him on one of the machines, primarily because he had a little money on him and she claimed to have none with which to play on her own. Barry refused this offer/request in the following way·

BARRY: No. I don't wanna go on that.
GIRL: Go on!
BARRY: I want *some'in' fe eat.*
GIRL: Jess put one in.
BARRY: No. *I wan' som'in' fe eat.* [He counts his money.] Two, four six
 . . . I wonder where Frazer is then . . . *Tarra, man!*
 [He turns to the woman serving behind the counter.] Can I
 have, er, rice with some coley on it, please?
 [The woman serves him.] How much is that?
 [He pays. As he does so he sees another girl passing by outside
 in the street and calls out to another girl inside the shop
 doorway.] *Eh, tell 'er fe com!*

In a second exchange, which takes place some minutes after the last, the girl in the shop again tries to get money from Barry. He had just complimented her on her new hair style. She replies to the compliment with:

GIRL: For that, Barry, you can lend me 7p.
BARRY: *Move ya bloodclaht!*
GIRL: No. You can lend me 7p.
BARRY: Sorry, can't do them things.

In these examples, the competitive and the cultural modes are both present, with the competitive/strategic utterances functioning *within* the over-arching cultural reference. In the first example Barry's initial refusal of the request is framed in terms of his lack of desire to play the game. When the girl repeats her request with 'Go on!', he produces a second reason for refusing: that he needs the money to buy food. However, he bolsters his refusal by strategically slipping into the creole form, using the infinitive 'fe'. The request is made a third time and he maintains the same reply, although slightly increasing the creole content by uttering 'wan' instead of 'want'. He also adds 'No' at the beginning of the utterance.

The second example is very similar to this, for here again Barry employs the London Jamaican form 'Move ya bloodclaht!' to express *emphatic dissent*, a usage already observed in the example of the two schoolgirls above. He does so again to deny the request for money. When he is unsuccessful with his use of the common formulaic expression, 'Move ya bloodclaht!', he moves back into white vernacular pronunciation with 'sorry, can't do them things', although 'them things' is also ambiguously an anglicised rendering of the creole 'dem tings'. The whole phrase, therefore, does not represent a total retreat from the previous strategy, although it serves as a contrastive reformulation.

There is, of course, a sexual subtext beneath the banter over money: the girl forcing Barry to pay attention to her and striving for a submission of will – the very struggle over which constitutes the substance of the sexual play – and Barry enhancing his masculine identity through a language associated in part with street machismo.

In contrast to these strategic uses, his expression of annoyance at his friend's failure to arrive, 'Tarra, man!', indicates a rather different function, as does his use of the infinitive, 'fe', and his creole pronunciation of 'com', in 'Eh, tell 'er fe com'. These are non-strategic with regard to the immediate interaction, although the latter is perhaps employed to give additional authority to the command. 'Tarra, man!' is not directed at anyone in particular, and is more in the nature of a reflective exclamation of annoyance than an instrumental utterance. In this absence of immediate strategic uses we may see delineated the purely cultural marking, separated out from the competitive mode. Creole here bestows a cultural patina on the language.

The strength and frequency of the kind of cultural marking observed in these examples varies greatly, from the occasional inflections of speech that are merely suggestive of black culture, to extremes in which, as far as possible and in permissible contexts, an imaginary 'black' identity is fully embraced. The kinds of impediments placed by white friends in the way of such an adoption, if such appear, are very different from those encountered in the exchanges with black friends, discussed in the next chapter. It is important in this regard that the employment of a strong creole pronunciation, which is for many blacks a highly sensitive aspect of white creole use, is much more common in creole utterances exclusively between whites, than by whites in the company of blacks. Here, unimpeded by the possibility of provoking hostile reactions, young whites who choose to do so may enter as fully as they are able into the imaginary identity they assume.

In the following extract two white reggae enthusiasts, one of whom was the only white member of a group of boys who ran an amateur sound and who called himself 'Papa Danger', are conversing in the street about Papa Danger's role as toaster in relation to another member of the sound. The conversation then turns to a discussion of the relative chances of different commercial sounds in a forthcoming competition. The dialogue contains some very free play-acting, of a kind that would be difficult to negotiate with black friends. It becomes relatively simple, with a white friend prepared to collude:

A: *'im wan, 'im wan, i: seh wan dat. 'im soff!*
B: He wants everything!
A: *'m soff, though. Jackson seh Papa Danger com fe toast tonight!*
   [They enter a tobacconist where they make purchases in white
   vernacular. They leave the shop.]
A: *Yeah, bwai, Papa Danger com fe nice op dis area!*
B: Who d'you reckon'll win the cup?
A: I fink Shaka. *Shaka gonna mash . . .*
B: Yeah, but Shaka's gotta watch the Frontline, *innit*?
A: Yea, but Shaka's one fool. 'e ain't got a brain.
B: I know, I know.
A: All 'e deals in is juss pure bass line. Drum an' bass, 'e's got electric
   drum, goes 'budoom boom', like that, right, but Frontline,
   Frontline's top sound in Brixton, so . . . I think Sir Coxsone,
   Sir Coxsone could walk it.
B: Yeah, yeah.
A: 'Cos Sir Coxsone's got the music . . .

This is an identification with black youth culture at an unusually high level for both boys, although boy B uses no creole forms other than *innit*, in his third utterance, and this much was in any case part of the local multi-racial vernacular. Boy B merely demonstrates his strong interest in what is primarily a black adolescent concern. Boy A, on the other hand, actually adopts a black persona, and all of his complaints about the other member of the sound – ''im wan', ''m soff' – and his boasts – 'Papa Danger com fe nice op dis area' etc. – are unashamedly uttered in heavily accented creole. He drops the unmixed London Jamaican, however, when boy B asks his opinion about the competition, but his language continues to contain creole forms and expressions: 'Shaka gonna mash', 'Shaka's one fool' etc., as well as common black adolescent idioms such as 'deals in' and 'juss pure bass'. There is no conflict between these boys, although boy A, who was the leading cultural innovator of the two, is certainly making plain his mastery of the culture. However, the immediate *strategic* uses observed elsewhere above are totally absent. A form of positioning is, to be sure, taking place but not *between* the boys. Rather it is a positioning *of* the cultural, an implicit reflection of a view of the relative statuses of black and white cultures as they are felt and experienced: a re-evaluation which accords to black culture (or rather, to that part of black culture to which they are relating) a significance and efficacy above that of the white culture which is their 'natural' inheritance.

Although the incorporation of creole forms into the speech of white adolescents is most widespread in areas of densest black settlement, adolescents, such as boy A here, who attempt almost to 'become black', and who project that identity through the strong use of London Jamaican, are not restricted to areas of this kind. They are found, usually attached to groups of black friends, even in areas of quite diffuse black population, where many of the influences of creole noted above are totally absent from the speech of white adolescents, and where their activities cannot be taken as part of any mainstream linguistic trend. They do, nevertheless, represent one *extreme* of a process of cultural attraction which *is* more common, and which occurs elsewhere at a lower level of visibility.

While questions of 'personal identity' are inevitably raised by evaluations such as that displayed in the example above, their *social* significance resides more importantly in their contribution to the emergent folk taxonomy of the relations between social groups, implicit in the spread of these and other similar, less visible, practices. The existence of creole forms that are, in specific contexts, *unmarked* for ethnicity, described earlier in this chapter, is necessarily preceded by the use and absorption of these same forms, ethnically marked to some degree. The observable 'sociolinguistic patterns' produced by the impact of creole on white London vernacular are, therefore, a linguistic embodiment of sociocultural evaluations, running counter to the dominant assessments of the relative prestige of black and white cultures. This can be read as a map of perceived sociocultural relations, revealing *implicit* folk taxonomies as they are acted out in a multitude of often minute linguistic adjustments.

As was seen in the case of individualistic/competitive functions, however, the employment of creole forms can be very selective, limiting the choice of markers to those which relate only to functionally specific uses of the language, and not necessarily implying any wider cultural valuation. Because of this variability in function, the sociolinguistic 'maps' require careful and discriminating reading. What has been said above concerning the erosion of racist ideology, for example, is but a small aspect of the social machinery surrounding some uses of creole by whites, and remains a potential only occasionally realised. On the other hand, the conscious use of creole between whites does at least open up the possibility of the interplay of social and cultural forces through the social semiotic generated at street level by the real social interaction of social beings. The influence of social structure on the nature of that semiotic field is, of course, crucial, relating as it ultimately does to the issue of race and class. The foundation of any enquiry into that relationship must, however, be the examination of the real and everyday interactions in which signs are generated and exchanged. These important issues will be returned to in Chapter 6.

In this chapter I have described a range of creole influence on white adolescent speech, extending from unconscious incorporations of often minute features, through the conscious use of marked items in game and game-like contexts, to the openly displayed adoption of black language and speech styles by whites wishing to identify themselves unambiguously with black youth culture. All of the examples were taken, however, from recordings in which whites were in the company of other whites. The ambiguous cultural practices of some white adolescents provide us with a unique access to an interplay of social and cultural forces which more commonly remains opaque.

The most complex social issues arise, however, not in these white-to-white uses, containing as they often do a strong play-acting element, but in the negotiation of creole use by whites in interaction with their black friends. Here, inevitably, much more is at stake, and the social meanings attached to creole use become far more evident than in the relatively simple white-to-white uses. Except for unconsciously imported elements, usually forming part of the local multi-racial vernacular, white-to-white uses of creole are always either in the strategic/competitive mode or in the exhibitionistic/cultural mode, because creole is not an established language of communication between whites in Great Britain. It is, therefore, employed as a stylistic device within only a limited set of functions. Only in white-to-black speech, and then only under very specific conditions, may creole use be non-positional in either of these senses.

5

White creole use in inter-racial contexts

I

The effect of demographic factors on the distribution of creole influence, discussed in the two previous chapters, is particularly relevant to the discussion of creole use by whites in interaction with their *black* friends. The demographic differences between Areas A and B are significant because, at an early age, white children in Area B are more likely to be exposed to such creole as is employed by their peers and by older children, both in junior school and in the local neighbourhood. Thus while they may – like children in Area A – come to hear language that is creole-influenced in school, for them it is more likely to be reinforced by what they hear *outside* the school. Even at junior school age, when fewer black children use creole forms, some white children from Area B may already have picked up odd words and phrases, or at least may have come to understand what limited creole they hear in the playground and in the street. Thus, by the time they reach secondary school age, when more black children themselves choose to use more creole forms, such children often already have a context and a history for this aspect of their language experience. White children living in Area A, on the other hand, and even black children too, may have heard little or no creole before they reach secondary school age, having been less exposed to it both in and out of school when young. It is more 'exotic' to them, and the functions which they see it serving amongst black adolescents are also more limited than the wide range of daily uses observable in a community in which there are more black people.

As was observed above, differences of area also affect the nature of the local vernacular. The penetration of creole-derived features into the local vernacular is far greater in Area B than in Area A. In other words, the border territory between creole and non-creole speech is wider, and

150

in Area B the very existence of a *multi-racial* local vernacular facilitates the further incorporation of creole-derived features. In Area A the linguistic contrast is more stark, and items are more heavily marked as belonging or not belonging to speech associated with black people.

White adolescents in Area B often attempt to appropriate words from London Jamaican, and they use the multi-racial local vernacular as an umbrella under which to do so. They do this because many black creole users – and non-creole users – are sensitive to the use of creole forms by whites, suspecting in such use an element of derision, or simply because they dislike what they regard as the devaluing of culturally significant markers by outsiders. As one black girl expressed it:

> It's offensive 'cos, like, a white boy might say something in joke to another, and then he'll see a black person and say, 'Wa'appen', or make some joke, or say 'Oh, rass!', but he's taking the piss out of you, you know? So when you hear two of them talking it, you think, 'What they trying to do now? What they trying to prove now?'

Because of such suspicions, the lexical traffic across the borderline of creole and non-creole speech is always regulated by very specific local conditions, giving rise to great differences in the practices of adolescent social networks even within a single demographic location. As was observed in Chapter 4, what is regarded by one group of black and white friends as unmarked with regard to ethnicity may, in another group in the same locality, be regarded as marked, and therefore possibly as the subject of special negotiations in inter-racial usage. If a white youngster wishes to use a certain word, therefore, he or she may have to make it appear 'natural' to their speech if they are to avoid the possibility of being challenged, or of being thought to be appropriating a language which they have no right to use. The existence of a vernacular which already contains a number of creole-derived features provides a useful alibi, a kind of smokescreen through which words may be smuggled into white speech. This kind of activity is inevitably much more difficult in Area A than in Area B, where the local multi-racial vernacular is broader and more flexible.

A prerequisite for transposing a word in this way, in either area, is the abandonment of any hint of Jamaican pronunciation. Failure of attempts to 'slip in' black forms often occurs because of the use of Jamaican accents. This partly emerges in the following extract from an interview with a sixteen-year-old black girl:

> We used to say 'hours', when we were going home, instead of 'later', you know, like they say 'later' we used to say 'hours'.

And everytime Timmy (a white boy) was going home from this club he used to say, 'hours', and he knew David couldn't stand it. And he used to say, 'later', and 'w'appen' and ''ow's tings?', and all this, and he sounded a right berk ... typical English guy.

As has been observed in Chapter 3, pronunciation especially is treated as a marker of ethnic group membership. Thus those whites wishing to avoid the imputation that they are attempting to claim such membership take pains to avoid using anything but white South London pronunciation when employing words which may be marked for ethnicity. They must appear to be aligning their speech with that of their interlocutor merely as a member of the same *peer group* and not the same ethnic group. Their alibi is in effect, 'This is the language of the neighbourhood. I've just picked these words up but I don't know where from. To the best of my knowledge they carry no ethnic reference.' What is being avoided, in fact, is any positional inflection of the kind described in the previous chapter.

Warrants for such use can be fortuitously provided where items that might have been regarded as ethnically marked are used by a black speaker to a white speaker, hence legitimating the return of the same item by the white, as in the following example:

WHITE BOY: Eh, Floyd, eh, guy ... where 'ya goin'?
BLACK BOY: Goin' to see Davis.
WHITE BOY: Where 'bouts?
BLACK BOY: 'p 'is *yard*.
WHITE BOY: Up 'is *yard*?
BLACK BOY: Yeah.

Here the use of the Jamaican word *yard*, meaning 'house', or 'place where one lives', is easily and naturally taken into the white boy's utterance, legitimated by the fact that the black boy has used it to him and that it is repeated as part of an apparent request for clarification. His use of it cannot, therefore, be challenged. The same word used by another white with other black friends, even on the same estate, might well provoke hostility, as, indeed, may its use by this boy on another occasion.

The contrastive relations between types of speech is what is of significance in particular interactions, not any absolute or 'objective' standard of what actually constitutes a speech variety. These contrastive relations are always subject to some local negotiation, despite more widely held and over-arching concepts of languages or dialects and their cultural and social associations and meanings.

This question of contrastive relations is also important in other respects. Although there is often hostility from black youngsters to the deliberate use of creole by whites, some young whites *do* manage to negotiate for themselves the right to use it with their immediate circle of black friends. Both this opposition and the process of negotiation will be examined more fully below. Here, however, it is relevant to note that demographic factors again are influential – in this case on the level of white creole acquisition. In Area A, where the black population is small, very dispersed and spread across a wider class spectrum, black adolescent friendship groups may themselves have little support, at home or in their immediate neighbourhood, for creole acquisition. As was seen in Chapter 4, many, indeed, even *most*, may know and use very little creole, and the fragments they use within their friendship groups as part of their generational group language are often limited to a few formulae employed within a limited set of functions. Certainly, any group of black youngsters from Area A displays a range of different abilities with creole, commonly extending all the way down to zero. The language employed within group interactions will inevitably reflect this, and those whites who become attached to such groups will often be in a very similar position, with no creole inputs other than those which constitute the common currency of the group. What little creole they use may, nevertheless, be treated as strongly marked, and their black friends may regard them as a 'creole speaker' simply because their creole use has parity with that of the group. They use the marked forms associated locally with black youth, and are accepted by their friends as doing so. Linguistically, their employment of creole may be of negligible interest; symbolically, it may be extremely important.

In Area B, on the other hand, for a young white to be regarded by his (or her) black friends as 'a creole speaker', his knowledge and use of the language would need to be far greater. In fact, the number of white youngsters who know and use creole to the same degree as the specialised 'creole-speaking' adolescents of Area A may be so high that, geographically transplanted, such whites from Area A would be unlikely to be regarded as 'creole speakers' at all. It is always these contrastive relations which are of importance over and above any 'absolute standard'. This difference in areas is particularly clear in the following interview extract. The black informant had moved, two years earlier, from Brixton into Area A, and was struck by the differences in local creole acquisition of both blacks and whites:

> I know a lot of [black] kids who have . . . not led a sheltered
> life, but didn't really mix with a lot of other young black kids.

> When they sort of speak, you *know* that doesn't come natural
> to 'em. Like, it's like a white kid trying to talk black. That's
> how it sounds to us, hearing another person talk when it's
> wrong. And then I know white kids, that when they speak
> black to you, like Danny, when he's gonna speak black to you,
> you just ... you wouldn't look at him and say 'that's a white
> man', 'cos he's been in the environment, Brixton. He came
> from Brixton with us up here, and when he's ready to talk to
> us you have to just listen. You have to mask [to maintain a
> serious expression], you know. You have to listen to him.

At secondary school, children are brought together in much larger
numbers than at primary and junior school. Here, possibly for the first
time, white and black youngsters may come to hear creole spoken, or at
least hear language containing creole elements used between black
youngsters, and even by the occasional white. In Area A this exposure to
creole is often restricted to the school context. Unless a white or black
child has close black friends out of school who speak creole, or unless
they are in some way exposed to it through their family, the uses made of
creole within the school are likely to be the only ones learned – if, indeed,
they are attracted at all to use creole themselves.

One school, with a wide catchment area and situated not far from the
border of the two areas, included children from Areas A and B.
Consequently the school contained *some* white children who knew far
more creole than many of the black children in the same school. Both
black and white children in Area A pass through secondary school
hearing little or no creole. A few, in small friendship pockets, employ
some creole with their friends for specific purposes – most commonly
those arising from the real or play rivalries described in Chapter 5. A
common use of creole by white secondary school children, and one which
excites no objections from their black friends, is where it is used
deliberately to exclude and mystify teachers and other adults in authority. It is, of course, a form of positional employment in which the value
of creole as a 'secret language' becomes taken up into the pupil's felt
conflict with those with obvious power. As one white boy explained:

> In school, if the teacher gets on your nerves and they don't
> know what you're talking about, and you tell 'em to, say, 'dig
> up' or something, they don't know what it means but *you*
> know what it means.

It is, perhaps, this very specificity and limitation of use within the
strategies of an oppositional pupil culture that accounts for why this form

of white creole use is usually not objected to by black fellow pupils. It is not simply its status as a 'secret language' that fits it for this purpose, however. 'Back-slang' would do equally well if that were the case, and many adolescents can speak one of the numerous forms of 'back-slang' with great speed and fluency. It is the specific association that creole has with a vigorous youth culture, itself often equated with opposition to hierarchical authority, that gives it its peculiar resonance. This, and the more common peer rivalry uses, often mark the extent of creole use in schools in Area A. In Area B, such uses are also apparent, but are present alongside more varied functions.

Gender also intersects demographic features with consequences for white creole use. Because in areas of diffuse black population, such as Area A, black girls tend to speak less creole, to use it less often than boys, and to use it in slightly different ways, this has some consequences for how often and to what extent *white* girls also use it. As a result of the prohibitions against female adolescent creole use which are more apparent amongst black families in Area A, and the smaller size of female adolescent peer groups in comparison with male adolescent peer groups, black girls tend to know and use less creole than boys, and to teach it less to their white girl friends. Furthermore, the little creole that is transmitted by black girls to white girls in Area A tends to be less organised around the competitive positional mode, because verbal and other competitive forms are generally less predominant amongst girls than amongst boys. Here, what is a major function of creole and the most common cause of code-switching amongst boys is, although not absent, certainly far less apparent. The little creole that is employed between girls is, in consequence, more low-key and matter-of-fact, less used both for competitive interactions and for display. As one black girl told me:

> Girls don't talk it like the boys do. They don't go up to
> teachers and say it. Boys are more outward going, but the girls
> ... You wouldn't go up to a teacher and say 'w'appen sah!'
> You wouldn't, you just wouldn't. But boys would. We just
> chat it amongst ourselves [. . .] With our black mates it just
> comes out. It's not a show. You don't put on a show and start
> talkin' it. It comes out naturally.

And, as another commented with regard to using fragments of creole with her white friend: 'We don't really think of it. We just walk along an' chat together.'

Furthermore, because of the 'fashion' for white girls to have black boyfriends, black girls were often very vigilant about penetrations by white girls into black youth culture. Hence there was a further incentive for white girls with close black friends to ensure that what fragments of creole they did employ were taken as an alignment with their black peers as personal friends, and not as an alignment with the ethnic group to which they belonged. Their use of creole items was more in the nature of unstressed and occasional inclusions, having the appearance of 'normal' and 'natural' speech and decidedly not in the nature of a display. The display use of creole by white girls in interaction with or in the presence of black boys was, however, frequently mentioned by black boys themselves. It was seen as part of a mode of behaviour which included dressing in black styles and claiming allegiance to black music in order to attract the attention of black boys, with a view to 'going out with them'. In group discussions between black boys it was spoken of in very disparaging terms. Black girls were also strongly aware of this use of creole by white girls, and it undoubtedly contributed to their attention to the maintenance of cultural boundaries. Indeed, white girls were strongly discouraged by black girls from using creole in any way suspected of being part of flirtatious display, and were also discouraged from this by black boys who were actually in relationships with white girls. In the flirtatious exchanges between black boys and white girls not yet in a relationship, however, black boys did sometimes enjoy the playfully dominating role of creole language 'tutor', despite their generalised hostility to white girls who 'try to act black'. But within the confines of a 'teenage romance', white girls often reported to me that their boyfriends made it very clear that they did not like them using creole. It appeared to be seen, in fact, as rather 'unfeminine'. Simple, non-amatory relationships between black boys and white girls suffered less from these constraints, as did very close relationships between black and white girls, but there is no doubt that in Area A, the convergence of demographic and gender factors decidedly influenced the distribution of creole use amongst whites.

The code of appropriate sex role behaviour also transected black male and female exchanges, as the following extracts from a group discussion with several black boys and one white boy suggests:

SIMON (white): Sometimes, if you're wiv a girl, you don't speak it.
PAUL (black): Yeah.
SIMON: Unless it's a girl who speaks it and says it to you first. You
   know what I mean?
[later on in the discussion]
PAUL: Like some white girls . . . you know what I mean, they think
   they're one of us sometimes. 'Cos you know they come singin'
   all dese dread songs what we know, innit. They can't sing it.
   They think they try to impress us or something like that.

DENNIS (black): Yeah, and when we start talking an' we start rabbitin'
    on, they start sayin' 'Cor, whyn't you speak our language?'
    You know what I mean? An' they ask for it.
    [...]
DENNIS: That's the way it is.
    But you said earlier that you wouldn't talk to girls in it anyway.
    Do you mean you wouldn't talk to black girls or white girls?
PAUL: I wouldn't talk to black girls.
    [...]
DENNIS: In a way it all depends if you like the girl, innit?
PAUL: Yeah.
DENNIS: If you respect the girl you can't. You know what I mean?
SIMON: Like if the girl's getting on your nerves, then you'ld say it
    wouldn't yer?
    Oh, I see, I mean, you'ld use it ...
SIMON: You'ld say, 'Go dig up!'
(*Others all laugh.*)
    How about with another black girl who knows it well?
JEFF (black): Yea, we'd speak it.
DENNIS: Yes 'cos they speak like that.
PAUL: Yeah. They speak it to you and you speak it back, innit.

If these observations do indeed reflect actual practice, it would seem that
the further factor of black boy/girl relationships and their appropriate
codes of behaviour may also affect the gender distribution of creole use
amongst blacks and therefore also, indirectly, amongst whites.

These gender-related factors are of course also influential in Area B,
but are far less pronounced, because the greater linguistic support
provided by the larger black community, together with the greater
concentration of working-class black families, tends to counteract the
effect of any familial discouragement of creole speech by girls.

Although not emphasised by demographic factors, some of these
gender-related patterns can also be traced in Area B. In particular, the
prevailing competitive modes of male language play are certainly
influential. Ritualised verbal abuse is predominantly a male activity
(Abrahams 1963; Labov 1972*b*; Maltz and Borker 1982), and in Area B a
white boy may learn the use of creole even at junior school age:

WHITE BOY (fifteen years old): What we used to do most of
    the time we used to sit over the park – there's a park just by
    [our estate.] We used to sit over the park and talk an' that,
    and that's when I first, ever, started to pick it up.
    How old were you at that stage?
    About seven. Six or seven.

And what did they think when you started using those words?
At first they used to laugh at me. You know, they used to start
laughin' if I said somethin' funny. Whereas then, after a while,
if someone said somethin' to me in that language, I could give
'em a sentence back that would mug 'em up. An' they used to
say, 'that's it, you tell 'im.' And they'd say, 'Don't say
anything to 'im 'cos 'e'll slag you down even worse.'

This ability to hold your own in a slanging match can be especially
important once a boy moves into adolescence, and to do so the language
has to be right:

A black kid, right? Say 'e tries to slag me down. I can slag 'im
down. Whereas if I'm wiv black kids I can give 'em some slang
and slag 'em down in [local], like white-man's [local] – well,
you know the slang don't yer? I could slag 'em down in that.
Whereas, I tell you what, if I was sittin' 'ere and there was a
couple of black kids and they started callin' me, you know,
they started talkin' the way they talk and slaggin' me down,
an' say I said to one of 'em, 'Oh shut up you silly black cunt',
what would they do? . . . They'd laugh. They'd laugh because
they'd think, 'e can't talk, you know, 'e can't do it so 'e can't
slag us down. To them, English speakin' is rubbish now, they
don't care about that. [. . .]
When you go around with black kids and they're all speakin'
it, you've got a challenge. You know what I mean? You've got
a challenge to be equally as good as them. You 'ave to be
equally as good as them. So you 'ave to try 'arder [. . .] Out of
school you *'ave* to do it.

This boy was brought up in the heart of Area B, lived in a predominantly
black street and went to primary and junior schools with very high
numbers of black children. In adolescence most of his friends were black,
and he had little patience with the forms of racism of which he was aware.
The comments on verbal competition above should not be read as
relating to any black versus white opposition but as part of the normal
verbal sparring that the neighbourhood boys engaged in. At the same
time as developing throughout childhood such competitive skills, boys
from Area B may well also be building on other, less theatrical functions:
the kind of functions for which girls also might employ creole. The
interview with the same informant continued:

When I was about ten I started to use it seriously.
And what sort of times and occasions would you use it?

> Well, if I was wiv me mates and, say one of 'em said, er,
> 'We're goin' so an' so', then I'd use it. If I didn't wanna go, I'd
> use that language to say 'I don't wanna go.' Whereas, if I did
> wanna go I'd use that language to say I was gonna go. It's
> funny, if I'm wiv white kids I won't do nothink, I won't say
> nothin', I won't talk it. Whereas sometimes I come out with
> the odd word, but when I'm wiv black kids I 'spose you 'ave to
> use it, in some ways, don't ya?

Some white *girls* from Area B also often regard some facility with creole as a normal part of getting on with their black friends; and if they have had black friends from an early age who use creole, they too may have developed sufficiently easy relationships to permit the extension of their creole use to newer friends. As one girl put it:

> Most of us go up this disco, and it's, like, mixed quantities [of
> black and white], and, sort of, you just get to know people
> there, but you all start mixing and they talk their language and
> you talk then, you know. You get on well like that.

This girl's comments do obscure the actual process of moving from the use of creole with close friends to using it with new acquaintances ('You just get to know people there'). This issue will be dealt with more fully below, but certainly the process is far easier, for both boys and girls, in Area B than in Area A.

The kinds of creole use found amongst white youngsters like these from Area B, and the uses of creole by boys and girls in Area A outlined above, are rather different in motivation from the culturally positional use of creole by whites who are strongly attracted to black youth cultural styles. 'Papa Danger', mentioned in Chapter 4, is typical of such adolescents and, as was mentioned there, they are found in both areas. There are some areal differences, however. In Area A, adolescents attracted to black youth culture tend to pass rather quickly through a phase in which they display their cultural allegiance. With little local support and the strong possibility of inviting hostility from both blacks and whites, they often only dabble with the little creole they manage to pick up. In Area B, the likelihood is increased that they will attach themselves to a group of black friends who will object to their behaviour far less than the more isolated black youth of Area A. One common activity for such whites is, like Papa Danger, becoming part of a 'sound', assisting in the lifting of speakers, the setting up of equipment and so on. They may even progress to toasting if they prove themselves to be good at it, although this is fairly rare. In contrast many whites, also from Area

B, who pick up creole from an early age and use it with their friends, do not even like reggae music and have no interest whatever in imitating black styles. This was true, for example, of the white boy quoted above. This creates complications for our analysis of particular texts because, unlike in white-to-white creole speech, where creole use is always positional in either the competitive or the cultural mode – and the absence of the competitive necessarily reveals the cultural – in white-to-black creole speech, the presence of the cultural mode is not so easily disclosed. The competitive mode may indeed be absent, but it remains to be determined whether an utterance is in the cultural mode or whether it is of some other kind not covered by *any* form of positionality. This problem will be returned to when we come to analyse particular texts.

Finally, in this general outline of areal differences it is worth recording what is common to both areas: that most youngsters who employ creole cease to do so at about the age of sixteen. There may be several causes of this phenomenon, including those discussed in Chapters 1 and 2 concerning the changing patterns of friendship at about that age, and the use of 'prestige youth languages' (Chapter 3). A few, usually the most fluent creole speakers, continue into their late teens and early twenties. Young women who develop a permanent relationship with a black creole-speaking man, especially where the couple live together, very often speak creole fluently (see also Pryce 1979: 86; Benson 1981: 118). Such young women are the most frequently occurring examples of whites whose creole use has expanded from adolescent contexts and continued into adulthood. For young men this continuation is even less common, although it can occur in the rare cases where a young white man has a close involvement with post-teenage black friends who also speak creole and are happy for him to do so. Such cases are very exceptional, however.

The phenomenon under discussion here is not extensions of this kind, but the involvement with creole speech by whites that occurs from the age of about twelve in Area A, from that age and sometimes considerably younger in Area B, and extends until the age of sixteen or so in both areas. The generalisations offered above concerning the differences between Areas A and B are appended by way of a background to the discussion which follows, and in which references to areal distributions will be only occasional. In the above comments I have attempted to highlight trends discernible in each area, so that the discussion concerning the interactive structure of white creole use might be given some approximate geographical context. It should be borne in mind, however that these observations represent *trends* rather than rigid topographical classifications.

II

Although the number of white youngsters who consciously use creole to any degree is very small in both areas, young blacks are extremely aware of and sensitive to the practice. Indeed, the notoriety of white creole use is far greater than the actual activity itself. Black adolescents will often report that white youngsters speak creole when what they mean is that certain people use a few creole expletives from time to time. In this way the incidence of white creole speech is consistently over-reported. This is certainly related to the symbolic role of creole within black youth culture, for white creole use is rarely remarked upon with any enthusiasm. The following statements are very typical of black attitudes to white creole use:

> They should stick to their own culture and not try to impersonate no one else.
> > (Black boy, fifteen years)

> I think they're taking the mickey.
> > (Black boy, sixteen years)

> It seems they are stealing our language.
> > (Black boy, fifteen years)

> The Rastas round our way say it's our identity. They identify their speech with their colour and their actual cult. And they say that somebody is trying to intervene if they copy their ways.
> > (Black girl, sixteen years)

> When I hear white girls talking like that it's poison to my ears.
> > (Black girl, seventeen years)

In none of these statements is the purely communicative function of creole addressed; in each case it is its symbolic status that is being invoked. The activation of 'ethnicity' involves the employment of cultural resources for social and political ends. The need for boundary maintenance where cultural resources appear to be losing their ethnic specificity is, therefore, of central importance. While black culture provides a range of elements – some of them linguistic – which constitute the semiotic raw materials of an active ethnicity, the socioeconomic history of black/white relations, and contemporary structural inequalities, ensure that the semiotic itself is suffused with the logic of positionality. The 'ethnicity' realised here is no mere discrete location upon a wider cultural landscape but a dynamic production of social and economic engagements manifested and realised through cultural as well as other contexts. 'Ethnicity' is, in this sense, essentially a positional concept, for it has its existence only in relation to other cultures bound within specific political and economic systems. With regard to the symbolic importance of creole indicated in the above quotations, it is significant that throughout expressions of this kind two themes were especially apparent, and clearly located creole as a cultural resource or marker of ethnicity within a *specific* historical/economic frame. These were that white creole use was regarded (*a*) as derisive parody, and hence as an assertion of white superiority, and (*b*) as a further white appropriation of one of the sources of power – 'It seems they are stealing our language.' The cultural semiotic brought to the fore by white creole use is structured by the logic of inequality, and is itself, therefore, an essentially positional manifestation.

In opposition to this contrastive semiotic there is, however, another influential factor which is situated within shared class positions, is fundamentally integrative and is based upon inter-personal relations. This is productive of the apparently anomalous conditions in which, despite the generalised hostility to white creole use, the practice is acceptable in the case of particular white friends. There are in fact two quite different and contradictory principles at work here, bearing in upon the same cultural practice. Informant explanations of this anomaly always indicate the exceptional circumstances of the particular instance at hand: 'Oh, he/she's different', 'We know he/she doesn't *mean anything* by it', etc. Indeed, occasionally some may even state explicitly, but usually in private, the heretical opinion that they actually like their white friends to use some creole:

> Half the time when white people speak I don't like to speak their language. I like to speak my way, and if they can speak, if they can chip in here an' there with the words, I feel at home. I feel more better.
>
> (Black boy, fifteen years)

Evidence of the contradictions of group ideology and individual practice are, however, never far away, even from such confessions:

> I had this white friend that he could toast . . . He said he wishes he was black. That's the type of person he was. He *talked* you know, he did everything, you know what I mean. We used to like it, you know, in the fact that, you know, I like people like that. But some people used to say, 'beat 'im up', as 'e's speakin' black, even. You know what I mean. It really was sad.
>
> (Black boy, seventeen years)

This contradiction was so pronounced that often the same adolescents who verbally condemned creole use by whites would themselves have close white friends whose use of creole they would tolerate or even encourage. Notably in group discussions, white creole use would be roundly criticised even by those who permitted it in interactive contexts. While group consciousness dictated the exclusion of whites from this key area of racial/ethnic identification, in the privacy of close friendship it was both accepted and engaged in as a marker of intimacy and an instrument of friendship.

The 'private arrangement' is, of course, not untouched by the social meanings involved in creole use. Indeed, the activity itself constitutes a specific approach to the positionality which charges creole with so much of its semantic power. It will be recalled that, in white-to-white creole speech, two modes were apparent, both involving a form of positionality. One of these was the competitive mode, the other was the cultural, and congruent with the specific emphasis given to 'ethnicity' here. In the broad discussion of white-to-black creole use given so far, a third possibility has also been alluded to in passing – that of the inter-personal, where, for example, certain white girls strictly avoided Jamaican pronunciation in creole interactions with their black friends, thereby aligning their speech towards the person and not towards the ethnic group. However, while such uses of creole may involve a certain amount of pre-negotiation, they are possible primarily because the most sensitive markers of ethnic group – especially the phonological – are avoided. Whites who are involved in a 'private arrangement' with close black friends may be permitted, as it were, 'full rights' with creole, involving none of the avoidances associated with maintaining a low ethnic profile. Indeed, within close friendships the clear distinction between the cultural/positional and the inter-personal is sometimes obscured by a *collaborative* exercise, in which the social and cultural dimension becomes taken up as an instrument of the friendship and is subjected to a process of neutralization. (The contrasting terms, positional/inter-personal, are, of course, adapted from the early writing of Basil Bernstein (Bernstein 1971). However, while the general concept of positionality is the same as Bernstein's, it will be evident that the notion of the 'inter-personal' is less specific and less theoretically nested than in Bernstein's work. The contrast implied here, therefore, should *not* be taken as related to that which Bernstein has isolated).

While the cultural mode involves the public display of creole, its use in the kind of strategy described here involves the seeming contradiction of a private display between friends. The private display, like the public displays of people like Papa Danger, depends on the fact that the language can be used to 'stand for' the community with which it is associated, and it is because creole is the linguistic expression of the structural relationship between social groups that it *can* be employed in this way. In this case, the use of creole by the white friend is treated as a kind of 'dumb show' or prefiguring of intended relations between that individual and the wider black collectivity. It is the substitution of a relation to language for the more complex relation to the black community. By temporarily freeing themselves from the constraints of their respective groups, the friends can achieve in language a fictive social relationship over and above their personal relationship of friendship. The cultural context of the friendship is established through a 'willing suspension of belief' in the ethnic boundaries which are treated as external to the friendship.

The fictive social relationship in question involves cognitively transcending the actual structure of racial group relations in which the interactants are embedded, and replacing the positional inequality encoded through their memberships of different racial groups with a relationship of positional equivalence. This fictive positional equivalence is formally similar to, and reflects in reverse image, 'fictive kinship', i.e. the social convention found in many societies, by which individuals may stand in a kin-like relationship, marked by the use of kin terminology. (In English society, for example, adult friends of a child's parents may be addressed and referred to as 'aunt' and 'uncle'.) In the case of such fictive kinship, characteristics of the positional are superimposed upon the interpersonal. Within a fictive social relationship of the kind described here, the interpersonal is superimposed upon the positional. Furthermore, while the forum of fictive kinship is public, the forum of the interpersonal is essentially private.

Whilst it is rare to find informants able to reflect on this dimension of inter-ethnic friendship formation, the following extracts from an interview with a seventeen-year-old white boy, Steve, who had ceased to use creole, may be illustrative. The informant is looking back on the period during which he employed creole. From the age of eight he had had a close black friend called Johnny. When he first entered secondary school the number of his black friends increased, and this initiated an identification with black culture:

> I started going round with black kids when I was eleven and
> then I got this thing in me about being black in a white
> person's body. Then all me friends used to speak patois and I
> just kind of picked it up.

His primary source of information with regard to creole was Johnny. He explained that they would go to black parties together and Johnny would answer his questions about the language that he heard:

> When you're a young kid you ask your parents, 'What does that mean? What does that mean?' Well I was asking Johnny. My friend Johnny, he really used to like to tell me about these things, about what they all mean . . .

At this time, he explained, he also fabricated for himself false ethnic credentials: 'I went around saying I was born in Jamaica, my grandmother was a half-caste woman and all things like that.' Indeed, he did his best to assume the position of a young black male: 'I used to suck my teeth but I wouldn't dream of doing that now.'

By seventeen he had come to regard this period of his life as an immature 'stage' of his early adolescence, conducted with Johnny's complicity because Johnny too was 'going through a phase':

> At this time we was both young – we were exactly the same age – so we were both going through the same thing. Probably thought it was cool for me to speak it . . . but we both got older.

He explained the end of this period in the following way:

> See, at that time I was about the only white boy on that particular scene. Then, when I got to the age of about fifteen, sixteen, more white boys started coming round with us and Johnny used to say to me, 'When you hear them speak, you never hear them speak patois.' He used to say, 'They're cool. They don't try and copy.' And then I decided maybe it was stupid, you know? That's when I started coming out this stage. It was when he kind of turned the tables and said, 'Well, you sound stupid, a white person speaking patois.'

Most dyadic friendships of this kind do not involve a reconstruction so radical as to include a fictitious ancestry; but the element of private conspiracy from which wider creole use is generated is very common. Where the friendship base of creole speech extends firmly beyond a dyad, the edifice of social identity may be both constructed by a slightly different process and dismantled – where it is dismantled – in more complex ways. Nevertheless, what is true here for dyadic friendships is also often true for whites within constellations of black friends which have gradually become part of such 'conspiracies'. There is, in such cases, a core group which has a similar function to that of the single close black friend in dyadic relationships. Such an extension of the dyad is inevitably more flexible; but the underlying principle of a conspiracy – free from wider group pressure – within which fictive social relationships are achieved through the use of creole, remains the same. Whether a fictive social relationship or merely a pre-negotiated use of creole is involved, the same *contradictory* movement of the interpersonal and integrative on the one hand and the positional/group and insulatory on the other is evident. Given the difficulties in mediating this ground contradiction, it is not surprising that the contradiction itself should have been productive of a set of *rules* governing linguistic interactions. These rules, it is important to note, are speaker observed and speaker expressed. They are, therefore, very clearly 'emic'. Their primary function is to deal with the difficulty involved for a white speaker in increasing the number of possible black interlocutors.

Because both pre-negotiated uses and fictive social relationships enacted in language are a matter of private establishment, they cannot, by definition, extend automatically to others. This appears to be a linguistic manifestation of a phenomenon described by Gerry Suttles in his account of inter-ethnic relations in Chicago:

> Where ethnic and kin unities are insufficient to fill the normative void between them, residents may take things into their own hands and establish a 'personal relation'. In this way people create a safe little moral world that is based on private understandings rather than public rulings. Necessarily this means a relationship where assumed individual proclivities map out the range of permitted behaviour. A most serious limitation, however, is that a personal relation requires a massive exchange of information and cannot be extended beyond the immediate participants. In fact, individuals must be felt out one-by-one without assuming very much about those connected with them.
>
> (Suttles 1968: 26)

The rules produced by the governing contradiction are essentially concerned to facilitate this process; to make it possible to extend both the number of potential interactants in creole, and the range of uses to which creole might be put with particular established interlocutors. These rules are of course informal, in so far as they are unevenly recognised in the white adolescent community; and they are often only discovered when they are not observed. This is, perhaps, in the nature of adolescent social learning. Nevertheless, they have been noted by numerous native informants, both white and black; and furthermore, it is apparent that those who do not observe them are very likely to suffer very obvious forms of censure which in themselves betray the underlying rule. The simplest option for any adolescent with black creole-speaking friends is not to use creole at all. Some whites with close black friends and an ability to use creole in interactions with *white* friends, refrain from using creole in the company of any black person. As one such boy expressed it to me: 'Well, it's their language, ain't it?' Those who *have* chosen to use creole and have negotiated for themselves the right to use it in certain ways – in games or game-like situations, say – and with certain friends, are likely to refrain from speaking it if they are in the company of black adolescents whom they do not know well. As pointed out in Suttles' account above, 'individuals must be felt out one-by-one', and whites will often not use creole until the new friendship is established to such a point that they can feel confident about not provoking hostility by using it. As one girl put it:

> When you meet someone they may not speak to you [in creole] and they may give you dirty looks an' that, but, you know, you can start, if you're gettin' to know 'em better, you can start talkin' how you wanna talk with 'em.

The same need for caution was also emphasised by black informants:

> I don't really care [about certain white friends using creole] but they might use it with me and I laugh with them an' chat with them in the same thing, but then they might move out to a certain group and use it again and they find the hostility in other people.

The rule which is applied to this situation is, therefore, that where a speaker is in the company of black adolescents whom he does not know or whom he knows only slightly, he will not speak creole until the friendship is established to such a point that he feels confident about not provoking hostility by using it. This was regarded as 'common sense' by most of the whites I interviewed. Each extension of the number of permissible interlocutors has to be earned; creole use cannot automatically signal friendliness, and the only cases that have been reported to me of white adolescents using creole to black adolescents who were unknown to them or only slightly known resulted in the provocation of hostility – even where such use was intended in a friendly way. The following account is a case in point:

WHITE GIRL (fourteen years): When I was in a home once I saw fighting over it [i.e. creole use by a white].
Yeah? What happened?
But what made me laugh, though, this white girl I know, she started talking patois an' that to this coloured girl. An' then the coloured girl turned round and said, 'Oh look she's trying

to speak like a black girl now.' She said it right pure English
and they sort of got into a fight over it. 'Cos they think you're
takin' the mickey out of them. They think you're takin' the
mickey out of their language and the way they speak.

It is interesting to note that this un-negotiated use of creole provoked
both a display of exaggeratedly 'correct' English, as a significant counter
to any potential for cultural stereotyping, and a rather less symbolic
divergence in the form of simple physical violence. The dramatic
dissociation of the black girl's speech simultaneously distanced her from
any element of parody suspected as having been intended, *and* rejected
the intimacy which the initiation of creole was attempting to effect.
Clearly the rule mentioned above was not a rule for this white speaker, or
perhaps she believed that she had already established sufficient intimacy
with her interlocutor to be permitted to use creole with her. Certainly the
generality of the rules influencing white-to-black creole use often failed
to cover a wide range of marginal cases.

The same is true of a second rule, similar to the first, which most black
and white informants said they adhered to and/or usually observed in
others. This rule may be stated as follows: where a white creole user is
with black friends, and they are joined by one or more black friends who
are unknown to the white speaker, the white speaker will refrain from
using creole. This emerged from informants' answers in reply to a
hypothetical question beginning either: 'If you were with your black
friends and were joined by another black person whom you did not
know . . .' or: 'If you were with a white friend [usually named] who was
using creole with you and you were joined by a black friend whom the
white friend did not know, do you think your white friend would
continue to use creole?' In nearly all cases the reply from whites was, 'I
would know not to use it' and from blacks, 'He/she would know not to
use it.' Furthermore, the implicit ruling was also often mentioned in
interviews unsolicited by the interviewer. Speaking of a white boy who
used creole with a certain group of black friends who met regularly at an
adventure playground, one black girl told me:

> While we're there [at 'the Adventure'] 'e can let it off, but 'e
> knows when to do it from when not to, 'cos, right, 'e sees me
> out in the street, 'e'll say, 'all right?'. Whereas, if we're in the
> Adventure 'e says, 'wa'appen'.

Most whites whose close black friends permit their use of creole seem
to manage to act entirely within the confines of these rules without
specific instances of violation and reaction needed to remind them to do

so. It seems that they accurately intuit what are likely to be the social
pressures on their black friends that might make it embarrassing for them
to be seen allowing whites to join them in this culturally significant
activity. Whites who can be relied upon to act this way earn the
confidence of their black friends by their caution, and by their understanding of the social context in which pre-negotiated creole use takes
place. This implicit understanding of boundary-maintaining practices
and the reasons for them often provides an important condition for really
strong inter-racial friendships in adolescents. However, the imprecision
of this rule, like that of the previous one, does occasionally lead to
trouble. The following example of a serious failure in extending the
interlocutor base beyond the immediate sanctioning circle was recounted
to me by a black girl:

JUNE: There is this girl, Elaine Wilson. She goes round with Sandra
      Johnson, Jackie Walcot [both black girls]. They live on her
      estate and I know her as well. And she does it, she does it, she
      put it on [i.e. creole]. Pauline [also black] got a shock 'cos she
      tried talkin' Jamaican. Pauline just laughed in her face. She
      didn't know she did it. . . .
MARGARET: (black girl, age 14] And all of them are used to it so they
      didn't say nothing. I was really shock when I heard she said it.
      . . .
      When Pauline heard her and laughed did she know her?
JUNE: Yes, she knew her.
      Oh, she knew her she just hadn't heard her talk it?
JUNE: No. She goes something like, 'Mudder gon' kill me.' She came
      out with something like that and Pauline just laughed, and her
      brother turned round at her – 'cos Pauline was with her
      brother – 'cos he knows she talks like that but Pauline didn't.
      She just laughed in her face and the girl felt shamed and she
      shut up.
      What did Pauline feel then?
JUNE: Pauline felt embarrassed after 'cos everybody else knew and she
      never, an' so she just laughed.

Pauline, however, did not feel in the wrong for her response, even
though on this occasion she was the only one in the black group who was
not in on the licence extended to this white girl. In the following chapter
this event will be recounted again, this time by Pauline herself. It is clear
from *this* account, however, that the white girl felt quite secure in her use
of creole and was not anticipating any challenge. All of the black
youngsters knew her quite well, and all but one of them had long since

come to accept her use of creole. The one girl who had not heard her, however, was clearly sufficiently angered publicly to 'laugh in her face' and 'shame' her. It is obvious, therefore, that even the application of this rule may be insufficient to cope with instances involving very strong boundary vigilance. Furthermore, events of this kind also convey to the other black youngsters involved the 'group' strictures concerning boundary maintenance. Interestingly, one girl 'spoke for' the racial/ethnic group, while the *actual group* of black youngsters present did not. From such events all participants learn social facts, even if they are not all the same social facts.

Apart from these rules relating to interlocutors, there are also explicit rules concerning the *modes* of creole interaction. Only two modes are recognised within this folk taxonomy, the 'joking' and the 'serious'. According to this classification, white creole use is in an either/or relation to the two modes. If the use is a 'joking' use it cannot be 'serious', and vice versa. Given this simple classification, white creole speakers may claim (*a*) that they always only use creole 'jokingly', 'just mucking about', or (*b*) that they use it seriously on all occasions, or (*c*) that they use it jokingly on some occasions, seriously on others. Note that in (*c*) the determining factor is said to be the nature of the occasion; reference is not made to interlocutors. The rule here is one of simple limitation, and is reported in the form of a practice grounded in 'commonsense'. Thus many whites will claim that they observe the rule, 'only ever use creole jokingly', and black adolescents will also say, 'X uses creole but only mucking about. He/she wouldn't do it seriously.'

Although the exact scope of these terms is difficult to establish, it is at least clear that within the 'joking' mode would certainly fall the game and game-like competitive uses described in Chapter 4, except that here they would be carried out in the company of black friends. When employed by whites in the company of blacks with whom such a use has, by trial and error, been negotiated, then the possibility of a challenge to any subsequent use *within that mode* is excluded. Thus, if the language use can establish itself as 'playful'/'not meant', or is already so established by past usage, or by the nature of the friendships involved, then not only will censure be avoided but the 'play' enjoyed and participated in by the black friends present. Such is often the case where a white speaker employs creole within the enactment of a specific dramatic role, recognised as a 'play' role by the other participants. Other functions which fall within the folk category 'joking' are, for example, the using of creole in ritualised insults and in most kinds of banter. What seems *not* to be included under this category are the kinds of uses found within developed fictive social relationships such as that described for 'Steve' above. The *observable* modes of white-with-black creole use will be discussed more fully below; however, it is certainly the case that, just as the self-reported rules relating to interlocutors influence practice, even if they do not determine practice, so the 'joking/serious' classification and the rules relating to these modes also influence practice and for very similar reasons: the same desire not to provoke hostility by breeching cultural boundaries is encoded in the exclusive use of creole in 'joking' ways. The 'joking' use preserves the alibi: it provides the 'cover story' and avoids any possible challenge. For the same reason, whites who are well established in their black friendship groups and fluent in creole will claim never to use creole 'jokingly'. It seems that to claim otherwise would admit to the merely borderline status from which they are at pains to distance themselves.

Curiously transected by both interlocutor rules and mode rules is the issue of pronunciation. Within 'serious' fictive social relationships, London Jamaican pronunciation will be employed freely by whites; but where those same whites use creole with blacks outside that relationship, pronunciation is the first element to be jettisoned. Similarly, in movements from a game context, in which Jamaican pronunciation is sanctioned, a white employing creole to any extent may again jettison the phonological before any other class of marker. This appears to be related to the specific semantic value given to pronunciation amongst young blacks discussed in Chapter 4. It is taken as a specially sensitive marker of ethnicity, and is therefore perhaps inevitably implicated when the rules derived from the central cultural contradiction of white creole use are evoked.

It is important to note here that, although the rules described are 'folk rules' of behaviour, expressing intended practice, if not determining practice, they are nevertheless very influential. The rules concerning interlocutors and modes are actually realised in speech events, including, for example, the nature of pronunciation briefly discussed above. It is possible, therefore, given that the source of these rules is also known, to model the relationships between the various levels of the description, and to produce a diagram of the model from the most general level to the most particular (see Figure 1). From such a model the social and cultural relationships, together with the economic context which evokes and structures them, can be explicitly located, not in the conditions of each instance of white creole use, but in the 'sociolinguistic patterns' evident in collections of such instances.

III

It is now possible to relate the observable forms of white-with-black creole use to this model. I will be concerned initially with what I have

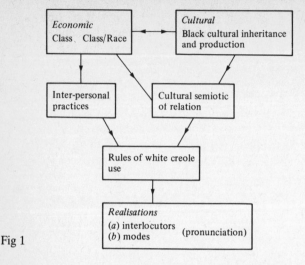

Fig 1

termed the 'pre-negotiated' use of language marked as 'black' or 'patois'. By 'pre-negotiated' I mean that the practice of whites using fragments of creole and creolised 'black' speech within specific interactive contexts is legitimated either by the prior existence of a tradition of the practice within the immediate adolescent community – in school, for example, this may be the class or year group or a fraction of such groups – or by past occasions on which, by trial and error, a white has come to use creole forms with specific friends and has been allowed to do so. Thus a tradition may exist either for particular individuals or within particular groups. Clearly, too, the latter can only become so established through many instances of the former.

Games provide a useful model for displaying this tradition at work. Furthermore, an examination of game interactions also helps to clarify an aspect left intentionally vague in Chapter 4, the area of overlap between the competitive and the cultural modes. It became evident from an examination of a large number of interactions within table games that the use of creole forms to mark and establish positionality within the play was also often synchronised in complex ways, with a limited *cultural* marking of the game itself which was *collectively* arrived at. That is to say, the vocabulary of play used by most of the players was frequently inflected with creole items apparently within a wider semiotic practice concerned with the enactment of cultural images of masculinity; this collective practice was often functionally synchronised with the use of creole items to mark, establish and enact competitive positionality within the game.

The practice is related to the question of 'roles'. Within such games the group identity of the players is achieved through the collective alignment of their speech with that of an idealised target which has its cultural existence in sets of stereotypical roles. (Such stereotypical roles are, of course, not simply 'given', but are culturally derived through perceptions of social relations – class, ethnic, racial, gender – achieved productively through ideological struggles over power, and hence represent refracted social definitions.) It is necessary, however, to distinguish between 'position' and 'role'. 'Position' I take to be a node point within a set of structural relations, for example kin, economic or game. Any evaluations placed on particular nodes are extra-structural and essentially ideological. The products of such evaluatively contextualised positions are *roles*. In a manufacturing works, the position of foreman or manager may be evaluated in one way in one socioeconomic system and in quite another way in a different system. When they are so evaluated, certain attendant attributes will be superimposed on the position; and these will be elaborated from the sociocultural context, with its specific sets of power-inflected social relations from which the role derives its morphology.

The dramatisation of positionality within games can take many forms; the use of creole by whites, however, is a significant and highly detectable tracer of this process. The 'black' roles that are invoked and referenced as part of positional strategies within a game serve culturally to clothe that position and to provide it with attendant functional assets, with respect, for example, to shaming other players, covering embarrassment at setbacks and losses, celebrating success, and so on. At the same time, unless a player is alone in such cultural referencing, there is a collective dramatisation of the interactive space (i.e. the game itself) derived from the same cultural source. Thus the cultural referent and its associations are invoked in *two* capacities simultaneously: first in a dramatisation of individual position within the game (formal position is converted into specific role); secondly in the collective dramatisation which constitutes a cultural and 'ideological' contextualisation of the interactive space itself. (The semiotics of a game of pontoon are not the same as those of, say, a bridge party.)

These two forms are complexly related and inter-dependent, for it is not possible for the cultural referencing of the interactive space to be effected except through the roles assumed by individual players. However, these roles need not be positional only vis-à-vis the relationships which structure the play at any given point. Indeed, creole utterances in which positional strategies are not evident are often also employed, and must be taken to indicate the presence of the cultural mode collectively engaged in. This cultural mode is, of course, perfectly congruent with the evocation of the external cultural referent for the purposes of competitive positional marking. Thus it is possible for an utterance both to serve a competitive/positional purpose and to be part of the *collective* cultural contextualisation of the game.

Because of this established dual function of creole use within games, games provided one limited context in which the permit to employ creole was granted to whites with relative ease. Indeed, I recorded no examples of any challenge to the use of creole by whites within formal games, nor were any such challenges reported to me in interviews. However, it should be stressed that all the examples of card games were gathered from all-male groups, and that the evocation of masculine imageries within these practices clearly underwrote them in such a way as to appropriate the ethnic/racial reference for a semiotic of gender.

The competitive mode in white-with-black creole uses within games functions exactly as it does in white-with-white uses. Some use of creole, it appears, easily becomes regarded as a shared resource for the stressing of competitive positionality within the game. Challenges, complaints, the covering of embarrassment, attempts to undermine the confidence of other players and self-celebration are all marked, at times, in this way. In the numerous card games that were recorded, all of these uses were frequently present. One of the most common occurred in games of pontoon (a very popular card game with boys), where a player whose turn it was to get as close to twenty-one as 'the luck of the draw' allowed would be harangued by other players each time he requested an additional card from the dealer. This was a strategy for undermining the confidence of the player and building up the tension surrounding the decision to 'twist' another card or 'stick' with the hand as it stood. Sometimes it was the dealer himself who engaged in this heckling, sometimes it was one of the other players who also stood to gain or lose by the outcome. In the following example of a game between four boys, one of whom was black, the player who is requesting cards from the dealer is subjected to an interjection counterpointing each demand. The creole utterance (the first utterance below by Player B) is merely one of three such interventions. (All creole or creolised utterances, including pronunciation features, are italicized in the texts that follow.)

A: Twist.
[The dealer deals a card.]
B: *Irie bos'-op!*
A: [To dealer] 'gain.
[The dealer deals another card.]
B: Oh no!

A: Twist.
[The dealer deals another card.]
B: What?
A: Twist.
[The dealer deals another card.]
A: Stick.

The creole utterance 'Irie bos'-op!' has exactly the same function as 'Oh no!' and 'What?'. It is employed to induce trepidation in the player and to fog his judgement.

When a player actually *does* fail, creole terms are again often used by other players, black and white, to celebrate the downfall. On the other hand, players who are already out of the round and who therefore no longer have anything at stake in the hand, may actually encourage and support other players at that point in the game. In the following extract Aubrey (black) and Peter (white) behave in this supportive way, whilst Eddie (white), who is still in the round, celebrates Terry's eventual 'bust', switching to creole to do so. The dealer deals without speaking:

[The dealer deals two cards to Terry.]
ALAN: Show, Tell.
[Terry shows the cards to Alan. Aubrey and Peter also see the hand.]
AUBREY: Yeah, nice cards.
PETER: Yeah.
TERRY: Twist.
[Dealer deals one card.]
AUBREY: He's got eleven ... twennyone. No, nineteen.
TERRY: Twist.
AUBREY: No can't 'ave nineteen.
[Dealer deals one card which does 'bust' Terry.]
EDDIE: *Bos'-op! Mi' gi' you a bos'-op in your [*]*
TERRY: Twennytwo.

Similarly motivated switches into creole are often also evident in games of pool. Both black and white players commonly comment on the poor play of a partner with disparaging observations employing marked 'black' linguistic forms. On one such occasion, a black pool-player in a youth club badly miscued. His white partner, who until that point had used no creole terms, remarked sarcastically, 'Ya sof'! Sof', guy'. Expressions of annoyance at failing a shot in pool or at losing a hand in cards are often marked by a switch into black forms, especially where there is a need to cover embarrassment.

In each of these cases the code-switch to the 'black' form is clearly tied to the specific position of individuals temporarily established at that point in the play. In contrast to this mode is the use of creole by several players, black and white, in which a dramatisation of the interactive space is achieved collectively. Here there is a shared honorary 'black' identity assumed within the game.

As was apparent in some of the white-with-white examples in Chapter 4, the competitive mode can be taken up *into* the cultural mode and assume a dual function to speak, as it were, with two voices – one, that of the individual position within the interaction and another, that of the dramatised identity of the group. In the next example two of the players are white, two black, while a third black player looks on hoping to join in when he can get change of a note. The dealer, who is black, is very much in charge of the game:

BLACK ONLOOKER: You playin' for money? Money?
DEALER: Yeah, readies. It's two pence a game. Lay your dosh on the
    line. You playin'?
ONLOOKER: [Indicates 'no'.]
DEALER: Well go away you slut-lover. Two pence [said as he throws
    cash on the table]
ONLOOKER: I ain't got change, *wa'appen?*
[Everyone ignores this utterance.]
DEALER: Right, ready? [He deals.]
A (white): Yeah.
B (white): Twist.
[Dealer deals one card.]
B: Twist.
[Dealer deals one card.]
B: Stick.
C (black): *No black wid de brak back!*
B: [Examining his hand] *That's sweet!*

The hard, macho style of the dealer – 'Lay your dosh on the line', 'You slut-lover' etc. – and the creole inclusions of the onlooker and Player C, with his cryptic alliterative remark, prepare the context for B's similarly marked 'black' utterance 'That's sweet', which serves a competitive purpose whilst also being firmly integrated with the culturally marked language of the assembled group. Similar examples, such as the innumerable sequences of 'Twist / Twist / Bos'-op!' and the frequently employed Jamaican pronunciation in the use of the term 'burn', meaning to resign from the round, also appeared to place the competitive mode within the ambit of the cultural. The word 'burn' with the /r/ heavily pronounced, was consistently employed to maintain the 'face' threatened by the need to withdraw from the round at that point. Its use in some games was so common that it, too, appeared to be part of the collective cultural reference:

A (black): I'm getting a pontoon now. Don't need more than these two cards. These two cards are magic.

B (white): *Burn.*

C (white): *Burn.*

Several of the examples above have involved marked 'black' utterances consisting of single items only. The articulation of such utterances within long stretches of discourse is difficult to demonstrate within the confines of reasonable extract length. The following series of examples, drawn from different points within a single occasion, are presented here to show how several small instances scattered throughout a stretch of dialogue come together to produce a discourse in which the persistent but fragmentary use of 'black' forms functions as an unmistakable cultural diacritic synchronised at several points with the competitive mode.

These extracts are recorded from a game of pontoon lasting fifteen minutes, with five players – three black, two white:

Extract 1

[Player A has just 'bust' his hand.]

A (white): Really I'm only 2p down 'cos o' that *murderer.*

B (black): *Wicked one, bwai!*

A: *Giem finish!*

B: [laughs]

A: *Yer rass!*

B: [laughs]

A: *Ya murderer!*

B: [declaring his hand] Twennyone.

Extract 2

B: *Wicked.*

A: Twist.

[Dealer deals one card.]

A: Twist again.

B: *Raa'*

A: Twist again.

B: Oh my word! *Com op [**] fies?*

A: Could of blown it.

B: Oh my word! [**] That's three now ... Garn!

A: *Ooo dere's nice-ee!* [To B] What's that?

B: Twenny.
A: Twennyone. [to another player] How much you got?
C (white): Twenny.
A: [inaudible]
C: [inaudible]
A: You owe me again. *I wan' write it down.*
B: [laughs]
A: *Gimme piece a piepa.*
B: *Mi na gat piece a piepa.*
A: [inaudible]
B: Nice one dere. Nice one dere. Very nice.

Extract 3

B: [throwing down cards] Bung! Two, owe you one.
A: Owe you two, owe you one. *See I'm a very tight person.* [**] pound
   note [**] losing. Can't bank all that money. [Here he begins to
   sing a reggae song quietly to himself.] Stick.
B: Stick.
A: [singing] *Eh, eh, eh a-murderin' style.*
B: Twenny, twenny.
A: Twennyone . . . Twennyone [singing] *Eh, eh eh.*

Extract 4

B: Oh no.
A: Twist
B: [to another player] I owe you four now.
A: Five.
B: Five . . . Oh my word!
A: *Com on den. Gimme de card! Gimme de card!*
B: Twist?
A: Twist.
[Dealer deals one card.]
B: Stick . . . Twennyone.

This joint individualistic *and* collective aspect of certain game contexts
renders almost any creole or other marked 'black' utterance by whites
immune, it would seem, from the kinds of challenges that occur in less
obviously 'play' situations. Games provide a charmed circle within which
rules and conventions relating to white creole use do not appear to
obtrude.

Beside such formal games in which positionality is immediately
implied, creole is also used in a similar way in the 'informal' games in
which boys (again) specialise, and which involve ritualised displays of

aggression, sometimes including 'play' fighting, chasing and name-calling. For whites to use creole in this type of game is certainly more risky than in the kinds of games examined above; but where familiar black acquaintances are involved in the play, the game context provides a clear legitimation for the use of creole by whites. Such a case is seen in the following extract from a recording made of two groups of boys taunting each other from either end of a long corridor. A group of black boys stood at one end. They had just been fighting with two white boys, and there was a disagreement between the groups about who had won. The fighting and the name-calling which followed were 'friendly' and, despite the extremity of the language, all of the participants were actually close friends. As the abuse becomes more and more intense, one of the black boys switches into creole pronunciation, and this is responded to by one of the white boys also using a creole form. At this point the black boys approach and the fighting starts up again:

A (white): See! We didn't 'ave to call in our reinforcements, which was Mar'in Spriggs. We didn't 'ave to call in our reinforcements 'cos we was jus' good enough as we was.

[Black boys at the other end of the corridor call out jibes and peals of mocking laughter.]

B (white): [**] you shit.

C (black): You look like it! Ah ha!

B: You are it!

D (black): You eat it!

A: You bloody need it 'cos you live there!

B: Your carpet is coated with shit!

A: You fuckin' live there ya big ... You do live dere. You feed on it!

D: *Fock aaf!*

A: [inaudible]

C/D: [inaudible]

A: *Jes' com 'ere!*

[The black boys advance down the corridor.]

A: 'ere comes the shit breader! 'ere comes the shit breader.

The reflexive switch to creole pronunciation by the white boy does not, in itself, cause the renewed fighting, but it marks the direct invitation to come and fight again, 'Jes' com 'ere'. The fighting and chasing which ensued were also peppered with creolised abuse from the same white boy, with 'Fockin' bitch' and 'You fockin' shit you' pronounced in clear contrast to how the word 'fucking' was realised in other settings by the same boy.

In a similarly spontaneously created game, again involving boys only, a shoe belonging to one of a group of black and white classmates was being thrown around the classroom. A white boy caught the shoe as it was thrown over the head of its owner. As he did so he shouted out in a strong London Jamaican accent, 'Stylin' murder!' and ran off down the room. He stopped at the end of the room, and again shouted out victoriously, 'Stylin' murder!'.

Beyond the sanctioned world of game contexts, the employment of creole in the competitive mode is also apparent, as it was between whites, in non-game interactions which also possess some component of conflict or disagreement. Where this occurs in interaction with black youngsters, there is no doubt that the use of creole by whites is heavily dependent on there being an established closeness between all of the interacting parties. Here, although the context and nature of the utterance is less restricted, utterances are strictly limited with regard to whom they may be addressed to, especially if creole pronunciation is employed. Often close black and white friends have the kind of relationship that allows some freedom to use creole forms in playful, sparring banter. This may be considered a weak form of the kind of fictive social relationship described earlier in this chapter. Here white girls are often as active as boys in establishing with their black friends an easy 'playful' use of creole, although for both sexes this is with the proviso that a 'not meant' quality is preserved by the infrequency of use and other evidence of a lack of 'serious' intent. Thus a white might, as the following girl did, comment to a close black friend cheekily, 'Wa'appen chile, cat bit you?' and have such a comment be received with every appearance of amused tolerance, whilst to another black acquaintance the same remark might produce a hostile reaction.

Examples of such pre-negotiated non-game creole use by whites are not uncommon amongst whites with very close black friends, especially where the black friend also tends to use creole primarily in such 'playful' ways. This was certainly true of the following example, in which a white girl was spending her school lunch period in a classroom with several black girl friends. Her black friend, Beverley, had rubbed out part of a diagram that was chalked on the blackboard. The diagram was numbered 'sixty-one', and the white girl, who was about to copy it into a school-book, called out in mock annoyance, 'Cha man! See mi sixtyone rass-up! Ya bambclaht!' In doing so she employed a strong Jamaican accent, but her remark was not apparently objected to by Beverley or by the other black girls present. She explained to me later that they often 'carried on in that way'.

In school, dinner queues regularly provided a simple structure of competition which often promoted verbal sparring between pupils eager to get into the dining hall. In the next example, a white boy attempts to enter the line in front of his black friend:

BLACK BOY: You ain't commin' in front of me. You can wait for your food.
WHITE BOY: Come on. Let me go before you. Come on. Don't be like that, you savage! [Black boy pushes him out of the line.] *Jes' res' yourself!*

The address term 'you savage' was often used by whites to other whites, and here is unlikely to have been used even playfully as a racist term. It was also apparently not taken as such. This is indicated by the utterances which immediately followed, in which the black speaker asked cheerily, 'Oy, do you know a boy called Derek Jackson?' and the banter concerning a place in the queue immediately ceased.

There is a distinctive uniformity to the employment of such creole fragments in formal games (cards, pool, dominoes etc.), in improvised games devised around equally improvised conflicts, and in non-game bantering interactions. Such uses within the competitive mode are, however, *socially* constrained by specific relations with black interlocutors, and here are necessarily transected by the emic rules described earlier. The move from card table use to abuse game use may not be socially difficult, although there is no doubt that it would need to be handled with care. The move from either of these uses to a bantering non-game use, however, is far more sensitive, and entirely dependent on how an initial creole utterance is received by the black interlocutor. 'Black' inflected utterances by whites *between* the safe and well-established realms float vulnerably, without external support or guarantees. The penalty for such interstitial use is rarely as severe as the fighting reported earlier, however. Having an acquaintance 'laugh in their face', probably in a public context, may nevertheless be a sufficient warning to whites against attempting any further extension of the interactive frame or interlocutor base.

In the following playground exchange, a white boy who has a negotiated creole-using relationship with at least one black friend, employs a marked 'black' form to a black boy whom he knows quite well but with whom he had not established any such understanding. The black interlocutor contests the use of creole here by not responding with further banter, and by acting as though he had not clearly heard the remark – thus allowing the white boy an opportunity to replace the utterance with a non-offensive one. This opportunity is not taken, however, possibly because of the presence of another white boy who might construe such a replacement as a 'climb-down':

A (white): *You sof'!*
B (black): What?
A: You 'eard.
B: What?
A: *Sof'!*
C (white): Tell 'im, *dread.*
B: /

It is significant that the other white boy, C, positively encourages boy A in this exchange and, by his own use of the 'black' term of address in backing up his friend, 'Tell 'im dread', explicitly supports A's use of creole. As B apparently considers not only that A is not to be embarrassed out of this use of 'black' language, but also that A is supported by a second white boy also using a 'black' term, he simply expresses his scorn for both of them with a dismissive tooth-suck.

In blocked or challenged interstitial use of creole, the emic rules generated by black perceptions of racial/ethnic boundaries divide up the contexts and conditions of white creole use into discrete 'safe' areas. Perhaps the safest of such areas is that of the fictive social relationships described above. Here, furthermore, the use of creole is less restricted to the isolated phrases which slot so easily into spaces provided in the highly structured competitive mode. The sociocultural fiction into which the friends enter may at times also overlap with the competitive mode in a way that is closely related to the dualism observed in several of the card games examined above.

The text from which I will quote here is drawn from the same recording as that containing the 'fish and chip shop interaction' between Barry and several girls, quoted in Chapter 4. Here, however, Barry has been joined by his black friend, Fraser. Throughout much of the extract Barry is playing at the Space Invaders machine whilst Fraser stands at his side, looking on. Some of Barry's utterances form part of exchanges with either Fraser or the girls; others are comments directed at the machine, or rather, at the electronic characters that drift across its screen. Some of Fraser's remarks, too, are directed at the game, although, because he is not himself playing, he is freer to converse with the girls. Much of Fraser's conversation with the girls is concerned with a holiday hostel in Scotland which he and Barry had visited, and which the girls were also soon to visit. All of these exchanges were in local vernacular, and are explicitly abbreviated in the extract below.

BARRY: [to the machine] *'s it der Rasta!*
GIRL: Oh Barry let me play. [She tries to take over.]
BARRY: *Don't do dem tings, man!* [to machine] *Wa'appen.*

[Fraser and the girls talk about the hostel in Scotland.]
GIRL: And Sharon said she's goin'.
FRASER: Yeah?
GIRL: Yeah.
BARRY: Shellin' out again. Must be fuckin' mad.
GIRL: [to Barry, regarding a symbol showing on the machine] What's
     that mean?
BARRY: 'Extra' [inaudible]
GIRL: What do they dress like up there?
FRASER: Snowflakes.
BARRY: Weird. It's weird.
FRASER: Things like, mmm, some woman up there in 'er pyjamas.
GIRL: [laughs]
BARRY: [to the machine] *You fockin' pussyclaht machine nah!*
     [four-second pause] *What a fockin' fock-op machine!*
[several exchanges between Fraser and the girls about the holiday]
GIRL: 's'ave to wear these [**] anorak. Packed me wellies.
BARRY: Did yer?
FRASER: [apparently referring to the place in Scotland] There's a bum
     [man?] down there, innit. Bum [man? *] borin' plastic fings.
     You know what I mean.
BARRY: [to Fraser] *Whey, whey-no, whey-no Blood.* [inaudible] *Eh,*
     young Blood [inaudible]
FRASER: *I couldn't care if 'im fuckin' sister to bloodclaht. I still cuss 'm,*
     see, /.
BARRY: *But 'im is a boy. E's not a gyel ...* [singing] *In a rub-a-dub style.*
FRASER: [of the game] That's you dead, boy.
BARRY: *Nice-ee.*
FRASER: Nice.
BARRY: I know it was. Give it a bit of a chance. Let the little wanker go
     away.
FRASER: See 'im move.
BARRY: [**] go around.
FRASER: Nah [*]
BARRY: I play 'is serious.
FRASER: That'll [*] you twice. Now ... Next two shots. [Fraser takes
     over the play briefly.] Now ... Now ... No ... Yes.
BARRY: Get that big one?
FRASER: [Gives back control of game to Barry. Gives him an
     unidentified object.] 'Ere, Barry, look after this, right. It's in
     yer back pocket.
BARRY: Er ... Look you made me get blown up!

FRASER: What's a matter [**] It's in yer back pocket, right?

BARRY: Like I *Fockin* [***]

FRASER: I'm goin' in to about, about seven o'clock, seven, somethin' like that.

BARRY: *Yeah, cool. Cool Rasta, seh ...*

FRASER: *Gonna chip bwai* [Fraser opens door to leave]

BARRY: *Wa'appen mi bloodclaht frien', Jah. The cool school. 'm a cigarette?* [Fraser leaves.] [to girls] Gi's a fag. [inaudible]

GIRL: [offering cigarette?]

BARRY: Nah. Do' 'ant 'em. No bruv. [***] I know why you 'ad to buy dem. 'Cos out in the countryside, boy, all dem cowboys 'ave to smoke *dem tings*, innit?

While Barry's talk is mainly directed at the machine in a commentary on the play which gives rise to several expletives involving creole terms, Fraser's talk is mainly directed to the girls, and is in these exchanges free of creole items. Likewise, Fraser's comments on the game, even when he briefly plays two shots, do not involve any move to creole. He *does* use creole forms when he and Barry apparently disagree about someone at the holiday hostel, and again when he is taking his leave: 'Gonna chip bwai.' Barry also moves into creole at these points. At no point does Fraser challenge Barry's use of creole. In fact he was one of a group of several black boys with whom Barry had established an easy relationship in which he regularly employed creole to some degree, although usually with only a weak Jamaican pronunciation. As in the material quoted in Chapter 4, Barry's use of creole is, for the most part, notable for its 'display' quality. It is essentially theatrical, involving frequent use of marked terms of address – 'Blood', 'Jah', 'Rasta', 'Mi bloodclaht frien' – as well as common obscene expletives and formulaic fragments of reggae lyrics – 'In a rub-a-dub style'. All of these features do more to set up the cultural co-ordinates of the interaction than to contribute to the infor-mational/interactive content. Fraser's few creole utterances are less implicated in this cultural marking, and their significance resides more in the fact that they enact his collaborative assent to Barry's creole use. Not only does he not challenge Barry's use of creole at any point, he actively endorses it. Barry's use of creole with other black friends was rarely as explicitly and unambiguously culturally marked as it was with Fraser; and it was also clear from interviews conducted with him that his friendship with Fraser was especially close. Not only was this relationship the strongest of the several friendships Barry had with black boys in which he was permitted to use creole to some degree, but, in contrast to all his creole-using friendships, he also had a number of less close black friends with whom he *never* used marked creole forms at all. It was, therefore, not his only style of speech with black interlocutors.

Not all such special relationships necessarily display strong Jamaican pronunciation in the use of marked 'black' forms by whites, and the 'black' identity assumed by white adolescents may be indicated more simply in the lexis and style of utterance. One such very clearly marked utterance by a white boy to a close black friend which has this character is the following, in which a white boy reports, in a kind of fantasy re-run, an exchange with a teacher:

> See the way Matthews [tried to pursuade me] into doin' A level? That was 'ard. That was 'ard. That was well sweet. He goes, 'You're doin' A level whether you like it or not.' I said, 'Yes, star, yes! Well sweet. Sweet as a nut, twice as 'ard. Know what I mean.'

As with the competitive mode the interstitial use of items heavily marked for black youth culture can be interactively hazardous. I recorded no challenges to Barry's use of creole or to his other incorporations of black youth cultural style. It seems that he was amongst those who 'knew when to use it'. However, one instance of a girl who unsuccessfully attempted to move beyond the security of her closest black friendships in making claim to a 'black' cultural identity is particularly instructive. The attempted extension fell within an already contentious interaction, which added a further level of complexity. The girl in question was thirteen years old, and had several close black friends, with whom she employed some creole and who similarly endorsed her commitment to black youth culture. The incident took place when she was playing Space Invaders in a youth club one night. She discovered that the machine was faulty and would allow her to play endlessly without her having to put money in. A group of black boys of about her own age crowded round the machine and attempted to make deals with her as to when *they* could have a turn. They complained that she had been too long at the machine, and one boy began the sentence:

> By the time half-past nine come . . . [i.e. 'comes']

The girl quickly interrupted:

> Half-past nine *come* [i.e. 'has come']

She continued to play and the boys settled down, subdued by her determination. With eyes fixed on the screen as she played, she asked the boy who had spoken: 'Have you heard the school band? I'm in it. I play drums and I toast.' As toasting is always performed in creole and good toasters are highly respected, the girl was making a large claim about her familiarity with creole and with black youth culture. The boy, already feeling badly disposed towards her, replied: 'The only thing you could toast is bread.' The girl made no comment but, as she continued to play, registered each setback and loss in the game by using creole expletives: 'Ratid!', 'Bambaclaht', 'Rass'. She also fought off one attempt to usurp her position at the machine with 'Try it, bwai!'

Throughout this exchange the girl was obviously eager to establish her credentials as an initiate of black culture. She did not know the boy well, and her first attempt was in the *content* of what she said – her claim to be able to toast. She spoke, however, in standard English. When her claim was derided she continued her attempt *linguistically* by adopting creole forms. These were not used with direct communicative intent – which could have provoked a rebuttal – but were exclamations for display purposes, and were guaranteed in context by her obvious exasperation at the game.

Her apparent confidence in this strategy was related to the fact that she had a number of close black friends with whom she intermittently used creole forms, and was a well accepted follower of black youth culture within her primary (mainly black) peer group. None of her close friends was present during this exchange, however, and the situation was further complicated by the factor of gender. In the first instance she had refused to relinquish the game and was determinedly playing in the face of strong, albeit plaintive, opposition. She then assumed that the boys' continued attendance represented an acceptance of her control and an interest in the game *she* was playing. At this point she made her attempt to establish herself as an initiate of black culture. Her claim to toast was probably elaborated from some limited experience in school. Made in this context her boast was obviously misjudged, and provoked, not admiration, but derisive rejection put in sexist terms: 'The only thing you could toast is bread.' Her difficulty arose partly because she was attempting *two* socially provocative manoeuvres, and it became evident that neither of her aims – to maintain the position of control of the machine, and to establish cultural identity – could be achieved across cultural *and* sexual borders. She therefore forsook her gender role and adopted an essentially *male stance* in order to underwrite both manoeuvres simultaneously. This she did by her use of swear words, not directed at the group of boys but plainly employed for them to hear. The strategy went beyond any customary female role – even the 'facety' (cheeky) stance sometimes adopted by black girls in their dealings with boys. By adopting the language and posture of an older black boy she combined two strategies, one on behalf of her gender in defence of her control of the game, the other on behalf of the cultural identity she wished to establish. The defiant 'Try it, bwai' displayed a contempt written into the role itself, which pre-empted both the position of 'young male' and that of 'young black' that might have been marshalled against her by any of the boys. It proved a powerful combination. Her 'bluff' was not called and she continued to play.

Here the challenge was not to her use of creole, although it *was* to the cultural identification within which her use of creole was usually positioned. Her response was not to 'back off' however, because more was at stake than her negotiation of cultural 'rights'. By linguistically intensifying the cultural identification she effectively 'saved face' on this occasion but, despite the tactical success, the warrant which she sought was actually *denied* by these particular interlocutors. The encounter represents a further example of the potential hazards of interstitial acts of cultural identification by whites.

Between all of the 'safe' established locations of white creole use in (*a*) game contexts (formal and improvised) (*b*) bantering interactions in the competitive mode, and (*c*) cultural marking employed within fictive social relationships, interstitial employment consistently appears as vulnerable to challenge determined by the underlying structure of emic rules generated by structural social relations operating at higher levels.

There remains, however, the *interpersonal mode* alluded to above, in which characteristically creole pronunciation is either very weak or completely absent, and in which whites appear to be aligning their speech undemonstratively with that of specific black friends, rather than using creole as a linguistic corollary of certain roles emergent from structured game and game-like contexts, or as an explicit marker of cultural affiliation with an idealised 'black group'. While such undemonstrative uses of creole are, like other uses, restricted to particular interlocutors, it appears to be the case that they are also less likely to be challenged both because they are non-assertive, unlike utterances in the competitive mode, and because – unlike utterances in the cultural mode – they are not displaying linguistic blazonry as part of any claim to group membership. This use of creole seems to be accepted by black youngsters, not as something special and privileged, but as part of the normal convergence of co-operating interlocutors. The following extract, for example, lacks any competitive dimension, and the creole utterance shows only the slightest trace of creole pronunciation. It falls within a merely technical discussion over arrangements to do with sound equipment. The white boy employs a creole plural marker quite 'naturally', without any attendant theatricality, and without challenge or even apparent recognition from the black interlocutor:

A (black): Jes' see how it goes . . . If it ain't got the plugs on it, jes' buy the plugs for it then jes' tune it up my yard.

B (white): Alright.

A: 'Cos I got the amps. I could take the amps down your yard . . . or somethin' like that.

B: *Wha' 'bout de speaker-dem?*

A: Well . . . that means we're gonna 'ave to tune it at my yard. 'Cos that's the reason my ol' man [**]. 'Cos if I blow it I could pay thir'y quid to get 'em fixed.

Similarly, a white boy indicating to his black friends that he was going for a smoke in the lavatories used the phrase '*Mi a-go blango*' with no special stressing and with all the appearance of matter-of-fact conversation; and again, in the heat of the moment in a basketball game, a white player called to one of his black team-mates, 'Check mi de ball nah!' Often such unstressed creole forms are integrated into expressions in unmarked local vernacular, a feature which also seems to contribute to their 'low ethnic profile'. In another example, a white boy watching television with his black friend in a youth club turned to his friend and said, 'Come pictures tommorra night, check some gyal?'

Girls tend to use this undramatic form more than they use creole in game contexts, although – certainly in Area B – creolised banter between white and black girls is common. However, as in the last example, the mixing of creolised and non-creolised local vernacular forms also contributes to the ease with which such utterances appear to be accepted, as does the use of strong cockney accents in utterances employing creole forms. Both of these things obtained in the case of the following example:

GIRL A (black): 'Ow d'you get on last night?

GIRL B (white): Oh I got *mash-up bad*.

Because in this mode creole pronunciation is employed only weakly if at all, it is often not possible to draw any clear distinction between it and what I have called above the 'local multi-racial vernacular'. In fact, it is likely that no such distinction is linguistically legitimate in this context. It may be more correct to speak of individuals situating themselves in social space through the subtle semiotics of minor linguistic differences at particular times and in particular places. Meanings, connotative and social, become derived, therefore, within particular settings and between particular interlocutors. Here the symbolisms of overt cultural marking are abandoned, and instead a more fine-grained signalling takes place, in which the minutiae of *absent* details are as important as the presences:

A (white): Oy, you know I 'ad that tetnus [injection]?
B (black): Yeah
A: Oh I come up! Fuckin' bus' it up, boy.

Here, 'bus' it up, boy' appears as a kind of white shadow of the implicit
black form '*bos' it op, bwai*', with the latter merely indicated through the
phonology by the word-final consonant cluster reduction on 'bus''. In the
following example the 'black' reference is again indicated through
consonant changes:

[Two boys discussing a third boy who is sometimes inclined suddenly
to become vicious]
A (white): No, sometimes you gotta be careful of John 'cos he does . . .
        dunnee?
B (black): 's a good fighter.
A: He's a good fighter, you know . . . 'e jes' tu*r*n.

Here the absence of the final 's' tense marker on 'turn' and the roticity of
the postvocalic 'r' – both features of creole speech – have the effect of
also contextualising 'jes'', which, because it is followed by a word
beginning with a consonant, would be equally correct in local vernacular
as in creole.
    The same is true for ethnic ambiguities surrounding words in the local
multi-racial vernacular. Both 'sweet' and 'check' (a multi-purpose verb)
were marked 'black' forms between some interlocutors, although they
were treated unproblematically and as undemonstrative by others. The
following utterance by a white boy to his black friend is, on textual
grounds alone, difficult to place, except that the absence of creole
pronunciation which might indicate the cultural mode, *and* the apparent
absence of a competitive positional dimension, seem to suggest either
that this is an example of interpersonal speech alignment, or that both
speakers were simply using the local multi-racial vernacular.

A (white): That's sweet, boy. You should check that girl in the white at
        school.
B (black): She's askin' for it. [inaudible]
A: [inaudible] She's ripe!

While all speech activity is implicated in the semiotics of group relations,
certain modes privilege a heavy cultural marking which could be considered as especially exhibitionistic and 'symbolic'. In this mode, which I
have called 'interpersonal', the blatant symbolic 'group' reference relating to any membership claim by a white is absent as a contrastive feature
– as indeed it is in some competitive uses. As such, this form of white

creole use and its relationship to the multi-racial local vernacular is probably of more interest to linguists than the creole used within other modes. It is, conversely, probably of *less* interest to sociologists and anthropologists for the same reason. Nevertheless, before moving on it is perhaps worth re-stating that the borderline between the multi-racial local vernacular and white creole use in the interpersonal mode is at least as difficult to draw, if not more so, than that between the multi-racial vernacular and some forms of creole/English code-switching. Further-more, variations from speaker to speaker, and *within* speakers' reper-toires, differentially explored with interlocutor variation, probably make the concept of discrete dialect varieties nonsensical in this context.

In order to indicate something of the range that may be found within black-affected white speech, I conclude this section with two extracts from an interview conducted with a white boy. He was seventeen at the time of the interview. Unlike all the examples above, which are from recordings of peer interactions in street, school or club settings, in these extracts *I* was the interlocutor. I am white and over twice the informant's age; nevertheless his speech shows a range of influences from creole which were by no means deliberately affected for me. From my own and other informants' observations of this boy, what follows represented his normal 'English' style of speech at that time, although he also had a very good command of creole which he used with his friends, *all* of whom were black. Here, not only are prosodic, intonational and lexical features of creole-influenced London English all present, but also very obvious are certain creole *grammatical* features. The extracts have been chosen from deep into the interview and from a point where the informant was discussing matters of great interest to him concerning his own and others' relations with the law. Despite the cultural gap between this speaker and myself, therefore, the style is likely to be amongst his most 'relaxed', within the constraints of a formal interview situation:

> *Extract A*
> There was one time I was walkin' wiv my girl frien'. An', um, Li'lewoods . . . Li'woods shop was . . . de alarm bell was goin'. So anyway, we was standin' up by Li'lewoods shop, right, an' I 'ad this bag on my shoulder, so they come an' say they wanna search de bag an' dis an' dat, an' they wanna search me. An' I tol' 'em, 'Not gonna search me 'cos I don' like policeman searchin' me.' I tol' 'em I jes' come 'ere, an' dere's dis ol' lady standin' up by de bus stop as well that said I never done nothin' but they perzisted in searchin' me, you know? So I said, 'Ya not gonna search me'. So then they called for car to take me to police station an'

whatever. An' den my girlfrien's mum did come to the police station to get me out because they said I can't come out, I need bail, 'cos they di' charge me as well. They said that I . . . because when I was in the station der was dis one called [X] in dere, and 'e ask me oo I fink I am, or whatever, an' if I don't shut up 'e's gonna punch me in de face, an' 'e's gonna do dis and 'e's gonna do dat. So I jes' tol' 'im if 'e feel that 'e's bound fe do it, make 'im come an' do it. So me an' 'im di' 'ave a li'le scuffle, so they said I sor'ed a police officer out an' I 'ad to go [. . .] Court in the mornin'. You know, dem is slackness, them things dere.

Extract B
[The content of this second extract requires some comment. The tragic event it describes contributed to local white adolescent stereotypical images of young blacks; references to it occurred in a number of other interviews with young whites. This account is singular in attempting to take a view that is very different from that of most of the young whites I spoke to.]

What did 'appen, I mean, dis li'le boy called Dale, 'es a nex one, ya know. 'e's like, 'e was one o' dem soul-boys. 'e used to wear bright red trousers an' dese black poin'ed shoes, an' 'e always used to walk wiv de girls-dem. So 'e sorta jus' got to like reggae music, an' goin' blues, an' buyin' a few clothes, an, you know? So, like, I don' know, they, they all 'ad knives – li'le pen knives an' whatever – an dis boy must of come up to about my ches', 'was only a li'le small boy, an' dey was outside the [pub] and I don't know what actually 'appen, 'bout 'ow the fight star'ed, but anyway dis big white man did chase 'im. So li'le Dale jus' sort o' jus' bring out a knife an' just', I fink 'e jus' wan'ed to cut the man so 'e could run, but 'e's jus' unlucky the knife did, the knife did go in 'is 'eart, you know, an' did kill 'im. It wasn't really sort o' like, didn't, Dale didn't really go out that night to stab no one, or . . . it jus' the case tha' 'e 'ad a knife in 'is pocket an' . . . 'e was jus' trying ''elp 'imself.

The phonological features in the passages above can only be suggested in conventional type, but it will be observed that *both* the Cockney 'f' and the creole 't' are used in places where standard English would have 'th' /θ/. On the other hand, a range of realisations from /ð/ to /d/ inclusive are also present throughout the text. These have had to be represented as either 'th' or 'd', depending on which they most closely resembled. Glottal stops, common to both Cockney and London Jamaican, are present throughout, but very emphatic initial glottal stops on words such as ''appen' and ''eart', where standard would have 'h', are characteristic of creole-influenced London English. There are a very few lexical items that are clearly from a creole source. However, 'scuffle', 'slackness' 'a nex' (meaning 'another'), 'blues' (a reggae party at which guests pay) and 'make' (meaning 'let' here in the phrase 'make 'im come an' do it'), are all characteristically creole items.

At the level of grammar, indefinite articles are absent in some cases – 'they called for car to take me to police station' – but not in others – 'I sor'ed a police officer out', ''e 'ad a knife in 'is pocket'. The creole plural marker 'dem' is used once. However, as often occurs in London Jamaican, this is used together with the standard plural marker 's', thus: 'girls-dem'. Elsewhere, where 'dem' could be used, e.g. with 'soul-boys', it is not employed. Perhaps the most noticeable and systematically applied creole feature is the use of the past marker 'di', sometimes 'did', which appears throughout both passages. A further distinctly creole grammatical feature is the use of the infinitive 'fe' in the sentence, 'So I jes' tol' 'im if 'e feels that 'e's bound fe do it, make 'im come an' do it'.

This boy had apparently only ever chosen to have black friends, and was completely integrated into the local black late-adolescent community. He no longer lived at home with his parents, but shared a flat with two black boys of his own age. Two and a half years after this interview was conducted, I interviewed this informant again for a final time. In this interview his speech showed no creole influences whatever, although he still apparently used creole on some occasions with his friends, one of whom told me that when speaking creole this informant was indistinguishable from a Jamaican-born creole speaker.

IV

The modes of creole use described above, and the emic rules which divide up the interlocutor bases and folk modes into 'safe' areas, are socially and historically circumscribed. Thus, even though whites in other countries and in other historical periods have also been influenced by and (in some cases) have adopted black speech, the precise social meanings that the activity had and has in any one of those contexts is unlikely to be exactly equatable with the social meanings of 'the same' linguistic practices elsewhere. Furthermore, any study of these phenomena whose exclusive focus is language, rather than the whole gamut of social signalling conducted within specific material conditions, is likely to yield only limited and socially unintelligible results. The surface similarity between the use of the infinitive 'fe', in the expression 'I wan' some'in' fe eat', by a white boy in south London, and the phenomenon described by Raven and Virginia McDavid (1951: 15) in the following quotation is a case in point:

> From the Negroes – whether the form is in origin an Africanism or a relic of early English usage – many white folk speakers along the South Carolina coast have taken *for* as the particle with the infinitive of purpose, as *he come for tell you* rather than the standard *to* or the widespread folk form *for to*.

The racial contact necessary to produce this similarity is all that can be asserted. Both the nature of those contacts and the precise economic and sociocultural circumstances of the interaction productive of the similarity need to be considered separately and in detail before anything of a more general nature can be said about 'black/white speech relationships'. The speculations of McDavid and McDavid themselves indicate the starkly different conditions in this case:

> It may possibly be that the Negro playmates of well-to-do white children (especially boys) and the Negro servants to whom they have been accustomed are at least partially responsible for the more frequent occurrence and the higher degree of cultural tolerance for nonstandard forms in cultured speech in the South than elsewhere.

Different social and historical conditions evoke different parameters of interaction, different meaning systems and different rules of appropriateness. Specifically with regard to black/white relations, it must be added that the particular historical forms assumed by racism itself must also be taken into account.

The relays and production of racism within the south London white adolescent community have been described above in some detail, and related to those factors regulating white-with-black creole use. With rare exceptions, creole use by whites is limited in range and restricted to adolescents. This is related both to the fact that black youngsters themselves often reach a peak of creole use in their late teens and gradually come to use it less and less, and to the common drifting apart of white and black friends after the age of about sixteen. Both these factors are themselves related to the structure of social relations in Britain, and particularly to the inequalities of social power as they become manifested through historically located racial ideologies and practices. It is therefore theoretically possible to give a comparatively full account of the context of white adolescent creole use today.

In some respects and in certain modes, the use of black forms by whites in contemporary London may be demonstrably similar to practices elsewhere. Scattered reports of the use of 'Black English' by adolescent whites in the United States are certainly suggestive. Folb (1980: 53) quoted one of her young black informants in Los Angeles as follows:

> Most of my friends are black. Rafael, he Chicano dude I runs with sometimes. He cool. Simpson – he my partner – white dude live over on Avalon and 80th, he accepted like one of us. The way he got in good, he tried to get wi'd happenin's. Like he talk like one o' us – slang language. At leas' he caught on quick. He talk to brothers and sisters too. Sisters like him a lot. He got a nice personality. Since fellas see he's with some coloured dudes so he gets in good. So, if he play cool, act like one o' us, he's okay.

Suttles (1968: 65) also reported of his Chicago study:

> For the most part, syntactic and phonological differences divide the white and Negro residents in the area. An interesting departure is the use of 'jive'. This special vocabulary of argot or 'slang' terms is restricted according to both age and ethnicity, but its usage overlaps the Negro–White distinction. Negro boys are most expert at this sort of discourse, but the English-speaking Mexican and Puerto Rican boys are also somewhat conversant with 'jive'.

He adds in a note:

> The Negroes, Puerto Ricans and Mexicans are very eager to show they are hipsters, familiar with the most advanced of urban speech, clothing styles, and learning.

Silverman (1975), Labov and Pedraza (1971) and Wolfram (1972; 1974) have also written on the influence of black speech on the language of Puerto Ricans in cities in the United States, although an early observation by Oscar Handlin suggests that there may well have been a number of social cross-currents to this activity that have been overlooked in the sociolinguistic studies:

> The coloured Puerto Rican wished above all to avoid the stigma of identification with the Negro and he could do so only by establishing himself as a Spanish-speaking Puerto Rican.
> (Handlin 1959: 59)

Although the focus of my own research was indigenous white English adolescents, I also frequently encountered adolescents from ethnic minorities other than Afro-Caribbean who used creole forms to some degree. A number of Turkish boys and girls in Area B had a fair and sometimes very good command of creole, and in Area A, Asian teenage boys were occasionally members of black friendship groups and used creole with their black friends. Black youth culture was apparently felt to be so attractive an option for some Asian boys that they even artificially curled their hair, wore Rasta colours and attempted to 'pass' for black. Greek youngsters were reported to me on several occasions as using London Jamaican creole, and one of my black informants even had a close African friend who used an African language with his parents, standard English in school and London Jamaican with his black friends of Caribbean parentage. He was also a follower of Rastafari. Such cases may well parallel the adoption of black speech forms by Puerto Rican and Mexican youth in North American cities. Certainly the use of creole forms by young Londoners of Turkish and Asian origin would reward investigation.

'Jive' talk in the United States has a long history of influence on white speech, and its use by whites and others may be considered a similar development to the cultural mode observed for white and other creole users in South London. White jazz musicians in Chicago and New York in the 1920s, 1930s and 1940s were especially attracted to black speech forms; and the autobiography of white clarinettist Mezz Mezzrow (Mezzrow and Wolfe 1946) who identified extremely closely with black people in general and in particular with the black musicians he admired, is so dense with black language that it became necessary for the authors to append a glossary. David Dalby has also observed:

> since the popularisation of jazz and other forms of Black music from the beginning of this century there has been a steady flow of Black American vocabulary into the English language at large.

> (Dalby 1970: 21)

That the use of black language in urban contexts did, partly through its association with jazz, attract to itself a high cultural prestige is further reflected in the publication of popular books such as *Dan Burley's Original Handbook of Harlem Jive* (1944) and Lou Shelly's *Hepcats Jive Talk Dictionary* (1945). It is also worthy of note that one of the most accomplished narrator/performers of 'jive' talk was 'Lord Buckley', a white man who enjoyed a large following, especially amongst blacks in the 1950s and 1960s.

At more mundane levels, however, the imitative use of culturally prestigious black language by whites became so common in the United

States in the 1960s that it appears to have become a spur to further black innovation. As Claude Brown (1972) put it:

> it is not difficult to see why certain terms are dropped from the soul language. Whenever a soul term becomes popular with whites, it is common practice for the soul folks to relinquish it. The reasoning is, 'If white people can use it, it isn't hip enough for me.' To many soul brothers there is just no such creature as a genuinely hip white person. And there is nothing more detrimental to anything hip than to have it fall into the square hands of the hopelessly unhip.

He continues further on:

> Borrowings from spoken soul by white men's slang – particularly teenage slang – are plentiful. Perhaps because soul is probably the most graphic language of modern times, everybody who is excluded from Soulville wants to usurp it, ignoring the formidable fettering of the soul folks that has brought the language about.
>
> (Brown 1972: 137)

The view expressed here by Claude Brown may have been only one of a number of intersecting and controlling factors in the use of black speech forms by whites. It may be the case that such a view is related to the boundary-maintaining precepts of young black South Londoners but expressed through a different cultural complex. In fact, in the following chapter I will return to issues raised by young black Londoners that express in very similar terms Brown's view that whites actually ignore 'the formidable fettering of the soul folks that has brought the language about'; in general the problem of white attraction to black culture within a racist context is fraught with ambiguities (Hewitt 1983).

Whatever the similarities, however, the specific conditions giving rise to the modes of use and the interactive rules and social grammars need to be investigated each within their own terms. As the Trinidadian linguist Mervy Alleyne has remarked with reference to Afro-American cultures, 'There is obviously a need for more studies of socially embedded language functions' (Alleyne 1980: 9); and it is only through an understanding of such 'socially embedded language functions' within black cultures that the social significance of white appropriations can also be fully understood.

The range of historical contexts in which whites have adopted black language is so wide that by no means all offer themselves up for comparison in the way 'jive' talk does with the use of London Jamaican creole in the cultural mode. In contemporary Jamaica it is normal to find white Jamaicans who use creole. Indeed, the popular humorous dictionary *How To Speak Jamaican* (1981), published in Jamaica, was written by a white Jamaican, Ken Maxwell, and illustrated by a black Jamaican, Livingstone McLaren. The use of creole by whites in the West Indies is not a recent phenomenon. Charles William Day reported in his *Five Years Residence in the West Indies* (1852) that:

> Our captain, a white man from Anguilla, called himself an Englishman and hated everything French. Yet he had never been out of the West Indies and spoke a very singular dialect, all but negro.
>
> (Quoted by Dillard 1972: 189)

There is no shortage of similar reports by travellers prior to the twentieth century.

In the Caribbean islands, of course, blacks have long constituted the majority. In the South of the United States, however, where the economy, plantation system and demography were different, the process by which black speech patterns came to affect those of the white community would not only have shown differences with the Caribbean but also differences *within* the white community itself. The McDavids' speculations, cited above, about the 'well-to-do' white children learning black forms from their 'Negro playmates' and from the 'Negro servants' are borne out by a number of the authors cited by Dillard, such as Sir Charles Lydell, who reported a family in which black children were learning to read along with white children. He observed:

> Unfortunately, the whites, in return, often learn from the Negroes to speak broken English, and in spite of losing much time in un-learning ungrammatical phrases, well-educated persons retain some of them all their lives.
>
> (*A Second Visit to the United States of America*, 1849, vol. II, p. 20, quoted by Dillard 1972: 189)

Quoting Caroline Gilman's *Recollections of a Southern Matron* (1838) as follows: 'Although, at the time of which I speak, I preferred to talk to the Negroes in their dialect I never used it to the whites', Dillard argues:

> Statements of this type are legion during the period just before the Civil War. Before Emancipation the children of the slave owning class had plenty of opportunity to acquire Black English; individual families obviously differed as to whether the acquisition was welcomed or resisted.

He adds: 'Bidialectal switchers seem to have been primarily upperclass males.'

However, the use of black speech forms by white children does not appear to have been restricted to that class or that time. A British traveller to the American colonies wrote in the *London Magazine* as early as July 1746:

> One thing they [the English settlers] are very faulty in with regard to their children . . . is that when young, they suffer them too much to prowl among the young Negroes, which insensibly causes them to imbibe their manners and broken speech.

Furthermore, it seems that Dillard's assertion that the Emancipation brought whites 'for the first time into close contact' with blacks, is over-simple at the very least if Genovese's (1975) account of black/poor white relationships is accurate:

> actual relations between slaves and local poor whites were complex and included much more than mutual distaste and hatred. Many of the slaves who stole their master's goods sold them to poor whites at drinking and gambling parties, which could promote genuine friendships and encouraged a dangerous ambivalence on both sides.

And again:

> White men sometimes were linked to slave insurrectionary plots, and each such incident rekindled fears. By deciding that lower-class whites who associated with blacks were 'degraded', the slaveholders explained away the existence of such racial contacts and avoided reflecting on the possibility that genuine sympathy might exist across racial lines. They also upheld stern police measures against whites who illicitly fraternised with blacks, and justified a widespread attempt to keep white and black labourers apart. The circumstances of lower-class white–black contact therefore encouraged racist hostilities and inhibited the maturation of relationships of mutual sympathy if not equality.
>
> Such relationships of mutual sympathy between slaves and poor whites did exist. They remained few in number, but their existence was ominous in a society in which no sane member of the ruling class wanted to take chances.
>
> (Genovese 1975:23)

It would be surprising indeed if contacts between slaves and poor whites of the kind described here did not promote linguistic influences such as Dillard attributes to the upper-class plantation owners. Certainly it is a commonplace that today the language of black and white Southerners of all classes is very close indeed (Wolfram 1971; McDavid 1971).

Precise sociolinguistic excavation of past modes, embedded in their own social terrain and permeated by the various forms that racism has historically taken there, is no doubt now impossible. However, I have tried to indicate what a genuinely *social* view of such linguistic phenomena might look like. It may be the case that at certain levels the reiterated conditions of racism have produced interactive consequences at some points in the past which are very similar to those in the present. Certainly there is something dimly reminiscent of the situation described by Genovese above in the following quotation (my emphasis) from a community newspaper in South London, *The Peckham Pulse*, which reported in August 1979:

> The first week [of the month] here saw three SPG [Special Patrol Group] visits to the same GLC [Greater London Council] estate; on each occasion they interrogated and bullied black children and teenagers who were sitting on walls or playing. In one case they bundled one white boy into a waiting police car accusing him of *causing trouble by 'talking like a black boy'*. It was only when his mother arrived and told them that he came from a mixed family that he was allowed to go.

Clearly the social meanings attached to the use of black forms by whites may themselves vary from group to group within a single location, depending on their position in the social structure and the specific power interests they wittingly and unwittingly serve. Contesting and overlapping definitions continually draw existing signifiers up into hegemonic struggles; the use of creole by whites and blacks alike is only part of a process that extends out to embrace a much wider range of interactive and signifying practices. The lived daily realities of adolescents communicating through the available structures of signification – innovating and assembling into partial structures of their own the cultural fragments that constitute the given world, forging new signifiers and grappling with the contradictions of race and friendship – embrace, but are not restricted to, language in the narrow sense. It is to some of these contiguous and broader practices within which white creole use is situated, and through which its meanings shift and change, that I shall now turn.

6

Social semiotics and ideology

In his *Principles of Phonology*, Nikolai Trubetzkoi drew attention in passing to how the study of phonology as a system of significant phonic differences in language might be extended to analogous work in other areas of the social sciences. In particular he cited the potential for this kind of analysis with regard to clothing (Trubetzkoi 1969: 17) – a potential which was later explored in the work of a number of writers concerned with semiology, most notably Roland Barthes (1967; see also Sahlins 1976:179–204). It is evident, however, that the process by which items of clothing, their colours, material, styling etc., are selected and manipulated within a system of differences to indicate class, gender, generation, ethnicity and many other things, is not merely analogous to certain aspects of language behaviour but is in fact continuous with them. They are both in certain respects manifestations of the same process, a process which can be seen across a wide range of cultural activities. It would appear that any set of cultural entities, from garden flowers to vowel variants, can become the site of systematic social marking, indicative of the same scale of coarse and fine social differentiation. It is in this sense that the use of creole by white adolescents can be situated in the wider arena of social semiosis alluded to at the end of the last chapter. It is important, however, that the position of the individual in the establishment, and the exploration of these processes, should be properly understood if a confusion of social marking of this kind, with some notion of individual, context-free 'markers of identity', is to be avoided – a confusion to which the signification of 'ethnicity' seems particularly prone (see Giles 1979). Before proceeding, therefore, it is valuable to examine certain ideas in sociolinguistics which relate to this issue.

Much sociolinguistics has been concerned with language and 'social class' – particularly with the issue of 'social dialects'. The notions of social class with which sociolinguists have worked, however, have been amongst the least rigorous in the social sciences. Nevertheless, the usually broad and untheorised notions of class employed are often deemed to be vindicated by the sociolinguistic findings themselves. Thus Trudgill writes that a comparison of groups of speakers in Norwich, England and Detroit, USA,

> suggests that the division of society into two main class groups, 'middle-class' and 'working-class', a division made largely but not entirely on the basis of the difference between manual and non-manual occupations, is of some validity and importance since the social barrier is clearly reflected in language.
>
> (Trudgill 1974: 44–5)

The leap from what is found in language to the assertion that here a 'social barrier is clearly reflected' is, however, too readily made, and ignores any possible intervening agencies. At the very least it ignores the question of the internal perception of class relations – not at all identical with any *actual* class relations – which may be encoded in the language practices of social groups related through power. What sociolinguists might assert with more certainty on the basis of such evidence is that the patterns of speech revealed by sociolinguistic techniques reflect per-ceived relations enacted and encoded in linguistic exchanges by social groups involved in a process of mutual definition – now distancing themselves from some, now indicating perceived affinities with others. The perceived class and group relations may or may not correspond to any actual relations obtaining. It is apparent, therefore, that the class relations 'reflected' in daily language use may at best be considered as betraying folk taxonomies of the social order – folk taxonomies enacted in many ways, including but not restricted to linguistic ways, and forming part of ideologies as they become encoded in cultural practices.

Specifically with regard to phonology, a major contribution of socio-linguistics has been to show the ways in which variation exists within social groups and within the speech of individuals. What sociolinguistic study has done is to describe how, within a speech community, variants come to serve an indexical function. What is indexed, however, should not be mistaken for any 'objective' categorisation of classes and groups but, more phenomenologically, the *group* perceptions of class relations betrayed in the distribution and frequency of socially marked variants. It is here that ideologies may enter into the processes of social dialect construction to mediate social groups and the language that they display, in just the same way that ideologies influence the mutual evaluations and perceptions of social groups displayed in other cultural practices. Thus Labov's account of the distribution of certain phonological variables in his Martha's Vineyard study (1972*a*) clearly indicated *not*, say, the formal economic relationships between seasonal visitors and young islanders, but how those relationships were perceived by the younger generation of Martha's Vineyard inhabitants and how those perceptions were reflected in language use. Similarly, the growth of the use of glottal stops in the speech of young English middle-class radicals in the 1960s and 1970s was indicative of a perceived unity with the 'working classes', expressed at the phonological level, and could not be taken as indicative of a unity that might be credited with any 'objective' status.

In the light of the discussion in Chapters 4 and 5, the phonological shifts in the speech of white upper-class Philadelphians, reported in the work of A. Kroch are also relevant here. Labov (1980*b*) analyses these changes as a reaction by those white speakers to changes in the social location of 'new ethnic and racial groups' in the community, such that certain phonological ranges were avoided and others explored in re-action to the phonological spectrum of those minority groups. Whatever – in social and economic terms – the structured relationship between 'upper-class' whites and the 'new ethnic and racial groups' might be, the phonological shift exhibited the encoding of an evaluation of that relationship as perceived at some level by the whites. The encoded perception may or may not be 'correct', but the evidence of it cannot be taken as a warrant for any 'objective' social categorisation, any more than the use of glottal stops by young English radicals can be taken to indicate any 'objective' formal unity with 'working-class' interests. What is of importance here is how the folk taxonomies of the social order betrayed in certain aspects of language use are implicated in wider cultural and symbolic systems. The reduction of linguistic social markers to simple and inert 'indicators of social status' or beacons of 'social identity' must be avoided if the scale and context of signification is to be fully accredited.

Part of the theoretical problem at the heart of the sociolinguistic endeavour stems from assumptions often made about the relationship between social stratification and linguistic variation. Although Labov has often been at pains to stress the normality of linguistic variation *within* groups, there persists in the writing of some sociolinguists a somewhat mechanical view of society, language and the 'causes' of variation. The following hypothetical postulate by Halliday (1978) reflects the view that social dialects are the products of societies in which divisions within the social order stimulate the varieties found:

> Let us postulate an ideally homogeneous society, with no division of labour, or at least no form of social hierarchy,

whose members (therefore) speak an ideally homogeneous language, without dialectal variation.

To emphasise the hypothetical nature of his comments, Halliday adds: 'There probably never has been such a human group' (1978: 178).

Such a construct of a 'homogeneous society' having (therefore) a homogeneous language cannot imply, however, that variation at the level of the individual speaker would not exist. This is born out by linguistic evidence from the society commonly held by anthropologists to be the most notable example of non-stratification – the San of southern Africa. Anthropologists who have studied these hunter-gatherers all attest to the lack of stratification in and between !Kung bands (the San about whom most is known), the scrupulousness of their resource sharing, the equality of the sexes and the deliberate employment of strategies to avoid the differentiation of groups within the band on the basis of status. Linguists, however, have had a very difficult time in analysing the phonemes of the various San languages. Researcher upon researcher attest to the baffling quantity of variation in pronunciation amongst the San. Ernst Westphal describes how it was

> extremely difficult to establish the phonemes of !Xũ [!Kung] since a great deal of time was taken up with the attempt to record all the variations of pronunciation occurring with single words. Those who have examined Dorothea Bleek's *Bushman Dictionary* will understand this difficulty. They will find e.g. some 20 or so vowel symbols being used in the description of one language where none seems to have more than 7 vowel phonemes and perhaps only 5. (Snyman 1970: editor's preface)

In societies such as that of the !Kung San, where meanings are universally available, variation at this level needs no explanation. Any process of standardisation would need explanation in social terms, as would the development of any distinguishable group varieties within or between the bands. Such features could only emerge from social changes which brought stratification and differential rewards for specialised social roles. The diversity would be replaced by a number of standardising processes, as social groups defined themselves in relation to others and the perceived boundaries become encoded within linguistic forms. Halliday implicitly assumes that social divisions create linguistic variety, and that without such divisions variety would diminish. However, if social divisions annex varieties as social indicators and 'standardise' them, this 'ideal homogeneous society', as with the San, would not display a uniform language but, within the limits of intelligibility (no doubt set much higher in a society without cultural divisions) would be likely to display a *high* level of variation. What would prevent this variation from becoming standardised would be the absence of power groupings to marshal or annex this variation into a codification of social difference, solidarity and relation. Variation itself is clearly not a *consequence* of social division, although it seems to be the case that the standardisation process (within social groups) is such a consequence. In more complex societies the 'available variation' employed in this way, and the varieties already established within society as in themselves indexical, are those which become capable of expressing perceived relations.

What is clear from this is that, while particular variants found in the speech of individuals are in no sense determined – i.e. there is, within the confines of denotational intelligibility a clear potential for individualistic and even eccentric variation (Trubetzkoi 1969: 19–20) – at the *social* level, the level of group or class, powerful influences generated from group relations do enter in, making some variants more likely than others within groups taken *as* groups. It is the patterning of such 'more likely variants' on the basis of group relations that gives social significance to any individual case and betrays the limitations of any reduction of social behaviour to aggregations of individual states. It is the misunderstanding of the difference between social facts and facts about individuals that so commonly leads to the misapprehension that any form of social determination also implies a deterministic view of subjectivity.

Returning to the issue of the refracting mechanism by which social divisions generate intra-group standardisation in signifying practices, it is important to bear in mind that while, as we have seen, some variants come to express the perceived relations between groups, and do so under the influence of actual divisions within society, the relationship between particular signifying practices and the distribution of power is always likely to be positioned and mediated by the wider ideological context and the symbolic orders within which they are embedded. This has particular consequences for the 'ethnic sign', and especially for the 'ethnic signs' of those groups occupying subordinated positions in the social formation, for, at the point of their inception, such signs are pre-positioned by the very act of selection itself. They declare simultaneously, 'I am strong' *and* 'I am weak'. It is this basic ambiguity that makes the issue of subordinate minority language use in institutional contexts (e.g. the status of creole in British education) the cause of such confusion and division even within the minority communities themselves. Signification is always vulnerable to its essentially social nature, and attempted redefinitions of low-status languages and dialects are always confronted by this obstinate fact. There is, in other words, always a limit to what a social group can achieve with regard to the dominant definitions of the status of its language, *without* exterior, structural support – a support only available through a repositioning of the group within the social structure or through a total transformation of all social relations.

It is for this reason that the employment of a strongly defined 'ethnicity' for politically strategic purposes may be simultaneously beneficial *and* limiting. By attempting to resist dominant social definitions, the subordinated ethnic/racial group may also over-define itself (through the codes its history has generated, codes often forged in social and political struggle) and substitute one form of pre-positioning for another. Thus, for example, where 'black people' are simply equated with 'black language', the *institutional* recognition of 'black language' becomes posited as enabling the 'success', usually in socioeconomic terms, of 'black people'; whereas it may be the case that only by resisting *any* construction of 'blackness' may the underlying problems of powerlessness and racism be approached. This remains, nevertheless, a paradox which is likely to continue to generate confusion for black social and political activists as much as for others less aware of the dimension of racism.

As a mechanism for group solidarity and for the sharpening of sociopolitical objectives, however, the articulation of a politically pointed racial ethnicity is clearly treated as important by some sections of black youth. The selection and manipulation of powerfully charged ethnic signifiers by black youngsters 'at street level' is also free from many of the paradoxes that beset such acts of group self-definition in institutional contexts. At street level, the distinctive voice of black adolescents is 'I am strong', and the 'I am weak', audible in the wider public area, remains unheard.

The distributions of racial/ethnic marking across a range of code bases – linguistic, sartorial, musical, kinetic, etc. – and the role of marking within boundary-maintaining practices is particularly evident in inter-racial adolescent relations, and is continuous with the kind of processes observed in black/white creole language relationsⁿips described in Chapters 4 and 5. As was seen there, the ambiguity of such marking practices by whites springs from the conflict of personal friendship and group membership. This is an area in which individual friendships and structured social relationships come face to face: where friendship, facilitated by approximately shared class positions, becomes transected by the perceived racial divisions within the economic order.

To demonstrate how such 'struggles within signification' with regard to creole language use are treated as situated within a wider range of signifying practices which have their own ideological contexts, the following extract from a group discussion is instructive. The extract shows clearly how a racial/ethnic code, generated from the structure of power relationships in which blacks have been positioned, is taken up into the interactive arena, and is activated to produce group conformity organised around sets of ethnic/racial signifiers.

Present in the discussion at first were three black girls, Claudia, Margaret and Pauline – the girl referred to in Chapter 5 who was reported to have 'laughed in the face' of Elaine, a white girl, for using creole (see p. 169 above). Also present were two white girls, Sharon and Susan, who both speak only once. In this discussion I was questioning Pauline about the event involving Elaine, to establish her version of the story. Elaine was a close friend of Sandra, another black girl, who enters the room and joins the discussion some minutes after it has begun. The three black girls who were there from the beginning are united in their condemnation of Elaine for using creole and adopting other aspects of black culture. Because, on entry to the discussion, Sandra denies that she had encouraged Elaine's habitual use of creole by denying that she had ever heard Elaine use creole, the others increase the pressure of implicit and explicit criticism until she is forced, towards the end of the extract, to confess her part in Elaine's transgression of the cultural boundary. As the pressure is increased, the symbolic context of creole use is explored by the group, and the wider arena of signification in which creole use is situated is made explicit.

> *The thing I was interested in was, er, before June went away . . .*
> *I think it was June was telling me how there was a white girl*
> *who used to hang around with them, and she used to speak bits*
> *of Jamaican.*

SHARON: That was Elaine.

PAULINE: Elaine who?

> *She said you heard her say something one day and you . . .*

MARGARET: Elaine who goes round with Sandra . . . Wilson.

PAULINE: Elaine Wilson . . . Oh yes, we went to the fair. I can't remember what she said. I was just shocked. You know, she just came out with it. I just looked at her and I looked at the rest of them and I just laughed to myself, you know.

> *You can't remember what she actually said?*

PAULINE: She goes . . . I can't remember. Something about she's gonna get 'licks' when she gets home.

> *Oh yes. That's what they told me. The thing that interested me*
> *was that they said they all knew her and knew she talked like*
> *that but that you'd never actually heard her.*

PAULINE: No, and you know, I was a bit shocked.

MARGARET: And shamed.

PAULINE: And she's all . . . you see her in red, gold and green track suit. She don't care you know. She doesn't know if she's coming or going, poor girl. She's a bit mixed up.

MARGARET: [I've seen her too.] It shocked me as well from the way she was talkin'.
Does she talk it much?

PAULINE and MARGARET: Yes!

MARGARET: And things that people have told us about her . . .
[Enter Sandra, a close friend of Elaine Wilson]

PAULINE: [boldly] Yes she doesn't know if she's coming or going that girl don't. Who told you about Elaine Wilson, June?
I think it was June.

SANDRA: Elaine Wilson? What about Elaine Wilson?
[Silence]
We were talking about the fact that she uses bits of Jamaican.
Do you know her?

SANDRA: She doesn't.
Doesn't she?
[The other girls look accusingly]

SANDRA: She doesn't.

PAULINE: So you've never heard her say anything? Have *you* Claudia?

MARGARET: Have you Claudia?

SANDRA: You can admit it if you want to but I've never heard her say anything. Not in front of me.

CLAUDIA: We wouldn't know otherwise, Sandra, would we? [because they usually only see Elaine *with* Sandra)

SANDRA: Pardon?

CLAUDIA: Don't worry about it. I didn't say nothin' anyway.
[uncomfortable pause]
Well so what? The others who are used to hearing her talk it . . .

PAULINE: Yes some people have heard her talk it . . . Well most people.
[pointedly]
[The girls whisper amongst themselves below the recording level about this issue.]
[To Pauline] *When you first heard her speak it were you annoyed or shocked or what?*

PAULINE: No I was just . . .

CLAUDIA: Disgusted.

PAULINE: Disgusted. Disgusted, you know, really. 'Cos Susan here goes round with us but she doesn't try to talk it.

[Sandra mimics Pauline's words, reiterating them after her in a joking but deliberately disruptive way.]

SANDRA: I've heard Susan speak it once.

CLAUDIA: Oh yeah? Go away Sandra.

MARGARET: Oh no she didn't, Sandra.

SUSAN: [jokingly] Shut up Sandra Evans!

SANDRA: Shut up Susan Stinkstone! [a joking distortion of Susan's surname)

PAULINE: Anyway that Katy Harris, well! [They all laugh] She tries to speak it. I don't know what she thinks she's doing. I've told her off once. 'Cos she goes a bit too far. It made her *cry*. [They all laugh.]
Who did?

PAULINE: I only went, 'Don't speak like that'. She's a little soft person.

MARGARET: She's a bit highly strung you know.

PAULINE: She was goin' a bit over the limit, you know what I mean.

CLAUDIA: There isn't a limit. She shouldn't be using it at all.

PAULINE: No, but the way she was carrying on . . . She used it without knowing what it meant. I don't know if she wanted us to think she was hard or what . . . And a thing I don't like – I don't know about Sandra – Claudia and I don't like is, this girl was just playing reggae music . . . and she doesn't know what it means or anything like that. They just think it's some kind of fashion.

CLAUDIA: They just want to do what the other girls do. They want to be like us but no way, guy!

PAULINE: And you ask them what they're playing it for and they just say, 'I like it'.

MARGARET to SANDRA: [in the background] Are you *for* it, Sandra?

CLAUDIA: I asked her why, did she think, they only make it for black people, and she didn't really know. She was sayin' that the records always have a message and I said, 'Who's the message to?' So she goes, 'Black people'. So I goes, 'Right. So what's it got to do with you?' and she knew what I was talkin' about.

PAULINE: It wouldn't be so bad if they knew what it was about and they played it . . .

CLAUDIA: That's not the point, what it's about . . . it's . . .

PAULINE: [in a semi-joking, goading way] But *Sandra* . . . well . . . she thinks it's right.

SANDRA: I say . . .

CLAUDIA: They're just tellin' younger blacks like us about the times of slavery that our parents had to go through and really that's got nothing at all to do with them.

But then Lover's Rock isn't like that is it?
CLAUDIA: No. It is! Lover's Rock is for lovers and the rest of the music
is sending a message.
*So when you get white girls <u>dressing</u> reggae and getting into
it in that way does it actually annoy you?*
CLAUDIA, PAULINE and MARGARET: Yes it does!
PAULINE: Especially the way they carry on.
MARGARET: It's not just the dressing. It's the way they talk, if you know
what I mean, that annoys me.
CLAUDIA: And Bo Derek hair style. [A copy of black hairstyle] And
Jim Davidson. [TV comedian who imitates Jamaican voices]
It's just fun to them. They're just exploiting everybody. [...]
How many of the white girls you see at blues speak Jamaican?
PAULINE: Quite a few. Because they're there they think they have to
speak like everybody else.
CLAUDIA: But the point is no matter if they speak fluent Jamaican and
they dress just as well as us, they're never gonna be what they
wanna be. No way.
*But obviously if these girls picked it up they must have had
black friends who taught them.*
PAULINE: [pointedly] They *encourage* them.
SANDRA: I mean Elaine must have got some encouragement off of me.
CLAUDIA: Yeah.
MARGARET: Yeah.
PAULINE: Yeah.
CLAUDIA: If, well, if you've heard her speak it ...
PAULINE: Mmmmmm.
SANDRA: She must have had some encouragement ... and off my mum,
especially.

Here the final confession, 'Elaine must have got some encouragement off
of me' (and what Claudia sees as an essential ingredient in it, the
admission that Sandra *had* heard Elaine speak creole) brings to a close
the overt exploration of the meaning of racial/ethnic markers – black
styles of dress, black hairstyles, black music and creole speech – brought
to explicitness by this exercise in lateral pressure.

In a sense the event *reversed* the structure of the original event, in
which all of the black youngsters then present, except Pauline, had come
to accept Elaine's use of creole. On that occasion Pauline alone spoke for
the racial/ethnic group, while the actual interactive group did not. Here,
however, the whole group, except one, articulated the racial group
dimension until even Sandra ceased to deny her complicity and by her
confession implicitly rejoined the circle. Given the profound ambiguities

of the confrontation between personal friendship and group membership, it may come as no surprise that even Pauline, paradoxically, had a personal creole-permitting relationship with Sharon, and – despite the assertions to the contrary in this discussion – Susan, too, used some creole on occasions with this group.

The issue is not, therefore, one of differing personal responses but one of how a social code may become realised through the contradictory behaviour of group members under specific interactive conditions.

It is especially interesting to see how the precise definition of categories is refined in debate, with the strongest forms articulated by Claudia in response to Pauline's firm but slightly fuzzier-edged distinctions, while all, at different points, function as a kind of chorus. Thus when Pauline commented on the white girl's use of creole: 'She was goin' a bit over the limit', Claudia came back firmly with 'There isn't a limit. She shouldn't be using it at all'. A principle of total exclusion is being applied here, and the same powerful principle was also exerted a few moments later by Claudia to another fuzzy-edged remark by Pauline: 'It wouldn't be so bad if they knew what it was about and they played it.' Claudia replies: 'That's not the point, what it's about. [...] They're tellin' younger blacks like us about times of slavery that our parents had to go through and really that's got nothin' at all to do with them.'

Whatever the interpersonal basis of the unified attack on Sandra might be, there is no interactive reason why the most strictly insulating voice should attain dominance within the discussion more than any of the other gradations of criticism aimed to censure her. However, the specific articulation of the issue within the group actually brings the girls to co-operate in the joint realisation of the racial/ethnic code in a particularly clear form. The code informs and structures boundary-maintaining practices through the array of signifiers, yet is often obliterated. Here, the inter-personal and the inter-racial dimensions become uniquely synchronised.

Claudia's remarks about reggae music and slavery are very close indeed to Claude Brown's remarks concerning the appropriation of black speech forms by American whites which '[ignores] the formidable fettering of the soul folks that brought that language about' (see above, p. 196) – a clear indication that it is not simply a case of defending some identity-bestowing ethnicity that is involved here, but that the nature of the boundary maintenance itself is generated by the very specific relations of economic dominance and subordination which have historically characterised black/white social relations. Indeed, it constitutes a firm anti-racist practice.

The particular ethnic/racial code which is thus evoked is only one resource in the articulation of the politico-economic dimension. There are other codes which also moderate practices; and, at another level, there are black pressure groups, political organisations and community groups etc. which operate in ways which directly address themselves to economic, social and political conditions. For young people, however, although involvement in such adult organisations is an option sometimes taken, it is perhaps inevitable that the underlying issues should be manifested in less explicit ways, and lived out through the connotational language of social signifiers whose nimbus of meaning is rarely revealed or examined in detail. In this living-through of symbolic and semiological orders, young people share in, and contribute to, the often conflictual processes of culture.

The specific ethnic/racial code realised in 'boundary maintaining' anti-racist practices, in being but one resource available to and transecting the lives of black people, is sometimes as strenuously resisted by young blacks as it is endorsed and explored by others and, indeed, even resisted or bypassed on some occasions as vigorously as it is explored on others. There is, in other words, a moving in and out of focus and of prominence of boundaries and classifications – an ambivalence around such racial/ethnic signs – which here may have strategic recourse to this code and elsewhere may seek to avoid the over-determination to which the code may lead.

One black female informant (eighteen years old) explained, for example:

> My younger sister got into this big 'black' thing, although when she was at secondary school she had white friends but she outgrew her white friends at school [. . .] and so she went round with a lot of older black girls and she had this big 'black' kick, to be ever so 'black'. I mean she's not. I can see it in her now. I can see the way she fights it because she's not. She's just like me but she's had to . . . She's stuck in X and she's got a baby and now it's just what's happened to her, the way she's been led. Because, I think, I wanted to do something different. I wanted to dance, I wanted to do all sorts of things that took me out of it. I didn't get caught up in it. [. . .]
>
> I've always said that, alright I don't go along with it, but I've never claimed to not understanding it. Like, I do understand why these black kids act the way they do and I don't really condemn them I just know why I don't do it. I know why I don't wanna be part of it and I know why they do it but I do understand it. It's like the way people go on about, 'oh they

can't get jobs' and all the rest of it. I'm not sayin' it's true, 'all black people can't get jobs'. What I am sayin' is the fault lies in the fact that they have reason to think that in the first place. It's like this fire in Deptford. I mean whether it was a racist attack or not, that's not really ... The important point is that all those people felt it was. Why should they feel it is? That was the first assumption ... Nobody even knows [how the fire started] but I understand why they do. I haven't been in that situation much but the times I have it's been well frightening. To think that someone actually hates you for no reason at all and it's really hard to cope with. [...] I can understand and can really sympathise with other black people, but more so with black people of my parent's age than I can with other people of my own age because I know how they were brought up and all the rest of it but people of my own age I think should have come out of that by now.

The use of black racial/ethnic markers by *whites* is inevitably cruder and more superficial, being further removed from the source. In being but a coarse representation of 'black' ethnicity, such markers are perceived as a reduction into stereotypical forms which further contribute to the over-determined positioning of 'black culture'. This is certainly one of the motivations behind the kind of reaction to white appropriations displayed in the group discussion above. For those who felt acutely the political importance of black culture, such appropriations were experienced as a violation of the underlying code. For others, such appropriations may be experienced as functioning to over-define them within the terms of a code they already felt to be constricting. The informant last quoted continued:

[At school] I went around with one girl who was half Burmese and half English, so she was rather like me [The informant's parents were both black Jamaicans. She appears to mean that her ethnicity was not 'fixed' in any sense.] and there was another girl who was Jamaican Chinese. She was into this big 'black' thing as well. The other girl was black with an English-teacher father, so that helped her out, and the other one was Swedish. Now she just lived with her mother. She didn't have a father and I think she always found things to cling to and when she went round with us she was ever so 'black', ever so, ever so 'black' with us, you know. And it was funny because she had to prove more than we did. She went out with all the scruffy black boys we wouldn't have touched.

> She dressed in a certain way, and it was weird. And I think
> because she was insecure she had to prove to us that she was
> . . . not even, good enough to go round with us, but that was
> her idea of how we should be. She had a big stereotype in her
> head and so she reacted like that and we never did.

There are clearly differences amongst black youngsters both in the way
black ethnicity is perceived and in the way white appropriations are
perceived. Although the girl last quoted came from a working-class
home, she did aspire to being part of a new black middle class, and saw
the racial/ethnic code as circumscribing such ambitions. However, she
also expressed the belief that the option of social mobility was open only
to a few, that 'the system' restricted this option for black people in
general. Nevertheless, there is, in the perspective she brought to the
issue of racial/ethnic markers, a clear difference between herself and
those present in the group discussion.

Another informant, who was from a lower-middle-class black family,
told me of the parental pressures against any endorsement of 'black'
culture:

> My mum won't let me have my hair cane-rowed. She don't
> like the style. She thinks it's awful [. . .] [She] never talks
> Jamaican and my dad never talks Jamaican. That's why I don't
> talk Jamaican. 'Cos I'd feel stupid. 'Cos I was born here it
> doesn't reflect on me so I just feel it's stupid for me to talk
> that way. It's just like trying to talk French.

Even for those firmly within the black working class, however, the
articulation of a code of solidarity through the array of 'ethnic signs'
could be an ambiguous resource. Some black boys in particular had
difficulty in living up to an 'ideal' image of black youth generated from
the creative centres of the culture. They were marginalised both by white
domination *and* by a culture they felt to be both theirs as young blacks
and yet simultaneously not theirs. For such youngsters, white appropriations – which were sometimes no more nor less successful than their
own – could be particularly difficult to tolerate.

Whatever the paradoxes and contradictions surrounding the code
within the black adolescent community, its relationship to the specialised
signification of race was commonly the site of a vigilant boundary
maintenance, in terms both of the misplaced over-valuation of 'black'
signifiers by whites and of the *under*-valuation consequent upon any
trivialising of black culture by its association with 'mere fashion'.
Assertions that white girls 'try to be like black girls, you know, cane-row

their hair, put their hair in beads and talk black so they feel black' are as much concerned with the process by which social meaning is drained from signifiers as they are with the violation of boundaries. Claudia's statement that 'they just think it's some kind of fashion' not only connects with Claude Brown's view of the trivialisation of black language by whites, but also resonates with the accusation by the white boy quoted in Chapter 1 of this book: 'It's a fashion but you'd never get them to admit it. "I-man, I dread, mi music, mi colour, my background, my roots." Fuck their roots – it's a fashion.' Clearly, if powerfully charged racial signifiers, forged in a history of struggles of the most serious kind, are at stake, it is not surprising that such signifiers should *themselves* be fought over. The informant here, belonging to a racist, masculine youth culture, clearly did feel that black ethnicity, defined in terms of social power, was something that needed to be taken seriously enough to be denigrated, and he chose to do so by what he felt to be the most telling means available. The seeming force of the accusation, and the logical sleight-of-hand upon which it rests, is derived from the common confusion between black culture as the sum of cultural and social creativity generated by black people, and 'black' culture as a specialised inflection of those cultural products which invests them with an ultimately political meaning. There can be no doubt that the black contribution to 'fashion', as well as to many other aspects of commercial culture, has been substantial. Furthermore, it would be a travesty to reduce *all* black culture to expressions, reflexive or otherwise, of the conditions of political and economic struggle. There are, therefore, of course, many aspects of black culture which are not invested with powerful 'roots' or other political meanings. However, those which are and those which are not so invested are, within crucial interactive contexts, a matter of close and complex negotiation. There is no fixity in such signification, but a constant process of manipulation through socially structured interactions mediated by the ideological terms within which they operate. There is nothing generated within black culture which cannot become inflected for strategic use in specific social interactions; but those elements which are so used may vary from place to place and time to time even within the same group of interactants. What varies far less are the conditions of subordination and domination in the wider social context which predispose inter-racial contacts towards certain forms.

I found that this absence of fixity led to some confusion amongst white friends of black youngsters, seemingly bewildered about how the rules were applied at times. Sharon, one of the white girls present in the group discussion above, having been told by a black friend about an occasion on which *Sandra* had reprimanded a white girl for cane-rowing another white girl's hair, commented:

> But the thing that puzzles me is that they [her black friends] ask to do it in my hair. And I asked Pauline why, once, an' she says, 'Because you're friends'. But maybe the other person had got black friends who they wanna do it in *their* hair, so it goes in a circle, don't it?

Despite such bewilderment, some general rules were evidently conveyed, because she followed this point with: 'I was down Lewisham wiv my mum and I see this white girl with all different squares [in her hair] and she had beads in an' I thought, "I wouldn't like to be you".'

It is clear, however, that such difficulties operating where friendship and group consciousness intersect, while being of some educative value for whites with respect to the complexities of 'race relations', are ultimately not enough in themselves to effect a broad understanding of the issue of racism. Indeed, the realisations of a code *produced* by struggles against racial domination in no way guarantees the effectiveness of that code as a cultural tool in any less specific challenge to the wider ideological structure of racism itself. The rigour of the code gives it a specificity which in fact limits its usefulness in the kind of ideological deconstruction required by a broad-based anti-racism and, in its interactive manifestation, *can* even produce a closure of possibilities for truly penetrating the terms within which urban race relations are lived out. As one boy, who came from neither of my research areas, once commented to me: 'Round my way it's not blacks against whites – it's blacks and whites against Pakis and Turks.' The negotiation of the relationship between black and white adolescents is apparently no panacea for adolescent race relations, even if it can assist in the establishment of some advances; and the validation of black youth culture amongst whites *can* be ultimately of little meaning when it remains locked within the purely connotational realm of signification. There are evidently many senses in which the 'fictive social relationship' established in some inter-racial friendships, and permitting the use of marked 'black' forms by whites, are isolated from their wider, 'real' social context. The fragile building-up of structures within personal relations are forced by the sheer weight of their environment to remain short-circuited, incomplete and gestural, 'ghettoised' within their own fictive realm.

The contradictions and complexities of the cultural realm, which seemed to offer to some youngsters an escape from the stark world of articulated 'opinion' and articulated racial ideology, are even more acute where signifying practices are transformed and warped – as it were, against their will – by the wider ideological landscape.

The specific revaluations of black culture expressed by young whites are stimulated from a convergence of sources which includes: (*a*) the local ideologies and activities generated within the black communities themselves – that powerfully contrastive cultural output which itself is a challenge to white evaluations and to racist ideologies, (*b*) the friendships and other forms of association within which the privileged employment of racially marked signs by whites occurs, and (*c*) the external positioning of black people and black culture in the broader social context. It is in the articulation of this third factor, and the semiological exchanges between black and white adolescents, that further limitations and contradictions enter in and tend to contribute to the short-circuiting of any over-arching anti-racism.

The external ideological positioning of black cultural products takes a variety of forms, many well known. While, for example, black cultural and political resistance to white domination classically becomes re-interpreted as a law and order issue, the *productivity* of black people is filtered by racism in the labour markets in such a way that not only negative stereotypes but (pertinent to the attraction of white youth) an over-specialisation of positive stereotypes is also generated in the commercial sector. This over-specialisation is especially manifested in the validation of blacks in the entertainment industry, which inversely affects the distribution of black validation in other professions. However, a further – and here more relevant – effect of this over-specialisation is that in itself it generates other categorical grids within the racial imagery of 'white' culture. For example, just as Asian classical culture is often perceived by middle-class whites as contrasting with a putative Caribbean high-culturelessness, so black popular commercial culture, with its continuities and inter-relations with white commercial popular culture, is seen within the white working class as exposing the alienness of the Asian community – evidenced, according to some informants, especially in the absence of Asian music in the record charts, and by the rarity of popular Asian television entertainers and sports personalities in Great Britain. Indeed, the class distributions of racial imageries within the white population are fed by, and feed, the over-familiar constructions operating through the media at the national level, in which Asian cultural *difference* (for example linguistic, religious and sartorial) is stressed alongside Asian 'conservatism', 'hard work' and educational and professional success. (It is interesting to note how the same contrast is formulated in the North American context, where it is the *Caribbean* community that has been characterised as 'frugal, hard-working and entrepreneurial' (Sowell 1981: 219) by 'libertarian' right-wing race theorists, and used as a means to reproach the North American-born black population for 'their' economic failure.)

The white perception of these specific stereotypical qualities inevitably varies greatly with different class locations. Within sections of the white urban working-class, however, one consequence is a convergence of racial hostility towards Asians, and a rejuvenated *class* hostility; for the stereotypical 'Asian' virtues are also the ideologically preferred markers of the white middle class. Where this figure is reiterated in adolescent groups, either in the extreme forms of fascist youth cultures for whom Asians have long provided an especially intense object of hatred, or more generally in the diffuse forms evident in the undercurrents of dislike displayed more routinely, it contributes much to the blunting of such anti-racist sentiments as are generated within social contact, and stimulates instead a hostility to Asians capable of affecting black and white working-class adolescents alike. (See, for example, black and white adolescent attitudes to Asians displayed in Turkie 1982.)

Thus variations in the forms of racism in the labour market *and* in the distribution of white racial imageries help to produce a buffer to, and limitation on, any broad-based and articulate anti-racism capable of going beyond that expressible through a narrowly specific culture of contact. It is indeed this wider ideological in-forming that can produce realisations of 'blacks and whites against Pakis and Turks', and can limit the growth of those tentative structures of deviant white anti-racism built up within local communities. The very diffuseness and conceptual open-endedness of the connotational realm of culture permits of its re-modelling *away from* the kind of principled formulation necessitated by the distortions exerted by unequal positioning within the structures of power.

Despite some highly localised real advances, therefore, the inherent instability of those bridges built across the abyss of racism by *cultural* means alone, and the re-semanticising to which the cultural is suscept-ible, render the 'cultural mode' of white appropriations a flawed and only partial site for the generation of any over-arching anti-racism amongst young whites. The 'connotational realm' is too variable, inarticulate and open to distortions to provide a reliable counter to racism generated and reproduced at other levels, because those levels themselves conspire to infect the local with paradox. In these ways the 'folk taxonomies of the social order' encoded in signifying practices become vulnerable to – because they are formed within – their specific ideological setting.

The employment of creole forms by white youngsters falls squarely within this paradoxical and heavily mediated realm, betraying in the minutiae of its action how social location structures signification, on the one hand by simply providing as pre-given the associated primary language bases upon which secondary semiological operations are performed, and on the other by moderating, through its differential axes of power, the 'public' and consensual scope and meaning of those operations. The fragmentary and fragile structures of semiosis built up within the equally fragmentary structures of association challenge only on this basis, groping towards a more tenacious hold on their cultural and social setting, seeking a more benevolent environment through which to speak.

7

Transmission and intervention: racism and anti-racism in communicative practices

Throughout this book a number of cultural aspects of inter-racial contact have been examined. However, with regard to the countering of racism itself, the qualified efficacy of cultural means has led us ultimately back towards problems posed at the outset. What was especially addressed in the previous chapters was the way in which social relationships are enacted rather than spoken, for in casting its light through the language of black/white social relations, the semiotics of black/white cultural contact are finally inseparable from it. However, the central problem of how white adolescent reactions against racism declare themselves in concrete practices remains opaque.

Some aspects of the distortions and contradictions involved in the conscious adoption of 'black' social markers by whites, discussed in Chapter 6 and earlier, were apparent to white youth in both research areas, and such cultural means were deliberately *avoided* by many whites with black friends and acquaintances. While this avoidance removed one channel through which an affinity with black youth might, with whatever interactive delicacy, be expressed, a positive gain was evident in the side-stepping of a commitment which could limit non-racism or anti-racism to a cultural formula restricted to Caribbean-based cultures. Those whites who were content to remain 'white' in their cultural projection, yet who had black friends, were far less susceptible to the difficulties and paradoxes that have been examined above; and yet, even in these cases, the exact ways in which such individuals processed the racism in their environment were by no means simple or obvious. It is also certainly true that most young whites do not address themselves directly to such matters, any more than do most adults. In looking, therefore, beyond the dimension of 'social semiotics', it is necessary to return finally to issues raised in Chapter 1, and to examine more closely some of the processes of *transmission* evident in the adolescent communities.

Consider the following text, drawn from an interview with a boy from Area A who had a few black acquaintances but who had come, at the time of this interview, to have strong feelings of hatred towards black adolescents in general:

> *Text 1a*
> When I was nine I looked at a black person and thought of them as a person exactly the same as me. And yet now when I've looked on the proper, commonsense side of it and I've looked at a black person I've thought, look at him: they hate whites. They kill whites. They stab whites. They do not talk to whites if they are proper dreads [. . .] That is why I've got . . . Look at them. They treat us like shit. We must treat them like shit. That's my view.

This quotation has to be considered in its social and historical context of male peer group association described in Chapter 1. The informant's appeal to 'the proper, commonsense side' deserves closer scrutiny; and in another interview with this same informant, some clues to how the 'common' came to be so constituted emerged:

> *Text 1b*
> When I was talking to Nick Randolph about a year ago – I still just thought of 'em as human beings – and he goes, 'You know, you're walking along the street, you used to know 'em and they just stick their nose at yer.' And because he thinks that he is better than them, that they are inferior, it's not their country, they should keep in line, and they have, what he says, 'the audacity' to not even nod at you, to think that you are the shit . . . and the audacity . . . And the hatred builds up with him and if that happens he'll just go over there and kick the fuck out of 'em if he can.

A further text to which I will refer comes from an interview with a boy from Area B who had several black friends. The tone and form of the racism evident is different to that in the other texts above, but the issue of transmission is equally evident:

> *Text 2*
> There's a poem about, er, fingies, coloureds.
> *What's that?*
> It's a racialist joke.
> *Oh is it, yeah . . .*

Shall I tell it?
All right, go on then.
It's a sort of rhyme thing. It goes ... I don't ... I've never ...
I've never used it. I picked it off some kid, right ... He's not a
racialist but 'e got it off 'is old mates an' that ... an' 'e goes
... 'e goes:
> The wonderful fing about niggers,
> The niggers are wonderful fings,
> Their lips are made of rubber
> And their hairs are made of springs.

It's only stupid. And if you told it to 'em they'd just laugh.
They'd probably make one up about you.

Neither Text 1*b* nor Text 2 can be assumed to describe accurately the way
in which, in the case of 1*b*, the opinions and, in the case of 2, the rhyme
was conveyed to the informants. Both texts display with certainty only
the conversational strategies which were employed in interview with me.
Both constitute *accounts* of how their content was conveyed. They
nevertheless do indirectly tell us something about the process by which
racism is transmitted.

Much could be said about Text 1*a*. However, it is primarily the
conjunction of the biographical and 'rational' elements which are relevant here. The 'rational' explanation that is tendered in this passage is an
explanation of the 'commonsense view' which, according to the informant, must imply the acting out of hostility to blacks: they hate and exclude
themselves from whites, and therefore whites should do the same to
them. This 'commonsense view' is deemed to be arrived at through the
process of growing up. The growth of hostility is equated with growth
into maturity. This biographical/explanatory dimension is textually
dramatised by the linking of two identical events taking place at
'different' periods. 'I looked at a black person' (1) and 'I looked at a
black person' (2). In the biographical lacuna between these events, the
'view' ('That's my view') became established by the intervention of an
unspecified but definitely social agency constituting *common* sense. The
process by which the speaker came to be articulated with the community
for which such ideas constitute 'the common' implicitly indicates a gap
between actual experience and idealisation (stereotyping) which is,
unusually, not resolved in this case by recourse to denying counter-
evidence (by denying or excluding, for example, evidence that most
blacks *don't* behave in this way), but by reference to an imputed black
self-definition: 'They do not talk to whites *if they are proper dreads.*' This
itself constitutes part of a 'knowledge' about society, and was by

implication gained by the same process as that by which the informant came to participate in 'the common'. It has, of course, specific reference to adolescent society and adolescent rivalries.

In 1*b*, the same periodisation as is evident in 1*a* is maintained – 'I still [state of innocence/ignorance] just thought of 'em as human beings' – but the social dimension is focused on a single exemplary event: an act of transmission of social opinion/evaluation from a friend to the informant. This permits the enumeration of the series of ideas which constitute the 'opinion' and which explain/justify the hostility. It provides the opportunity to expand on the putative foundations of racial hostility whilst simultaneously avoiding direct *personal* responsibility by making 'Nick Randolph' the representative of a locally *public* opinion which is ultimately the arbiter of 'common' truth. As the passage opens, the narrator moves away from centre stage, allowing 'Nick Randolph' to speak as the voice of the peer group and of 'the commonsense side'. Indeed, the meaning of what is said and the exact terms through which that meaning is expressed are totally dependent on the 'social' life that is implied in the person of Nick Randolph. (A singular feature of the passage also lies in how it draws attention to the act of transmission. While racism is relayed within and between peer groups in a variety of ways, it seems to be the case that the processes of that relay may be dramatised and condensed into an imagery in which 'the common' is itself able to appear.)

The content of this 'explanation' should recall the ethnography of Chapter 1. Here, in Text 1*b*, the 'audacious' style of black adolescents is not treated as sufficient to explain the feelings it is 'proper' to feel. It needs, apparently, to be brought into relationship with certain well established and externally guaranteed tenets of racism, especially that 'they are inferior; it's not their country; they should keep in line'. At the level of content, it is apparent from this part of the account that such adolescent racism is not merely the result of adolescent rivalries but of the juxtaposition of adolescent organisational modes on the one hand and racist ideology available in the culture on the other. In this passage the cultural property (racism) is pressed into service, and becomes the means of apprehension of specific and local adolescent relationships. The racism per se is not the product of those relationships, even if hostility might be. (Even with hostility, indeed, it is difficult to 'know the dancer from the dance'.) Such an account does not ignore the fact that some white boys may have had the kind of experience referred to (black kids, too, sometimes reported on the 'arrogant' manner of other black kids), but it *can* serve to investigate why such experiences should be selected out of the totality of inter-racial experiences to express and even guide more general attitudes. It is also important to keep in mind that white behaviour to blacks is frequently 'arrogant' but is not highlighted as such for young whites, because it is generalised through the culture and because the racial structure of social power constitutes such behaviour as normality.

Text 1*b* works to explain an emotion – the emotion which is said to lead to the most overt acts of racial violence: 'And the hatred builds up in him and if that happens he'll just go over there and kick the fuck out of 'em if he can.' The emotion is treated as deriving from the conjunction of typical experience – 'you used to know 'em and they just stick their nose at yer' – and *accepted* opinion – 'they are inferior; it's not their country.' Both the experiential and the ideological bases of racist feeling are legitimated by, and referred to, the 'public' realm of the peer group as the essential (social) *other term* bestowing meaning.

The combination of a specific 'society' constituting such an 'other term', with the 'code' (formed here by racist notions and motifs) is in fact a feature of *all* codes, social, cultural and linguistic. Roman Jakobson's isolation of 'addresser' and 'addressee' within his well known account of the elements of communication (Jakobson 1960), involves, in this respect, a certain obfuscation of 'the social'. Just as his concept, 'message', necessarily involves the 'addresser'/'addressee' relation, so 'code' necessarily involves 'the social': both 'code' and 'message' are essentially dual-aspect entities; and if the inventory of elements necessary for communication should include 'addresser' and 'addressee' as well as 'message', it should also include 'society' as well as 'code', for 'addresser' and 'addressee' are to 'society' as 'message' is to 'code'. All meaning within language is only guaranteed by the accord of code and social 'knowledge'. 'Code' and 'society' are thus not independent terms. Where natural language is concerned, it is at least the case that the latter is entailed in the former.

In the case at hand, the inventory of formulaic 'opinions', the accompanying sets of unstated assumptions and the stereotypes which function like motifs in social narratives of race, *together* constitute the cultural materials (the 'code' in the sense in which I have been using it here) generated from social and economic relations (and from other cultural materials autonomously) which return as a *resource language* through which 'race relations' are perceived. This code is dependent for its meaning and capacity for transmission on a specific social context (or on a confluence of several such contexts). Furthermore, the code may be augmented and expanded by items which, generated from local and specific conditions, have themselves become formulaic. In Text 1*b*, the sentence 'you used to know 'em and they just stick their nose at yer', which closely resembles some of the utterances quoted in Chapter 1 and others which I collected, appears to be a candidate for a position within the set of motifs forming, along with other elements, a local language (dialect?) of racism in Area A. Certainly it is through a process by which social experience is parsed by ideology that new signifiers become generated in the language(s) of racism and come to gain wider currency.

The stereotype of the audacious, 'arrogant' black adolescent takes up its position in the array of motifs and symbolisms available to the narratives circulating within the white adolescent communities, and narrators can point to the 'tradition' from which it flowed to validate its special kind of truth. In this instance, attention was drawn to the 'other term' by the informant in his interaction with *me*. It was, in fact, an interactive strategy to secure the *social ground* of and for the particular racist view expressed. As such it constituted part of the 'struggle over signification' in which all socially significant meaning is engaged. (It was, indeed, a way of 'doing racism' by drawing on one of the codes of racism present in the culture to produce a 'well formed (racist) utterance'; here such an act of doing racism is, to the racist code on which it draws, as an act of speaking is to language.)

There is little doubt that the views expressed in Texts 1*a* and 1*b* would, by most criteria, be classed as examples of 'intended racism'. The content of Text 2, however, calls into question the clarity of the distinction between 'intended' and 'unintended' racism, for the informant disclaims responsibility for the racism of the words of his rhyme, and furthermore suggests that its content should not be taken as having any *social* meaning at all: 'It's only stupid. And if you told it to 'em they'd just laugh.' Yet he is well aware of its objective significance because he himself calls it 'a racialist joke'. He is saying in effect: 'This is a rhyme which is enjoyable for its humour and form. It uses the language of racism to achieve its effect, but don't assume that those who tell it are racist.' It is knowingly racist but is not intended to convey racism.

The justifications that the rhyme has 'no social meaning' are evidently adduced with a view to my likely response, and his hesitations and false starts are partly indicative of his nervousness in this respect. This informant knew very little about me, however, and it is equally evident that he was acutely aware that if the objective (social) meaning of an utterance is racist, then, ultimately, no amount of disclaiming can obliterate the fact. Indeed, Text 2 exemplifies the fact that intentionality is always a poor guide to meaning where a public language is concerned.

What is of special interest is Text 2's legitimation strategy, for it effectively makes the same appeal as did Text 1*b* – i.e. an appeal that there exists a *constituency* from which the rhyme has arisen. In this case the text is legitimated as a cultural form which, like all jokes, rhymes etc., has other claims to existence beyond its referential meaning. As is often the case with jokes suspected by their tellers of being socially sensitive, individual responsibility for the meaning content is elided by appeals to the fact that 'it's just something that people pass round for the fun of it'. Its self-evident racism is treated as the unimportant means to an end, and in order to indicate *how* it is able to be so treated, its pedigree in other 'unmeant' contexts – extending into an historically and socially misty realm – is added: 'I picked it off some kid, right . . . He's not a racialist but 'e got it off 'is old mates an' that . . .'. We also have in this text exactly the same strategy seen in 1*b* of putting the words into the mouth of another: 'an' 'e goes . . . 'e goes . . .'.

Besides such social contextualisation of the form, the informant also includes what is intended as corroborating evidence that its 'racialist' meaning can be ignored: 'It's only stupid. And if you told it to 'em they'd just laugh. They'd probably make one up about you.' Here there is recourse to the familiar notion of the democracy of humour: the belief that a joke about a black person by a white has the same social meaning and effect as a joke about a white person by a black – as though social intercourse existed in isolation from any meaning-bestowing contexts.

The fact that the rhyme existed in the local (white) culture, and had been evidently 'going round', meant that – although the informant in Text 2 was very different from the informant in Texts 1*a* and *b* with regard to his inter-racial friendships and his expressed racial attitudes – where his local 'common' culture contained such items, he could find himself 'doing racism' simply by reproducing – with little questioning but also with little conviction – the culture of which he was a part. (What is different from Texts 1*a* and *b* is the use of phrases such as, 'it's a racialist joke', which, in conjunction with the apologetics, provide clues to the anti-racist ideological strands in Area B culture.)

Such a 'common' warranty is, of course, also true of many racist term and traits. Such terms are often so ingrained in white cultures that they may be unquestioned and used even by those who would not wish to be regarded (or to regard themselves) as racist. Simply by living out the cultures in which racist codes (ideas, stereotypes, narrative motifs and language) are embedded, participants often 'do racism' through even the simplest and most mundane acts of communication, and sometimes with only the dimmest recognition of what is occurring. Thus, when in a situation where such communications are called into question, they have recourse both to rational legitimations – 'It doesn't *mean* anything' – and/or to appeals to the collective source of individual utterance, as was true with both Text 1*b* and Text 2. In the latter instance the racism was very evident to the speaker. In many cases, however, racist forms may remain undetected as such partly because the assumed constituency of communication is white, and the impulse to monitor expression for offensiveness is not interactively established. Such instances, where racism is embedded in the very means of communication, provide the clearest examples both of 'unintentional racism' and of the more overt examples of 'intentional racism'.

The kinds of 'doing racism' located in transmission between whites are discussed here because our concern proceeds from an interest in the processes by which racism is relayed within adolescent communities, and in what strategies also exist which interrupt and subvert this process. Furthermore, racism which occurs in acts of transmission makes up the most common direct experience of racism for whites, because the *observation* of racism as it is interactively done *to* black people constitutes only a very small part of reflective white social experience. Acts of transmission, therefore, provide a primary potential site for anti-racist intervention.

Challenges and obstructions to transmission – where they occur – are often oblique because of the very nature of communication between peers, resting, as it does, on the assumption of collectively shared values, and on the notion of a consensual 'knowledge' guaranteeing the meaningfulness of the codes of communication themselves. However, intervention is not always necessarily so oblique. A discontinuity in attitudes to race *within* the terms of adolescent (school) peer communication was displayed in a number of ways in a long dialogue between two of my informants, parts of which I will quote here.

The occasion on which the dialogue took place was intended to be an interview. By accident, the two fifteen-year-old white male school friends – one of whom came from Area A, the other from Area B – came to be interviewed jointly. I had intended the interview to be about creole use by whites, and about their friendship groups in and out of school. They began by describing the racial composition of their out-of-school friendships as follows:

DAVID: I s'pose I've got fifty-fifty white friends as I 'ave black friends, but I go round wiv seventy per cent blacks and thirty per cent whites.

JOHN: I go about wiv hundred per cent whites and I know about fifty per cent blacks, but I hang about wiv white kids.

The nature of the occasion rapidly became transformed, however, as the informants argued about race, with John (who was also the informant providing Texts 1*a* and *b* above) consistently putting forward a racist position, and David (who was described in Chapter 2) attacking his arguments and attitudes. This discussion was considerably more interesting than the interview I had planned, and I took a back seat, only very rarely interjecting remarks or queries.

John's racial attitudes were well known to David, but in the earliest part of the discussion they were fairly soberly considering the ways in which some white youngsters establish and maintain friendships with blacks:

JOHN: Some white kid [round my way], 'e speaks – even to 'is mum an' dad – 'e speaks dread. 'E walks like a dread, 'e wears a dread 'at, which 'e never takes off, because 'e wants to be something an' 'e thinks the only way 'e can get it is bein' a dread, sort of. An' now that 'e's growin' a bit older it's sorta stuck wiv 'im. 'E'll never get rid of it.

[TO DAVID]: *But how come you're not like that . . . You don't go round wearing a Rasta hat and . . .*

DAVID: Some people don't 'ave to.

JOHN: It's not . . . You don't believe in no black religion, do yer?
     [. . .]

DAVID: Well . . . I 'ang around wiv 'em and if they say . . . Say like one of 'em says, 'the police picked me up', for some reason. If, if it's wrong why the police picked 'im up I'd agree wiv 'im but if it's right, I say, 'well right an' all! You should 'ave been picked up' – say they was distracting the peace or somethin' like that – I'd tell 'em, but they'd agree wiv me.

David gave this answer after several moments' thought. It seems that he was searching for a way of illustrating how his way of relating to black adolescents was not distorted either by racial hostility or by any special benevolence or cultural attraction – that his relations were, in such respects, just as they would be with whites. He then began to explain how his friendships became well established. In the course of doing so he used the word 'nigger'. His use of this word was consistently ambiguous throughout the discussion, for on the one hand he appears at first to be using it involuntarily, simply as a common word in the white working-class lexicon which he shared with John; on the other, he also seems to be *appropriating* its use in such a way as to deliberately undermine John's confidence in his own set of racist terms. Indeed, David's use of 'nigger', at certain points in the ensuing exchange, continues to annoy John until he forces a discussion of its meaning. What John appears to find so disquieting is David's use of the word whilst simultaneously challenging his own racist views. It is as though David were attacking his racism directly while also subtly uncoupling the relationship between the racist 'code' and the specific and assumed 'society' which bestows its meaning and resonance, an act of semantic subversion which John appears to find very disturbing:

DAVID: An' what it is is, the first time I ever really got in wiv 'em – 'cos around my street all the niggers used to do was sit on the wall, talk. They used to take the draught board out and play draughts, all this lot. Know what I mean?

JOHN: Yeah, but that just shows how much you don't . . . You're really not like that [white Rasta]. 'E really thinks black. 'E acts black. 'E thinks 'e *is* black in a way. Whereas [you go], 'those niggers'. See, you said, 'those niggers', where, meaning . . . You don't think . . . They're just black to you ain't they? An' you can speak their language in a way, an' you use it to create a laugh an' fings like that. That shows how different you are, 'cos when I'm wiv you [in school] an' you see a black kid actin' flash you go, 'look at that fuckin' flash nigger!'

DAVID: But then again, John right, it's different. When they're your mates an' you're wiv 'em you 'ave to be one of 'em. D'you know what I mean?

JOHN: But I still think – I don't know if you'd call this racialist but – I wouldn't lower myself to associate wiv a black person. 'Cos they fink they are superior to white people– or most of 'em do. I wouldn't associate wiv any black person who fought [thought] that. [. . .]

DAVID: Well I'll tell you what John, I may go round wiv seventy per cent blacks an' thirty per cent whites . . .

JOHN: You're a cunt.

DAVID: No. I'd *raver* go round wiv seventy per cent blacks an' thirty per cent whites. They're more reliable, I tell yer.
[. . .]
You've been sayin' you hate blacks 'cos of the way they think they're superior to us. Well perhaps they feel the same way as white people think *they're* superior to them.

JOHN: White people don't fink they're superior. White people . . . You should fuckin' know this. It's a constant battle to white people to get back on top, to know that *they* think they're superior.

DAVID: But then again John, you say niggers think they're superior to us. There's many white people who think we're superior to them.

JOHN: That's because they're older and harder [. . .] They are solid English and they think they 'ave no right to come over 'ere.

DAVID: Listen, John, you said you think niggers think they're superior
      to us?

JOHN: Yeah.

DAVID: Now do you think we're superior to them?

JOHN: In my mind yes we are, 'cos we're English.

DAVID: Well that's what I'm sayin'.

JOHN: You said . . .

DAVID: I said some white people fink they're superior to them. You,
      you think you're superior to them . . . Everybody's equal no
      matter what the colour.

At this point David seems to realise that it is particularly *young* blacks to
whom John directs his dislike. He starts, therefore, on a different tack:

DAVID: I'll tell you what it is, it's the *age*. Down B the niggers, right . . .

JOHN: 'Black people'.

DAVID: From fourteen, right, from fourteen they become dread. When
      they're fourteen they become dread. When they get to
      eighteen they don't worry about that no more, and then the
      next lot of niggers who come from fifteen, *they* become dread.

Their discussion wandered over a variety of issues relating to racism.
David consistently attempted to side-step the rigid views of black youth
with regard both to black youth culture and to the images of black
violence, which he saw as especially generated by the local newspapers.
At one point he illustrated this with the following:

> There was a kid murdered in B, weren't there? who went to X
> school, didn't they. 'E was a white kid. 'E went to X school
> and in the [local paper] the next day it said, 'so an' so' . . . Me
> an' Mark Greenwood was comin' 'ome from school that night
> an' we went down the road an' we saw the body in there, wiv
> all the police an' everything. An' in the [paper] on the
> Thursday it said, 'Youth Murdered' – 'e was slashed an' 'is
> clothes were taken an' everythink – it said, 'Suspicion on
> seven black youths'. Six weeks later they arrested a white kid
> who lives the next door along from me named Y an' I used to
> go around wiv 'im. An' 'e's in prison now for the murder, but
> straight away, 'cos they never 'ad nothin' to write in the paper
> they put, 'black kids'. They put 'black kids' in the paper.

After much discussion in which John consistently got the worst of the
argument, he sought for a solution:

JOHN: But anyway, let's just put it this way: we've been brought up in
      two different environments.

DAVID: That's it. It's the opposite, John. If I was brought up where you
was brought up an' you was brought up where I was brought
up, you'd be sayin' what I've been sayin' and I'd be sayin'
what you've been sayin'.

Although John had suggested this as a formula for agreement, he found
David taking it over and effectively robbing his position of what he
thought to be its 'moral' authority by rendering both of their positions as
totally dependent on lived social experience. To this he could not agree,
because he felt that he was still the one in possession of the 'truth' in this
matter. The argument, therefore, continued, and David recounted how,
like other white kids in his area, he found black kids not at all as John
claimed to find them but indeed very friendly. He added realistically,
however – perhaps, again, to avoid any over-idealised 'soft' view:
'Whereas, there again, wiv niggers, there's some niggers in B, there's
some white kids in B they just can't stand.'
    At this point his consistent use of the word 'nigger' became too much
for John who forced the following exchange:

JOHN: Why do you call 'em 'niggers'? . . . Why do you call 'em
    'niggers'?
DAVID: Well what d'you want me to call 'em then?
JOHN: They're people. They're black people.
DAVID: Well, all right, 'black people', then, right . . . [trying to continue
    with what he was saying]
JOHN: [interrupting] Do you like black people?
DAVID: Yeah, I do.
JOHN: So why do you call 'em 'niggers' then?
DAVID: Well what d'you want me to call 'em?
JOHN: What they are, 'black people', if you like 'em.
DAVID: But they're niggers an' all ain't they?
JOHN: 'Niggers' is a slang expression of not likin' a black person,
    'nigger' is. If I went up to . . .
DAVID: 'Nigger' – real word – means 'worker for the government'
    doesn't it, or somethin'?
JOHN: Bullshit! To a black person it means takin' the piss. If I said
    'alright nigger' to Gavin or any black kid 'e'd beat the hell out
    of me. *You* don't call black people 'niggers' so why should you
    say it to whites, if you like 'em?
DAVID: Alright, a 'black kid' right . . .

The variety of ways in which David not only counters John's racist views
but puts him on the defensive is impressive, even if his lack of political

sophistication makes some of his formulations somewhat tortuous in their expression. In fact the very *absence* of any intellectual facility with the issues makes his onslaught on John's racial hostility all the more significant, for he is speaking very much in the voice of his own neighbourhood and not in the voice of any learned political or moral creed generated from outside his material and immediate social conditions. It is, with all its confusions, paradoxes and impurities, the authentic voice of a white youth so closely bound up in his racially mixed social networks, yet still distinctively white and working-class – he did speak creole but did not like reggae or adopt black style – that many of the distortions imposed by racism stood out with absolute clarity for him.

It seems difficult at first to decide on the extent to which David's use of the word 'nigger' in this discussion was his 'doing racism' in using the white working-class lexicon, and how much he was performing an act of sabotage upon the word. Certainly he does appear to be doing the latter, once he realises how much his use of 'nigger' aggravates John, although his initial use of it may well have been a reflex of his longstanding friendship with John. Indeed, John explicitly refers to this fact when attempting to show how David's use of 'nigger' was the indisputable evidence that he and John shared the same view and the same values: 'You said, "those niggers", where, meaning … You don't think … They're just black to you, ain't they?' – i.e. *unlike* the white Rasta who 'thinks black'. He insists that, in using this word, David demonstrates his distance from blacks and that, specifically, when he had used it on other occasions (evidently on other occasions when his usage had *not* annoyed John) he had been equally demonstrating his affinity with the views expressed by John: "Cos when I'm wiv you an' you see a black kid actin' flash you go, "Look at that fuckin' flash nigger!"'

There is good evidence from the text, therefore, that David may elsewhere have used this word on specific occasions and to specific and exclusively white interlocutors, and that his *first* use of it in this text may have been in the same spirit – a shared white working-class language employed within the enacted assumption of a shared set of values. The *extent* of the sharing implied in his use of 'nigger', however, is limited, and it is this fault in the surface of their 'shared' culture that becomes apparent to John, for whom the use of 'nigger' has a more specialised meaning than merely being part of the common language of communication. It is, in a sense, a 'politically' meaningful word for John, and he attempts to prove that David's use of it indicates David's authentic and underlying racist voice, and that it displays the inauthenticity and hypocrisy of his anti-racist arguments.

Whatever weight must be given to the 'doing' of racism evident in

David's use of 'nigger' at the beginning of the discussion, it clearly does *not* betoken the presence of the specific set of ideas and values that characterise intended racism and/or racial hostility. His use of 'nigger' very plainly does not indicate anything *beyond itself* about his ideas, attitudes and practices with respect to race; and it is the realisation of this fact that so irritates John, who actually *corrects* him several times in the full text from 'niggers' to 'black people'. John is, in effect, policing the word – attempting to keep it reserved for meaningful (racist) use only: '*You* don't call black people, 'niggers' so why should you say it to whites, if you like 'em [i.e. if you like black people]?'

Perhaps one of the most curious exchanges in this part of the text is the following:

JOHN: Why do you call 'em 'niggers'?
DAVID: Well what d'you want me to call 'em?
JOHN: What they are, 'black people', if you like 'em.
DAVID: But they're 'niggers' an' all ain't they?

There is a range of possible interpretations of the final question. In the interpretation which would impute the most racism to David, the statement, 'they're niggers an' all [also]' might be re-stated: 'However much they may be respectfully called "black people" they are still inferior beings.' In view of David's other remarks, however, this interpretation can be ruled out. A second reading could be one which sees the utterance in *interactive* terms. Its 'meaning' in this sense would not be quarried from its possible reference but from what it said about what was *shared* between the boys, i.e.: 'When you and I talk we use the word "nigger" without question. This occasion is the same as other occasions.' This interpretation seems somewhat strained, and in any case seems to contradict what appears to be really happening, i.e. that David is undermining the common ground between them. Perhaps a more likely explanation is that David is referring to the *objective* existence of the word in the language, independent of any intended meaning or specialised use *and* independent of its place in the set of terms comprising the racist 'code'. He is, for reasons quite the reverse of those of the informant in Text 2 above, attempting to deny the social resonance and political meaning of 'nigger'. His denial of its social meaning is an interactive strategy to take the social ground away from John – for certainly he was not innocent of its social meaning even if this denial and his facetious statement, '"Nigger" – real word – means "worker for the government"' was designed to suggest that he was. Indeed it was this which lead John to explode, 'Bullshit! To a black person it means takin' the piss', and to tell David something which he already knew full well.

It becomes clear, therefore, that his use of 'nigger' in past exchanges did not signal a set of racist assumptions shared with John. In this exchange his 'shallow' use of 'nigger' in the past is 'found out' by John and David immediately takes advantage of this by strategically manoeuvring a severance of the word from any 'common' social ground guaranteeing its meaning.

Such semantic 'guerrilla tactics', operating below the level of expressed opinion, substantially served to strengthen the effectiveness of the anti-racist position argued for on several fronts by David during this discussion. Here he was not simply blocking or side-stepping the transmission of racism from John to himself, but effectively confronting it and calling into question the scope of its assumed 'constituency'.

The specific form which John's racism takes is as relevant here as David's anti-racism, for, as was seen above, the expression of John's racism is made up of a conjunction of local adolescent rivalries and non-local ideological materials – 'they're inferior' and so on – which together produce a local variant. David gradually came to address himself to the specific delineation of John's racism, and related the generative basis of his own anti-racism to it. In doing so, he also addressed himself to the 'local' constituencies wherein racism is elaborated. The conclusion of their discussion saw David focusing on what was the key issue underlying the form of adolescent racism which John expressed. Here David led John not into any mere logical trap for the winning of points, but towards an actual realisation of the nature of David's *own* 'constituency' and its relation to the anti-racist position he had been arguing:

DAVID: It's funny about what you say about blacks don't want whites 'cos do you remember about two year ago up Clinton Road [a street in Area B] wiv niggers vee whites?

JOHN: Yeah.

DAVID: Was you up there? Well I was up there [. . .] and I'll tell you what, at Clinton Road when the blacks were fightin' the whites, there was more whites fightin' for the blacks . . . there was more whites on the black side than there were whites fightin' against the blacks.

JOHN: It was not B whites who were fightin'. It was strictly National Front, British Movement and Nazi 88 . . . [. . .]

DAVID: But then again, at Clinton Road there was all them people that can't stand niggers, they come from all over London all them people, and the people who fought against them people, d'you know who they were? Black kids from B and white kids from

B. B joined forces then. Black or white they joined forces . . .
The white people were supposed to be comin' down on a
demonstration to do the niggers, right? or the 'black people',
or whatever you want me to call 'em.

JOHN: Well listen if white people came down to beat up black people in
A I would go wiv white people. It's as simple as that.

DAVID: No, but that would be different in B. [. . .] If you had a mate,
he was coloured and he was one of your best mates, an' two
white kids were goin' to beat 'im up 'cos they didn't like the
colour of 'im, would you 'elp 'im?

JOHN: I don't know 'cos I 'aven't got any black people I respect enough
 . . .

DAVID: Well I'm sayin', would you 'elp 'im? I'll tell you what, if Wesley
[a black school friend of John's] if Wesley . . . You like Wesley
a lot don't yer?

JOHN: Yeah.

DAVID: If Wesley was down the road an' 'e was gettin' beat up by two
white kids who you never knew, an' they was just beatin' 'im
up for 'is colour, an' you was standin' there, would you 'elp
'im?

JOHN: Course I would.

DAVID: Well then!

JOHN: Because 'e is a person an' 'e's a good mate of mine. Fuck 'is
colour, I would . . .

DAVID: Its the same fing! That's what I mean!

JOHN: . . . stick up for 'im whatever 'appens.

DAVID: That's what I mean. In B *all* the blacks are friends of the
whites. D'you know what I mean. There must be twenty gangs
of people an' you can guarantee fifty per cent are white and
fifty per cent are black.

What is for John the basis of his own local group loyalties – "e's a good
mate of mine. Fuck 'is colour, I would stick up for 'im whatever happens'
– and the organisational foundation giving cohesion to the notion of a
'common' constituency of social meaning, is revealed as also the basis of
David's very different views. It is, for John, an undeniable value – so
undeniable that, even despite the generalised attitudes to black youth he
had expressed repeatedly in the discussion, his statement 'fuck 'is colour,
I would stick up for 'im' is uttered without a hint of qualification. Thus
when David moves on to clinch the point with an effective hyperbole,
'That's what I mean. In B *all* the blacks are friends of the whites', the full
'ideological' consequences which would flow from such a state become
immediately obvious within the discussion.

However much, in this instance, the terms of the equation are pre-cast by the notion of an essentially *male* loyalty system the specific form of racism displayed, and the specific anti-racist interactive strategies employed in response, take place not in any pure, non-socially located *moral* terrain, but on a ground thick with the meanings, practices, contradictions and affinities constitutive of actual social location. It is, of course, on such ground that all social and political battles are ultimately fought.

The discussion between John and David was, in a sense, a discussion between different sites of ideological and symbolic transmission. John was speaking from one site of racist relay and symbolic production – the white adolescent peer group structures of Area A. David was speaking from the cultural and political terrain of redefinitions and political productivity generated within the black community, filtered by his own position in relation to that community. The capacity of individual whites effectively to challenge the racism in their immediate social environment, and the motivation for doing so, inevitably rests on exactly those constituencies wherein the meaning of their individual actions are defined. The relations *between* those constituencies are ultimately an effect of the economic and political order which provides the modalities through which historically constituted cultural codes become expressed and transformed. The power of challenges to the transmission of racism between whites is thus as mediated by the structures beyond personal interaction as is the semiological dimension conditioned by its ideological contexts.

Here the proximity of black community struggles, political action and cultural definition, evident in areas such as Area B, provides a key factor in the erosion of the ideologies which otherwise parse specific local conditions – whether they be adolescent group relations or, indeed, any of the conditions often purported to provide in themselves explanations of 'bad race relations' – turning them into the materials of local codes of racism. It is, however, local social composition and history that moulds the process of transmission from the black community to the white, and moderates the impact of anti-racist initiatives through the local structures of interaction. Partial alternative structures of association, of coding, of symbolism are thus engendered in the cultural and social contexts of inter-racial 'contact', and both black and white young people have to pick their way across a crazy-paving of mismatched practices and ideological fragments.

While racism is, as is often pointed out, 'a white problem', the distortions which it exerts on friendship are experienced by black and white alike, if not equally. As has been seen repeatedly in the earlier chapters, the paradoxes are often lived through in paradoxical ways and it is always *to* those friendships, and the frail structures they attempt to initiate, that the contradictions return. Despite the variety of responses white adolescents have to racism – reproducing it without reflection, boosting it in collective practices, avoiding its reproduction, challenging its relay etc. – there remains, finally, the irreducible knowledge of racism itself. Whatever the particular, individual attitude of white adolescents, and however much their friendship with blacks – their practices and attitudes – may be non-racist or anti-racist, the very fact of racism's existence, by whatever face it is known and however imperfectly it is perceived, forms a knowledge of which only the social ingenue may be innocent. Indeed the knowledge is itself part of commonsense, part of 'what everybody knows'. Racism is thus able to intervene in friendships not only as a set of linked ideas, practices and symbolic forms but as a fact about society, which overshadows adolescent inter-racial friendships as it overshadows all black/white social interaction. Interactively, *some* consciousness of what others – black friends for whites, white friends for blacks – know and are potentially able to think and feel is always capable of informing choices within interaction. This, indeed, is the 'bottom line' in the negotiation of inter-racial interactions – a dangerous presence lurking beneath the surface, always able to emerge and threaten those who might attempt to behave in innocence without attention to its proximity.

It is this inter-racially shared knowledge which is one of the most difficult for adolescents to deal with in friendship for it allows of no avoidance. Perhaps it is for this reason that rituals emerge which seek to expose as nonsense and absurdity that which their friendships also struggle to contradict. Especially in the form of abuse rituals, the individual-transcending 'social fact' of racism is dug out of its lair beneath the surface of interaction and exposed in a game of dare which skirts the dangers it attempts ritually to destroy. The 'playful' use of racial abuse between friends is very common, and constitutes a ritual reflex of that social knowledge which cannot be 'unknown'. The processing of that knowledge is removed to the plain of the dramaturgical, in 'dumb shows' played out in some logical space anterior to any anti-racism that might flourish on the uneven social ground of inner-city life.

In addressing itself to the codes on which the doing of racism relies, this response involves the construction of a meta-code of ritualised behaviour. Commonly such a method of processing the racism in the culture will be opaque to its users, although intimations of its deeper meaning may be traced in adolescent *accounts* of this activity. One white boy, having stated that he had no 'racialist' attitudes, qualified his statement with the following remarks:

Well . . . like, Denis [a black boy who was also his closest
friend], I've always got a racialist attitude towards him, and
Patrick, my other coloured friend. I've always got a racialist
attitude towards 'em but . . . they've got so used to me. I don't
mean it in the sense of racial*ism*, because all this skinhead an'
all this rubbish stuff is just not on. You get some bad blacks,
you get some bad whites, you get some bad Asians, and all the
rest of it.
*When you say you have this racialist thing towards them what
did you mean exactly?*
It's just the way I act towards 'em. I don't know why. It's just
my attitude I've built up while I've got to know 'em and I say,
'alright, nigger?' or somethin' like that and they say, 'alright,
honky?' an' we 'ave a good laugh. We do it as a joke. They
never take it seriously and I never take it seriously so it's just a
good laugh, like I go, 'alright, rassman?' an' he'll go, 'alright,
snowflake?'

What he appears to mean is that he has taken racialism up into his
relationships and transformed it into a plaything, in an attempt to
acknowledge its social presence while rendering it meaningless. Having
witnessed such displays between this informant and his black friends –
which were initiated sometimes by one party and sometimes by the other
– I was left in no doubt about the fact that it was, indeed, done 'as a joke'
for the participants themselves, however painfully its meanings might be
registered at other, less conscious levels. The practice is nevertheless a
complex one and itself a matter of negotiation and learning. A similar
report of ritualised abuse was made to me by a sixteen-year-old white
girl. Talking about her black, youth club friends, she outlined how she
alone out of her white friends at the club understood the 'unmeant'
banter of her black friends:

I love muckin' about wiv 'em, though. They call us 'porkhead'
– well, only me 'cos the other [white] girls go, 'No I'm not',
you know – and they say, 'snowflake', and I say, 'Shut up,
niggers. Get out of England. I hate the lot of you.'

However, *her* responses became qualified by her experience in this
practice:

And I used to write along the wall, 'National Front. Niggers
Out' and fings like that. And they used to come in and go,
'Jonesy's been in 'ere. Oy! Get in 'ere! What 'ave you written
on these walls?' sort of thing. And I used to have to watch it

when Robin was about 'cos he did used to get offended. He did used to get upset. Because, I didn't notice it at first but Eddie [a close black friend] sort of said to me, you know, 'Next time you say it, just look at Robin's face,' and I did an' 'e sort of went [making a serious expression] like that, so I just sort of had to watch what I said. I mean all the others knew that I didn't mean anything I said. And sometimes *they'd* say things and I'd sort of go, '[gulp] Did they really mean that?' and they'd sort of *know* and give me a massive great cuddle: 'I didn't *mean* it.' That's why I think, how can . . . you know . . . 'cos what *is* it? It's just a *skin* colour, innit. It's so stupid! I mean they're just as brainy as us . . .

The discrepancy in the type of ritual abuse available to whites and blacks, however, certainly qualified the activity. 'Snowflake' or 'porkhead' may be racial abuse terms, but they lack the social and historical weight of 'nigger', and their social constituency is far smaller. Thus, although blacks and whites can join together in such exorcistic activities, the dangers with which they toy are dangers to friendship and intercourse forged and initiated by the consequences of racism itself. They are not merely the inherent dangers of abuse in *any* form. Nevertheless, the desire to drive their knowledge of racism to an exposure of its absurdity (as that absurdity is experienced in friendship) is often to be glimpsed in adolescent inter-racial rituals, and even this inequality of abuse resources has been ritually approached by some groups of adolescents. In particular, one practice which I observed, and which was also reported to me by adolescents and youth-workers alike, constituted a dramatic inversion of racial abuse which resolved the interactively dangerous aspects of the rituals by emphasising the 'common' which is established in inter-racial friendships. In this variant, groups of black and white youngsters range themselves on opposing sides in school playgrounds or on the streets and hurl racial abuse at each other in the fiercest way. The difference with this ritual, however, resides in the fact that the black youngsters call the whites 'niggers', 'black bastards', 'springy-hair' and so on, while the whites call the black youngsters 'porkhead', 'honky', 'snowflake'. This practice, apparently quite common in Area B, seems to enact the experience of contradiction and attempts to consume it in a dramatic inversion which finally drains all possible meaning from the language of racial hostility, robbing even the play abuse vocabularies of their imbalance. It turns racism into a kind of effigy, to be burned up in an interactive ritual which seeks to acknowledge and deal with its undeniable presence whilst acting out the negation of its effects.

The modes of 'processing' racism evident amongst adolescents discussed above constitute a series of initiations. They are, in a sense, fragments of structures, fraily erected against the flow, and offering the possibility of elaboration. As such, they share with all rudimentary cultural and social elements the struggle of achieving a translation from the individual and local into the common and socially sure-footed. They are part of that structural under-life located beneath the similarly fragmented surfaces of culture and society and, as such, struggle against the biases which favour some initiatives just as surely as they repel and deflect others. It is, in this sense, the obstinate ordering of social power along racial contours that constantly qualifies the meaning of inter-racial friendship within any wider context. The responses to racism evident in inter-racial friend-ships, and the capacity for an opposition to racism displayed by some white youngsters, are thus both hopeful and tragically circumscribed. They provide, nevertheless, some indication that racism is not an inevitable feature of economic or cultural 'deprivation', not the neces-sary reflex of 'unemployment' or poor levels of education. On the contrary, the capacity of some white working-class adolescents to pene-trate the terms within which 'race relations' are often perceived by those more favourably placed offers an enviable reminder of the inadequacies of such comfortable views of the social location of racism.

Just as different forms of racism are evident in different social locations – whether they be the italics of a class emphasis or the specialised inflection of an institutional setting – so the need is evoked for differential responses and oppositional strategies. What is ideologically achieved by the associational relays established through inter-racial friendship provides the ground for one such area of response and opposition. It is, however, (not unlike the commonly *partial* nature of white creole acquisition) in need of sustained contact with the black communities if it is to avoid distortion and a mispronunciation of the syllables of their resistance.

References

Abrahams, R. 1962. Playing the dozens. *Journal of American Folklore* 75: 209–18.
  1963. *Deep down in the jungle: negro narrative folklore from the streets of Philadelphia*. Chicago: Aldine.
Alleyne, M. C. 1980. *Comparative Afro-American: an historical study of English based Afro-American dialects of the New World*. Ann Arbor: Karoma.
Allport, G. W. 1954. *The nature of prejudice*. Cambridge, Mass.: Addison-Wesley.
Ausubel, D. P. 1954. *Theory and problems of adolescent development*. New York: Grune and Stratton.
Bagley, C. 1969. Coloured neighbours. *New Society* 1: 213–14.
Bagley, C. and Verma, G. 1975. Inter-ethnic attitudes and behaviour in British multi-racial schools. In C. Bagley and G. Verma (eds.) *Race and education across cultures*. London: Heinemann.
Bailey, B. 1966. *Jamaican creole syntax: a transformational approach*. Cambridge: Cambridge University Press.
Barthes, R. 1967. *Système de la mode*. Paris: Seuil.
Benson, S. 1981. *Ambiguous ethnicity: interracial families in London*. Cambridge: Cambridge University Press.
Ben-Tovim, G. and Gabriel J. 1982. The politics of race in Britain, 1962–79: a review of the major trends and of recent debates. In Husband, 1982.
Bernstein, B. 1971. *Class, codes and control*, vol. 1, *Theoretical studies towards a sociology of language*. London: Routledge & Kegan Paul.
Blanc, M. 1982. Social networks and multilingual behaviour: the Atlantic Provinces Project. Paper given at the 4th Sociolinguistics Symposium, University of Sheffield.
Braha, V. and Rutter, D. R. 1980. Friendship choice in a mixed race primary school. *Educational Studies* 6, 3: 217–23.
Brandt, G. 1984. British youth Caribbean creole – the politics of resistance. Paper given to the Conference on Languages Without a Written Tradition, Thames Polytechnic.
Brown, C. 1972. The language of soul. In Kochman 1972.
Brown, P. and Levinson, S. 1979. Social structure, groups and interaction. In Giles and Scherer 1979.

Burley, D. 1944. *Dan Burley's original handbook of Harlem jive*. New York: Dan Burley.

Butler, D. and Stokes, D. 1974. *Political change in Britain*. London: Macmillan.

Campbell, A. 1981. *Girl delinquents*. Oxford: Blackwell.

Carter, D. E., Dentine-Carter, S. L. and Benson, F. W. 1980. Interracial acceptance in the classroom. In H. C. Foot, A. J. Chapman and J. R. Smith (eds.) *Friendship and social relations in children*. London: Wiley.

Cashmore, E. 1979. *Rastaman*. London: Allen and Unwin.

Cassidy, F. 1961. *Jamaica talk: three hundred years of the English language in Jamaica*. London: Macmillan.

Cassidy, F. and Le Page, R. 1967. *Dictionary of Jamaican English*. Cambridge: Cambridge University Press (revised edition 1980).

Cayton, H. and Drake, S. 1946. *Black metropolis*. London: Cape.

Centre for Contemporary Cultural Studies. 1982. *The empire strikes back*. London: Hutchinson.

Chambers, I. 1976. A strategy for living: black music and white subcultures. In Hall and Jefferson 1976.

Cheshire, J. 1982. *Variation in an English dialect*. Cambridge: Cambridge University Press.

Clark, K. and Clark, M. 1947. Racial identification and preferences in negro children. In T. M. Newcomb and E. C. Hartley (eds.) *Readings in social psychology*. New York: Holt.

Cloward, R. A. and Ohlin, L. E. 1960. *Delinquency and opportunity, a theory of delinquent gangs*. Chicago: Free Press.

Cochrane, R. and Billig, M. 1984. 'I'm not National Front myself, but . . .'. *New Society* 68, 1121:255–8.

Cohen, P. 1972. Sub-cultural conflict and working class community. *Working papers in cultural studies 2*. University of Birmingham: Centre for Contemporary Cultural Studies.

Cohen, P. and Robins, D. 1978. Knuckle sandwich: growing up in the working-class city. Harmondsworth: Penguin.

Craig, D. 1983. Review of Sutcliffe 1982. *Language and Society* 12, 4: 542–8.

Dalby, D. 1970. *Black through white: patterns of communication in Africa and the New World*. Indiana University: African Studies Program.

Daniel, S. and McGuire, P. (eds.) 1972. *The Paint House: words from an east end gang*. Harmondsworth: Penguin.

Davey, A. 1983. *Learning to be prejudiced: growing up in multi-ethnic Britain*. London: Edward Arnold.

Deakin, N. 1970. *Colour, citizenship and British society*. London: Panther.

DeCamp, D. 1971. Toward a generative analysis of a post-creole speech continuum. In Hymes 1971.

Dillard, J. L. 1972. *Black English, its history and usage in the United States*. New York: Vintage Books.

(ed.) 1975. *Perspectives on black English*. The Hague: Mouton.

Dollard, J. 1939. The dozens: the dialect of insult. *American Image* 1: 3–24.

Douvan, E. and Adelson, J. 1966. *The adolescent experience*. New York: Wiley.

Durojaiye, M. 1970. Patterns of friendship in an ethnicly mixed school. *Race* 12: 189–200.

Edwards, V. K. 1979. *The West Indian language issue in British schools: challenges and responses*. London: Routledge & Kegan Paul.

Eisenstadt, S. N. 1956. *From generation to generation: age groups and social structure*. London: Routledge & Kegan Paul.

Escure, G. 1979. Linguistic variation and ethnic interaction in Belize: creole/carib. In H. Giles and B. Saint-Jaques (eds.) *Language and ethnic relations*. Oxford: Pergamon.

Folb, E. A. 1980. *Runnin' down some lines: the language and culture of black teenagers*. Cambridge, Mass.: Harvard University.

Fryer, P. 1984. *Staying power: the history of black people in Britain*. London: Pluto.

Garrison, L. 1979. *Black youth, Rastafarianism and the identity-crisis in Britain*. London: Acer.

Geerz, C. 1973. *The interpretation of cultures: selected essays*. New York: Basic Books.

Genovese, E. 1975. *Roll, Jordan, roll. The world the slaves made*. London: Deutsch.

Gerard, H. and Miller, N. 1975. *School desegregation*. New York: Plenum Press.

Giles, H. (ed.) 1977. *Language, ethnicity and intergroup relations*. London: Academic Press.

1979. Ethnicity markers in speech. In Giles and Scherer 1979.

Giles, H. and Scherer, K. R. (eds.) 1979. *Social markers in speech*. Cambridge: Cambridge University Press.

Gilroy, P. and Lawrence, E. 1986. Two-tone Britain. In P. Cohen and H. Bains (eds.) *Multiracist Britain*. London: Macmillan.

Girdwood, B., Drummond, P., Martin, R. and Nicholson, H. 1982. Summerville adventure playground: play in a multi-racial setting. In A. Ohri, B. Manning and P. Curno (eds.) *Community work and racism*. London: Routledge & Kegan Paul.

Gumperz, J. 1978. The conversational analysis of inter-ethnic communication. In E. L. Ross (ed.) *Interethnic communication. Proceedings of the Southern Anthropological Society*, Atlanta, Georgia.

1982. *Discourse strategies*. Cambridge: Cambridge University Press.

Hall, S., Critcher, C., Jefferson, T., Clarke, J. and Roberts, B. 1978. *Policing the crisis: mugging, the state and law and order*. London: Macmillan.

Hall, S. and Jefferson, T. 1976. *Resistance through rituals: youth sub-cultures in post-war Britain*. London: Hutchinson.

Halliday, M. A. K. 1978. *Language as social semiotic*. London: Edward Arnold.

Hancock, I. 1976. Lexical expansion within closed systems. In M. Sanches and B. Blount (eds.) *Social dimensions of language use*. New York: Academic.

Handlin, O. 1959. *The newcomers: negroes and Puerto Ricans in a changing metropolis*. Cambridge, Mass.: Harvard University.

Hannerz, U. 1969. *Soulside: inquiries into ghetto culture and community*. New York: Columbia University Press.

Hebdige, D. 1976. Reggae, Rastas and Rudies. In Hall and Jefferson 1976.

1979. *Subcultures: the meaning of style*. London: Methuen.

Heath, S. B. 1983. *Ways with words*. Cambridge: Cambridge University Press.

Henriques, J. 1984. Social psychology and the politics of racism. In J. Henriques, W. Holloway, C. Urwin and V. Walkerdine, *Changing the subject*. London: Methuen.

Henry, J. 1963. *Culture against man*. New York: Random House.
Hewitt, R. 1982. White adolescent creole users and the politics of friendship. *Journal of Multilingual and Multicultural Development* 3, 3: 217–32.
　1983. *Black through white: Hoagy Carmichael and the cultural reproduction of racism*. Popular Music, 3, Cambridge: Cambridge University Press.
Hiro, D. 1971. *Black British, white British*. London: Monthly Review Press.
Husband, C. (ed.) 1982. *'Race' in Britain, continuity and change*. London: Hutchinson.
Husbands, C. T. 1979. The 'threat' hypothesis and racist voting in England and the United States. In A. Miles and R. Phizacklea (eds.) *Racism and political action in Britain*. London: Routledge & Kegan Paul.
Hymes, D. 1962. The ethnography of speaking. In T. Gladwin and W. C. Sturtevant (eds.) *Anthropology and human behaviour*. Washington: Anthropological Society of Washington.
　1971*a*. Sociolinguistics and the ethnography of speaking. In E. Ardener (ed.) *Social anthropology and language*. London: Tavistock.
　(ed.) 1971*b*. *Pidginisation and creolisation of languages*. Cambridge: Cambridge University Press.
Inner London Education Authority. 1980. Youth service provision for girls. Report of the Working Party set up by London Youth Committee.
Jakobson, R. 1960. Concluding statement: linguistics and poetics. In T. Sebeok (ed.) *Style in language*. Cambridge, Mass.: MIT Press.
Jansen, T. 1984. A language of Sophiatown and Soweto. In M. Sebba and L. Todd (eds.) *York Papers in Linguistics 11: Papers from the York Creole Conference*.
Jones, L. 1966. *Blues people: negro music in white America*. London: McGibbon and Kee.
Kawwa, T. 1963. *Ethnic prejudice and choice of friends amongst English and non-English adolescents*, MA dissertation, University of London Institute of Education.
Kochman, T. 1970. Towards an ethnography of black American speech behaviour. In N. E. Whitten, Jr, and J. F. Szwed (eds.) *Afro-American anthropology*. New York: Free Press.
　(ed.) 1972. *Rappin' and stylin' out: communication in urban black America*. Urbana: University of Illinois Press.
　1975. Grammar and discourse in vernacular black English. *Foundation of Language* 13: 95–118.
　1977. Review of Gage 1974. *Language in Society* 6, 1: 49–64.
　1983. The boundary between play and non-play in black verbal duelling. *Language in Society* 12, 3: 329–37.
Koslin, S. C., Koslin, B. L., Cardwell, J. and Pargament, R. 1969. Quasi-disguised and structured measures of schoolchildren's racial preferences. In *Proceedings, 77th Annual Convention of the American Psychological Association*, Washington, DC.
Labov, W. 1971. The notion of 'system' in creole languages. In Hymes 1971*b*.
　1972*a*. *Sociolinguistic patterns*. Oxford: Blackwell.
　1972*b*. *Language in the inner city: studies in the black English vernacular*. Oxford: Basil Blackwell.
　1980*a*. Is there a creole speech community? In A. Valdman and A. Highfield (eds.) *Theoretical orientations in creole studies*. London: Academic.

1980*b*. The social origins of sound change. In W. Labov (ed.) *Locating language in time and space*. London: Academic.

Labov, W. and Pedraza, P. 1971. *A study of the Spanish spoken by Puerto Ricans in New York City and Puerto Rico*. Mimeo, Columbia University.

Laver, P. and Trudgill, P. 1979. Phonetic and linguistic markers in speech. In Giles and Scherer 1979.

Le Page, R. B. 1975*a*. *Projection, focussing, diffusion*. Mimeo, University of York.

1975*b*. Polarising factors – political, cultural, economic – operating on the individual's choice of identity through language use in British Honduras. In J. G. Savard and R. Vigneault (eds.) *Les etats multilingues*. Quebec: Laval University Press.

1981. *Caribbean connections in the classroom*. London: Mary Glasgow Language Trust.

1985. *Acts of identity*. Cambridge: Cambridge University Press.

Le Page, R. B. and De Camp. D. 1960. *Jamaican creole*. New York: Macmillan.

Local, J. K., Wells, W. H. G. and Sebba, M. 1983. Phonetic aspects of turn-delimitation in London Jamaican. Paper given at York Creole Conference, University of York.

Lord, A. 1958. *The singer of tales*. Harvard, Mass.: Harvard University Press.

McConahay, J. 1978: The effects of school desegregation upon students' racial attitudes and behaviour: a critical review of the literature and a prolegomenon to future resarch. *Law and Contemporary Problems* 42, 3: 77–107.

McDavid, R. J. Jr 1971. Addendum. In Wofram and Clarke 1971.

McDavid, R. J. Jr and McDavid V. 1951. The relationship of the speech of American negroes to the speech of the whites. *American Speech* 26: 3–17.

McRobbie, A. and Gerber, J. 1976. Girls and subculture. Hall and Jefferson 1976.

Maltz, D. N. and Borker, R. A. 1982. A cultural approach to male–female miscommunication. In J. Gumperz (ed.) *Language and social identity*. Cambridge: Cambridge University Press.

Mead, M. 1928. *Coming of age in Samoa*. New York: Morrow.

1930. *Growing up in New Guinea*. New York: Morrow.

1935. *Sex and temperament in three primitive societies*. New York: Morrow.

Mezzrow, M. and Wolf, B. 1946. *Really the blues*. New York: Random House.

Milner, D. 1983. *Children and race: ten years on*. London: Ward Lock Educational.

Milroy, L. 1980. *Language and social networks*. Oxford: Blackwell.

Mirsky, J. 1937. The Dakota. In M. Mead (ed.) *Co-operation and competition among primitive peoples*. New York: McGraw-Hill.

Mitchell-Kernan, C. 1971. *Language behaviour in a black urban community*. University of California, Berkeley: Language Behaviour Research Laboratory.

1972. Signifying and marking: two Afro-American speech acts. In J. Gumperz and D. Hymes (eds.) *Directions in sociolinguistics*. New York: Holt, Rinehart & Winston.

Mungham, G. and Pearson, G. (eds.) 1976. *Working-class youth culture*. London: Routledge & Kegan Paul.

Opie, I. and Opie, P. 1959. *The lore and language of school children*. Oxford: Clarendon Press.

Palmer, P. 1981. *An investigation into the language use of children of Jamaican origin in Manchester.* MA dissertation, University of Reading.

Parkin, D. 1977. Emergent and stablised multi-lingualism: poly-ethnic peer groups in urban Kenya. In Giles 1977.

Patterson, S. 1963. *Dark strangers.* London: Tavistock.

Pearson, G. 1976. 'Paki-bashing' in a north east Lancashire cotton town: a case study and its history. In Mungham and Pearson 1976.

Pollard, V. 1983. Rastafarian language in St Lucia and Barbados. Paper given to the York Creole Conference, University of York.

Porter, J. D. 1971. *Black child, white child: the development of racial attitudes.* Cambridge, Mass.: Harvard University Press.

Prescod-Roberts, M. and Steele, N. 1980. *Black women: bringing it all back home.* Bristol: Falling Wall Press.

Pryce, K. 1979. *Endless pressure: a study of West Indian life-styles in Bristol.* Harmondsworth: Penguin Books.

Puskin, I. 1967. *A study of ethnic choice in the play of young chidren in three London districts.* PhD thesis, University of London.

Ramirez, K. G. 1974. Socio-cultural aspects of the Chicano dialect. In G. D. Bills (ed.) *Southwest areal linguistics.* California: Institute for Cultural Pluralism.

Rex, J. and Tomlinson, S. 1979. *Colonial immigrants in a British city: a class analysis.* London: Routledge & Kegan Paul.

Rist, R. 1978. *The invisible children.* Cambridge, Mass.: Harvard University Press.

Romaine, S. 1984. *The languages of children and adolescents.* Oxford: Blackwell.

Root, J. and Austin, H. 1978–9. Black music: white youth. *New Community* vii, 1 (Winter): 99–103.

Rosen, H. and Burgess, T. 1980. *Languages and dialects of London school children.* London: Ward Lock Educational.

Ryan, E. 1979. Why do low-prestige language varieties persist? In H. Giles and R. St. Clair (eds.) *Language and social psychology.* Oxford: Blackwell.

Ryan, S. 1981. *Rastafarianism and the speech of adolescent blacks in Britain.* MA dissertation, University of Birmingham.

Sahlins, M. 1976. *Culture and practical reason.* Chicago: University of Chicago Press.

Savin-Williams, R. 1980. Social interactions of adolescent females in natural groups. In H. C. Foot, A. J. Chapman and J. R. Smith (eds.) *Friendship and social relations in children.* New York: Wiley.

Schofield, J. W. 1978. School desegregation and inter-group relations. In D. Bar-Tal and L. Saxe (eds.) *Social psychology of education: theory and research.* Washington, DC: Hemisphere Press.

Schwartz, G. and Merten, D. 1967. The language of adolescence: an anthropological approach to youth culture. *American Journal of Sociology* 72, 5: 453–68.

Sebba, M. 1983a. Code-switching as a conversational strategy. Mimeo paper tabled at York Creole Conference, University of York.

1983b. *Language change among Afro-Caribbeans in London.* Mimeo, Department of Language, University of York.

Sebba, M. and Wootton, T. 1984. Codeswitching as a conversational strategy. Paper presented at Sociolinguistics Symposium, Liverpool.

Select Committee on Race Relations and Immigration 1977. *Report*, vol. 1, *The West Indian community*. London: HMSO.

Shelly, L. (ed.) 1945. *Hepcats jive talk dictionary*. Derby, Connecticut: T. W. Charles.

Silverman, S. 1975. The learning of black English by Puerto Ricans in New York City. In Dillard 1975.

Smith, A. (ed.) 1972. *Language, communication and rhetoric in black America*. New York: Harper & Row.

Snyman, J. W. 1970. *An introduction to the !Xu language*. Cape Town: Balkema.

Sowell, T. 1981. *Ethnic America*. New York: Basic Books.

Spiro, M. E. 1965. *Children of the kibbutz*. New York: Schocken.

Studlar, D. T. 1977. Social context and attitude towards coloured immigrants. *British Journal of Sociology* xxviii: 168–84.

Sutcliffe, D. 1976. 'Hou dem Taak in Bedford, Sa!' *Multiracial School* 5, 4: 708–11.

   1978. *The language of first and second generation West Indian children in Bedfordshire*. MEd. thesis, University of Leicester.

   1982. *British Black English*. Oxford: Blackwell.

   1984. British Black English and West Indian creoles. In P. Trudgill (ed.) *Language in the British Isles*. Cambridge: Cambridge University Press.

Suttles, G. 1968: *The social order of the slum*. Chicago: University of Chicago Press.

Thrasher, F. 1927. *The gang*. Chicago: University of Chicago Press.

Troyna, B. 1977. The Rastafarians – the youths responses. *Multiracial School* 6, 1: 1–8.

   1982. Reporting the National Front: British values observed. In Husband 1982.

Trubetzkoi, N. 1969. *Principles of phonology*. Berkeley, California: University of California Press.

Trudgill, P. 1974: *Sociolinguistics: an introduction*. Harmondsworth: Penguin.

Turkie, A. (ed.) 1982. *Know what I mean?* London: National Youth Bureau.

Walker, I. 1982. Skinheads: the cult of trouble. In P. Barker (ed.) *The other Britain*. London: Routledge & Kegan Paul.

Weinreich, U. 1966. *Languages in contact*. The Hague: Mouton.

Wells, J. 1973. *Jamaican pronunciation in London*. Oxford: Blackwell.

Willis, P. 1977. *Learning to labour*. Farnborough: Saxon House.

Willmott, P. 1969. *Adolescent boys of East London*. Harmondsworth: Penguin.

Wilner, D. Walkley, R. and Cook, S. 1955. *Human relations in inter-racial housing: a study of the contact hypothesis*. Minneapolis: University of Minnesota Press.

Wolfram, W. 1971. Black–white speech differences revisited. In Wolfram and Clarke 1971.

   1972. Overlapping influence and linguistic assimilation in second generation Puerto Rican English. In D. M. Smith and R. Shuy (eds.) *Sociolinguistics in cross-cultural analysis*. Washington, DC: Georgetown University Press.

   1974. *Sociolinguistic aspects of assimilation: Puerto Rican English in New York City*. Washington DC: Centre for Applied Linguistics.

Wolfram, W. and Clarke, M. (eds.) 1971. *Black–white speech relationships*. Washington, DC: Centre For Applied Linguistics.

Wolman, B. 1951. Spontaneous groups of children and adolescents in Israel. *Journal of Social Psychology* 34: 171–82.

Index

Note: Words in italic indicate creole-derived words or titles of books.